Changing Schools and Schooling Systems

Changing Schools and Schooling Systems

Tushar K Sinha

AUTHORSPRESS

Publishers of Scholarly Books

Worldwide Circulation through Authorspress Global Network
First Published 2010
by
Authorspress
E-35/103, Jawahar Park
Laxmi Nagar, Delhi-110 092
e-mail: authorspress@yahoo.com

Changing Schools and Schooling Systems
ISBN 978-81-7273-545-6

Printed in India at Tarun Offset, Delhi.

PREFACE

Schools are perceived as agents for transmission of knowledge, social values and customs to the younger generations. The expectations from the school are high as 'schools' being the major providers of education all over the world stand out to initiate and catalyse the process of change. The school takes in its inputs, namely younger pupils, funds, teachers, learning materials etc. from the society; gives out output in the form of older, educated pupils, service to the community, a livelihood for teachers and their families etc.

The major responsibility of a school is to socialise children and to equip them as future mature members of the society by developing a feedback mechanism between school and its environment. In this process the schools are influenced continuously by the changing educational philosophies and the ongoing technological developments. In the contemporary society, school has thus become the focus of different reform initiatives for ensuring provision of relevant and quality education.

Schooling systems all over the world are continuously adapting themselves to meet the challenges of globalisation. The demand for educated and skilled workers is on rise. In fact the speed at which these changes are influencing the environment in the local as well as global market calls for reassessment of preparedness in school and higher education institutions to meet these challenges. Moreover, for developing a knowledge society the availability of quality education assumes increasing significance in such a scenario.

Today, the key concern for educational policy makers is how to provide quality education that is sensitive to local context and at the same time responsible to the demands of the global market. Conventionally, higher education provides leadership-manpower for different sectors of national development and growth whereas school education, to be specific secondary education sector is the major provider of workforce for all spheres of national productivity. Therefore, the school's responsibility towards realising student's potential is further enhanced. Ensuring quality education at school level is essential because the quality of teaching, learning and nature of the knowledge transmitted are perceived as the central concerns of the knowledge society.

This book aims to provide a comprehensive information on the changing nature of school education in the post-modern, globalising society. It attempts to bring forth and discuss the various strategies adopted at institutional level for improving school functioning whether it is organisation structure, institutional management, classroom organisation, teaching-learning process and so on. It responds to the growing needs of educators and non-educators alike to have a concrete picture of the changing face of schools and information about the programmes to meet sufficiently the demands of fast-changing societies. This will be ar influential work and will set new trends of thinking in school education.

Tushar K Sinha

CONTENTS

1

CHANGING TRENDS IN EDUCATION SYSTEMS

1.1. INTRODUCTION

Human beings have given foremost importance to education irrespective of countries. Their incorrigible thirst for knowledge about nature helps humankind advance forward. Education formalises the process of knowledge acquisition within an institutional framework. Educational institutions also complement the creation of new knowledge by making existing knowledge available in an intelligible format.

1.2. FORMAL EDUCATION

The students who attend regular schools and collages for attaining education is coming under formal education process. Formal education is a process whereby the students attain education through a three level—primary, secondary, tertiary—national educational system, graduating, repeating or dropping out of the system in the journey. Education will only involve that imparted through a schooling system and will as such exclude the so-called 'lifelong learning' acquired outside the formal system. In addition to building a credential, formal education prepares the individual for the labor market where the potential human capital is utilised oftentimes with necessary modifications.

1.3. EDUCATION FOR HUMAN DEVELOPMENT

Education is a form of 'human capital' capable of generating high returns for economic growth. The high literacy rates of western countries suggest that investments in human capital contribute to economic growth by increasing labor productivity, just as a direct augmentation of physical capital employed in other productive sectors would do. It is widely believed that the failure to understand the necessity and extent of social intervention required for educating the individual left many nations. However, the replacement of the skill shortages by growing unemployment among the educated disillusioned developing economies already started questioning the economic value of education developing economies about the economic value of education.

Education is a means for human development. It helps to educate people and thereby eradicate unemployment. Empowerment, or the capacity of poor people to influence institutions, processes, and policies that affect their lives are other benefits of education. Educated women and their children enjoy better health than their uneducated counterparts, partly because they have better access to information; but also because they are more confident and assertive in demanding services.

The decline in infant mortality is a result of the increased educational achievement of the mother. Falling infant mortality rates lead to lower fertility rates, because families aim for net child-survival rates. For disadvantaged societies with low income households, female education doubles the return by providing an in-house teacher for the children. Education prepares poor to participate in markets on more equitable terms, improving the distribution of income in the process. Globalisation and the associated emergence of increasingly knowledge-based systems of production, is strengthening the links between education and poverty reduction, both nationally and internationally

According to Sen, education is an end in itself rather than being a means for growth. Elementary and secondary education, considered as the backbone of every nation's educational system, is available free of cost and attendance is mandatory for all children of certain ages (usually 6 to 16 years) in many of the developed nations. The early childhood and the tertiary levei programmes are not always free in these countries. Many of these countries achieved a close to perfect level of net primary enrolment already.

1.4. Gains from Education

Education helps to uplift a nation from its predicaments. The graduates of the formal education system add to the percentage of working age people (15 to 65 years) with different level of education completed. Even in the cases of near perfect enrollment rates it will take some time to reach an adult population with 100 per cent education. The following area graph for global percentage of primary, secondary and tertiary educated adult population during the period of last 40 years is obtained from the International Futures System, IFs.

1.5. Investing in Education

Education becomes unattainable if there is no money. A major portion of educational investment has to come from public sources considering the high direct and opportunity cost on the part of the individual. Without proper government actions to facilitate the diffusion of knowledge through the provision of, at least, the basic level of education, the newly created knowledge cannot add enough value to generate the required incentive. Investment in education is thus a critical decision that helps the nations in the long run. International comparisons of expenditures for education show considerable variation across countries in the share of national resources devoted to education.

1.6. Universal Trends and Education

Globalisation is a multi-faceted set of processes which include not only the changes which have flowed from the new information technologies and opening up of markets, but also new concepts which mean that 'shrinking space, shrinking time and disappearing borders are linking people's lives more deeply, more intensely and more immediately than ever before'. These global processes will not only make our societies increasingly multicultural and ever more intercultural as the interactions among cultural groups intensify, but also they will force shifts in our educational and development priorities as we assume multiple cultural identities.

Right of everyone to education was the major battle in the Twentieth century. But during this century the struggle was about the purposes of education for all. Whereas education must and should contribute to the productive life of every society, its fundamental purpose is clearly set out in Article 26.2 of the Declaration: 'Education shall be directed to the full development of the human personality and to the strengthening of respect for human rights and fundamental freedoms. It shall promote understanding, tolerance and friendship among all nations, racial and religious groups.'

While there can be no doubt that the destinies of individuals, cultures and nations are being increasingly shaped by the decisions and actions of global players, globalisation is neither new. Globalisation brings with it a mix of opportunities and threats for every nation, culture and educational system. On the one hand, the removal of barriers and new technologies create new possibilities for intercultural exchange and dialogue, but on the other, we face the danger of a new global imperial regime in which one political, economic and communication culture is unilaterally favoured over all others.

The global political and economic forces which lead to the collapse of the communist states can also unleash latent linguistic and racial tensions in states previously held together by force.

Global forces may contribute to the undermining of what Gunter Grass calls the 'Kulturnation,' the core values of the cultural, social and educational system of nations necessary for social cohesion and national identity. Global forces may liberate and empower people from all cultures and nations, but only if we use our new tools to empower the poor, to strengthen intercultural dialogue and to enable all cultural groups to participate in decisions affecting their lives.

1.6.1. Inequality and Polarisation

In the 21st century, at least three global trends pose challenges for education and will make the task of learning to live together ever more important and challenging: inequality, population movements and the new information and communication technologies. UNDP and others have warned that globalisation is increasing the gap between the rich and the poor, between the connected and isolated cultural groups. Inequality within countries certainly has increased dramatically over the past 20 to

30 years. As measured by the Gini co-efficient, the greatest income inequalities are in Latin America, while the most dramatic rises since the 1980s have been in Eastern Europe and the CIS countries.

Inequality between countries has also increased dramatically this century, the income gap between the fifth of the world's richest countries and the fifth living in the world's poorest jumping from 11:1 in 1913, to 30:1 in 1960, and to 74:1 in 1997. Thus today more than one quarter of the population, some 1.3 billion people live, in abject poverty on incomes of less than $1 day, while the assets of the three richest people in the world exceed the combined GNP of all LDCs. Despite the commitments made at Jomtien, Beijing and Copenhagen and the rapid increases in GNP per capita within the OECD countries, there has been a dramatic decline in aid provided for developing countries since 1992.

Private foreign investment and loans have replaced aid, but the UNESCO-ILO studies of structural adjustment show the burden of debt falls most heavily on the public education and health services available to poor and marginalised groups. The research clearly shows that the greater the inequality within a country, the greater the suffering of the poor and the greater the marginalisation of minority cultures.

1.6.2. Cultural Diversity

Increasing population movement is the result of global forces and thus to an exponential increase in intercultural interactions and exchanges. Most nations have long been a mix of cultures, and after years of struggle, the various tribes and cultural groups that now make up modern democratic states have learned to co-exist, even to celebrate difference as a fact of life. But as the extent of intercultural mixing and exchanges increase, we will face new challenges in learning to live together.

Globalisation is opening doors for a highly mobile, highly skilled international elite, it seems to be closing them for many others who will either seek to escape or remain locked in poverty. An estimated 130-145 million people now live officially outside their countries of origin, and there are at least as many illegal migrants. And over 23 million refugees struggle to survive: lacking papers, illegal immigrants, refugees and displaced persons face not only discrimination and exploitation, but also denial of human rights, including the right to education for their children. The sheer numbers of 'others' seeking a better life in another land creates irrational fears among the inter-culturally illiterate, fears too easily exploited by a racist far right.

The majority of people lived in rural areas. But global forces are also accelerating the process of urbanisation. The year 2000 marks a divide from a predominantly rural world to one where the majority of people now live in cities. Of the more than 400 cities with over 1 million inhabitants, 28 are mega-cities with populations of over 8 million, two thirds of which are in developing countries. In the latter, over one third are under 14 years, very poor and make up the bulk of the 30 million or more 'street children.'

The renewed concern for lifelong education stems from such rapidly changing global realities. One can no longer learn enough to be a fully functioning member of a society in one's youth. Extended life expectancy coupled with dramatic changes in economic, social and cultural situations mean that both individuals and societies must continue to learn—or be left behind and become marginalised.

1.6.3. New Information and Communication Technologies (NICT)

The spectacular development of information and communication technologies is the most visible symbol of globalisation and the creation of planetary networks with no structured organisation or centralised management. The NICTs constitute an extra-ordinary resource base for the storing, dissemination and sharing of information, and strengthen intercultural exchanges and democratic participation. They do offer new possibilities for providing access to education for large numbers and isolated communities with economies of scale, multiple channels of communication, visualisation and simulation, and powerful means for the exchange, processing and storage of information. While enhancing the free flow of information, the very openness of our new communication systems make money laundering and dissemination of paedophilia and the culture of violence and racism easier.

In the absence of controls, education systems can be expected to be called upon not only to help equip the young with the skills needed to use new information and communication tools but also to promote moral development and to make wise choices. The second issue of concern relates to the impact on cultures and languages of new technologies and media.

NICT can help preserve threatened languages and cultural products and promote inter-cultural learning and understanding. Amid the multitude of websites and programmes that celebrate travel, adventure and nature, we can find some which do attempt to build a deeper understanding of the cultures of others. NICT also open new opportunities for cultural minorities to interact in their own language and to support multi-lingual instruction.

1.6.4. Influence of Global Trends on Education

The influence of global trends on education lies in existing trends in the delivery of educational programmes. Educational programmes cannot operate without educational materials and equipment and in the absence of quality educational 'services.' Increasingly educational goods and services are being privatised. The Education and Training industry is now North America's second largest accounting for nearly 10 per cent of GDP.

In a highly competitive and polarised world, there has also been a significant growth in the 'shadow education system'—the world of private tutoring: more than half of the students in secondary school receive tutoring in countries like Japan, Mauritius and ROK. In ROK, spending on private tutoring in 1996 was half as much again as public expenditure. Such growth seems to be a social response to inadequacies in government support for education, both in quantitative and qualitative terms, and can only lead to further exacerbation of inequalities and polarisation. If current global trends continue, commercial activity in educational goods and services can be expected to grow substantially and education itself will become more 'globalised.' Highly capitalised educational publishers are shifting from marketing individual titles to marketing services to local publishers, while modern testing agencies are following a similar path.

1.7. Globalisation and Educational Rights

Most developing countries are making steady progress towards the goals of universal primary educational and reducing adult illiteracy, and that despite their limited resources, some developing countries have made surprisingly good progress.

The quest to provide education for all has made little headway in countries ravaged by armed conflict, crippling debt and rapid population growth. In particular, the data show a worrying increase in the number of out-of-school children in the poorest countries, especially in Sub-Saharan Africa.

Poverty can be alleviated through education. But the education offered to the poor and in poor countries is one of the first victims when resources are being cut. Unless the global forces impacting on these countries and their internal situation changes dramatically, our estimates indicate they will fall further behind during the next decade. While most countries have been able to keep pace quantitatively with the growth in numbers, few countries have been able to find the resources to provide a quality education for all. If anything, the quality of the education offered to the masses has suffered.

The transition to a market economy has been extremely difficult for most countries in the region, the economic downturn precipitating cuts in educational expenditure and with that a deterioration in the conditions for teaching and learning, to growing inequality in education and high drop-out rates especially in rural areas. The evidence also suggests that even in the rich countries, increases in income inequality are associated with increases in education and social inequality.

The impact of disadvantage on a particular child's education and subsequent behaviour depends on the cumulative effects of several risk factors including poverty, family breakdown, sustained patterns of impaired child-parent relationships, instability and disruption in key developmental contexts such as the family and school: The research suggests that irrespective of cultural context, it is difficult for families and schools to maintain the sustained care and interaction needed by a child to develop in conditions of poverty, conflict and constant change. There have been many attempts to ameliorate the effect of disadvantage on educational opportunities.

A strong negative correlation between most measures of social and cultural disadvantage and educational outcomes persist. Even a cursory glance at the league tables shows that schools and nations at the top are invariably those of the rich, and those at the bottom the most disadvantaged. Whatever changes are made at the school level or in the education systems of poor countries, their efforts will be constrained to the extent which inequalities within and between countries are structural and powerful mechanisms are maintained to reproduce existing hierarchies, and to the extent that 'social capital' continues to decline as relationships and supportive social networks collapse. The situation has been made worse by policies at national and international levels which deny the right of all to a decent education and thereby undermine the principle that education is a public good and the responsibility of the whole society, especially of governments.

To overcome disadvantage at the individual, national or international level, we need education programmes which respect the cultures and address the realities of the families and children to be served and give priority to the alleviation of poverty and building support structures for families and nations in difficulty. The stark facts on growing inequality and polarisation presented above drive home the reality that it is simply impossible to improve access to education or the quality of the education in poor countries without extra resources, and that within countries extra resources must be found to improve the quality and functioning of schools, families and communities, particularly those located in disadvantaged areas.

Governments and international organisations (public and private) must assume their national and global responsibilities and reallocate resources to meet targets—even if that means taxing the rich, cutting arms expenditure or putting people before profits.

If we do not assume a new path, life will be particularly difficult during the Twenty-first century for the already disadvantaged. At the World Conference on Education for All, we insisted on meeting the basic learning needs of all, the emphasis being on learning achievement, not merely attending school.

However, acquiring the knowledge and skills needed to participate in the life and work of communities in the Twenty-first century is possible only if the essential conditions for learning are present in the formal and non-formal education programmes. In the schools serving the poor and marginalised, these conditions are absent. Children cannot be expected to learn or to stay in school if they are sick, hungry and exhausted, if the school is overcrowded and unsanitary, if there are few or no books and teachers are unpaid and unqualified.

At best progress towards the alleviation of poverty will be slow if the present international economic and political order remains unchanged—if the poorest countries and groups are locked into a seemingly endless downward spiral of poverty, debt, conflict and misery and if inhuman traffic in weapons, drugs, arms, women and children continues unchecked. Education may be the key to the alleviation of poverty and to sustainable development, but not if the global economic order leads us to high quality private education for an elite and a poorly funded and inferior public education system for the masses. There will a global crisis in education if we allow our market forces to polarise the world of education, internationally and nationally.

1.7.1. Globalisation and Higher Education

Global wealth is concentrated less and less in factories and the land, and more and more in knowledge and skills. In the USA human capital is now estimated to be at least three times more important than physical capital. Participation in the rapidly changing knowledge society of the Twenty-first century demands new knowledge and skills and learning throughout life, and higher qualifications than ever before. As a result, the demand for higher education is growing constantly, higher education systems are under great strain to cope with dramatic increases in numbers without a commensurate increase in public funding.

Expansion, both public and private, has been 'unbridled, unplanned and often chaotic' in many countries. The results—deterioration in average quality, continuing inter-regional, inter-country and intra-country inequalities, and increased for profit provision of higher education—could have serious consequences' for developing countries and disadvantaged groups and the very concept of the 'university.' The World Conference on Higher Education sought to 'set the direction needed to prepare higher education for the tasks that await it in the Twenty-first century, and to help mankind and the community of nations to strive out towards a better future, towards a world more just, more humane, more caring and more peaceful' by establishing a few key principles and priorities for action.

The Conference showed the need to strengthen the traditional research and specialised teaching functions of the university, while at the same time to insist on its intercultural and international mission of higher education in the Twenty-first century.

Globalisation processes have led to an unprecedented demand for access to higher education while at the same time most governments are unwilling or unable to provide the necessary support to public institutions. Thus the dramatic growth in private and open higher education, the financial and identity crisis facing universities worldwide, and the intense and increasing competition for overseas students among the big league of internationalised universities and for adult learners from open and virtual corporate universities.

1.7.2. Globalisation and Teacher Education

Significant changes are needed in pre-service teacher education programmes if we are to select and prepare a new generation of teachers equipped with the knowledge, skills and values to help their culturally different and their socially disadvantaged students to learn, to resolve conflicts peacefully, to respect each other's dignity and cultures, and to become socially responsible citizens.

Learning to teach as a deeply personal activity in which includes activities designed to develop sensitivity to cultures, languages and lives of children coming from different social and cultural groups, and which provides constant and significant support, working with cohort groups, and a systematic long-term message which provides guidance and direction for personal development. The direction and culture of educational research must also change if we are to reform educational policies, established practice, curricula and teaching materials in ways which facilitate intercultural learning and ameliorate the problems created by disadvantage and discrimination in education and society.

The content and processes of education in traditional and contemporary cultural contexts; about the conditions under which intercultural learning and conflicts are resolved peacefully in different settings; about how best to select, prepare and support teachers and communities to cope with the realities and contradictions created by shifts in population, technology and policy; about the effectiveness of different approaches to combating violence, racism, substance abuse and suicide in our schools and universities.

The impact of different types of student and faculty exchange programmes, citizenship education, interactive multimedia packages and the web on intercultural sensitivity and the conditions under which various types of learning experiences transfer into acceptance of difference and tolerance in one's own community, school or university.

1.8. Intercultural Education

Global trends mean ever greater mingling of cultures and thus learning to live together, cultural identity and inter-culturality will become priority issues. Given the long history of violence as a means of resolving conflicts among cultural or religious groups, the Delors Report placed learning to live together not simply as one of the four pillars of education for the future, but as the greatest challenge facing education.

Every national education system must give priority in the Twenty-first century to learning to live together 'by developing an understanding of other people and an appreciation of interdependence—carrying out joint projects and learning to manage conflicts—in a spirit of respect for values of pluralism, mutual understanding and peace.' The Delors Commission met in a context in which many of the former communist states were falling apart: cohesion was imposed by an all powerful state apparatus rather than being the product of a participatory and educational process for building unity in diversity and for resolving conflicts. Even in the west, social cohesion seems under threat from a polarised and at times violent 'underclass.'

The most acute crisis facing many countries is that of social cohesion, a crisis fuelled by growing inequality, poverty and exclusion, and a sense of 'social crisis compounded by a moral crisis and the spread of violence and crime.' Its hope for a better future rests with the type of education which promotes cohesion while striving 'to take the diversity of individuals and groups into consideration while taking care that it does not itself contribute to social exclusion.'

1.8.1. Response of Education Systems to Cultural Diversity

One of the prime functions of education has been that of building a social cohesive society—one held together by shared values, purposes and activities in every country. While economic growth often seems to be driving government policy, building social cohesion still remains one of the main purposes of public education, and particularly as our societies become ever more multicultural. Historically, at least four different approaches to cultural diversity have emerged: (a) assimilation: imposing a common nationality (b) melting pot: gradually developing a national culture (c) differentialist: developing a common nationality but minimising interaction with and among minority cultures, and (d) multiculturalism: developing unity within diversity.

In the normative sense, multiculturalism represents a position about the place of cultural identities in contemporary society, stressing that acknowledging the existence of ethnic diversity and ensuring the rights of individuals to retain their culture should go hand-in-hand with enjoying full access to, participation in, and adherence to principles and values of the society. Nations adopting a multicultural approach to education have all sought to develop programmes in which children and adults have opportunities to develop to a reasonable level of competence, both the national language(s) and their mother tongue, and an understanding of the major cultures of the nation. Participation in the multicultural knowledge society of the future will demand even higher levels of language competence and cultural sensitivity as the world shrinks.

Countries adopting a multicultural approach generally acknowledge the need for greater knowledge and understanding of the major religions and other cultures and nations, their languages, history and values, and they increasingly employ staff from diverse ethnic backgrounds. The experience that has accumulated in these countries shows that neither special language programmes nor educational programmes may, in themselves, be sufficient to ensure equality in participation or mutual respect and understanding. The effectiveness of their policies for managing cultural diversity depends not on any one programme of policy initiative but on their cumulative effect. What has also become increasingly clear from a range of studies of social justice initiatives is that there is a need to change the way in which the system and its institutions relate to its students.

1.9. Unfinished National Agendas

1.9.1. Racism, Discrimination and Protection of Minorities

The UN Sub-Commission on the Prevention of Discrimination and Protection of Minorities regularly reports on current trends in racism, racial discrimination, intolerance and xenophobia. It notes with alarm the rise in serious incidents attributable to these phenomena especially in Europe and the tendency to deny the existence of malignant processes in one's own nation, community and life. It warns of the emergence of neo-racism not grounded on biology but on anthropology and of the dark side of an excessive ideological commitment to the virtues of difference which may lead us to believe that different cultures are incapable of learning from each other.

Our schools, universities, media and national leaders have intensified the problems. If OECD countries had expanded their vision of social cohesion, they may well have profited more from the opportunities presented by the end of the Cold War and globalisation. Recognition of the problem of neo-racism and wide public education about the psychology of racism and the impact of the confusion of identities which is taking place in a changing world should make it possible for leaders and educators alike to summon into the public forum what Abraham Lincoln called the 'better angels of our nature.' In no field of education does the issue of intercultural education as a human right have more poignancy than with respect to the rights of indigenous peoples whose languages and way of life is seriously threatened by globalisation and whose right to choose the form of education appropriate for their children has so often denied by assimilation policies.

These changes have eliminated centuries of injustice, prejudice and disadvantage, there is a growing acknowledgement, even appreciation, of the diverse cultures that make up national and global societies. Concurrent with this change have been significant changes within many indigenous communities in some cases a veritable renaissance among indigenous peoples in their cultures, languages, histories and traditional ways of learning.

1.10. Conclusion

The effective functioning of families, schools and educational systems is sensitive to the existence of supportive public policies at the community, national and international level: it has been the poor and marginalised cultural groups who suffered the most from the global economic and political ideologies which the led to the imposition of the structural adjustment, privatisation and cost-sharing programmes which they could ill afford and which have led to a deterioration in the education available to their children.

Education, being contained and utilised by human beings, the patters of demographic transition will influence the investment, achievements and outcomes of education quite heavily. This influence will be more pronounce on the largely populated developing countries, like China or India, which are expected to pass through the demographic transition within the coming decades. Adult education might be more important for these countries to achieve an overall increase in the percentage of educated in the labour force.

The responsibility for respecting human rights and for setting the framework for the educational reforms needed to actualise a shared national vision of education for the Twenty-first century rests first and foremost with governments. The pattern of public expenditure and taxation does have a significant effect on poverty reduction and on the quality and inclusiveness of the education available to all groups in a multicultural society. Our common future will depend on the degree to which we all become better world citizens, creating the unity within diversity which stems from an intercultural education which helps us to build strong cultural roots, to understand and respect the cultures of others and to learn to live together harmoniously in multicultural communities.

References

Barro, Robert J. and Jong-Wha Lee. "International Data on Educational Attainment Updates and Implications." Cambridge, Mass: National Bureau of Economic Research. Working Paper 7911. 2000.

Hicks, Norman. "Economic Growth and Human Resources". World Bank Staff Working Paper No. 408. Washington D.C. 1980.

Hughes, Barry B. *International Futures*. Boulder : Westview Press, 1999.

Lucas, Robert E. "On the Mechanics of Economic Development". *Journal of Monetary Economics*, 22: 3-42. 1988.

Psacharopoulos, George and Maureen Woodhall. *Education for Development: An Analysis of Investment Choice*. New York: Oxford University Press. 1985.

Romer, Paul M. *Human capital and growth: theory and evidence*. Carnegie-Rochester Conference Series on Public Policy, 32:251-286. 1990.

Schultz, T.W. "Education and Economic Growth". In *Social Forces Influencing Economic Growth*, ed., N.B. Henry. Chicago: National Society for the Study of Education. 1961.

Solow, Robert. "A Contribution to the Theory of Economic Growth." *Quarterly Journal of Economics*, 70:65-94. 1956

Wheeler, D. "Human Resource Development and Economic Growth in Developing Countries: A Simultaneous Model". World Bank Staff Working Paper No. 407. Washington D.C. 1980.

2

GLOBALISATION OF EDUCATION

2.1. INTRODUCTION

Globalisation is the buzz word in this new era. The life of people is also in a status of changing. Innovations and inventions in the path of human beings have changed their life a lot. Historic changes are transforming the lives of people in the developed countries and most developing ones. National economies and even national cultures are globalising. Globalisation means more competition, not just with other companies in the same city or the same region.

Barriers have no place in globalisation, which means, the national borders do not limit a nation's investment, production, and innovation. Everything, including relations among family and friends, is rapidly becoming organised around a much more compressed view of space and time. Companies in Europe, the United States, and Japan can produce chips in Singapore, keypunch data in India or the Peoples' Republic of China, out source clerical work to Ireland or Mexico, and sell worldwide, barely concerned about the long distances or the variety of cultures involved. Swatch now sells a watch that tells "Internet time," a continuous time that is the same everywhere in the world. Even children watching television or listening to radio are re-conceptualising their "world," in terms of the meanings that they attach to music, the environment, sports, or race and ethnicity.

Global economy is differed from world economy. World economy has existed since at least the sixteenth century. Rather, a global economy is one where strategic, core activities, including innovation, finance and corporate management, function on a planetary scale on real time. And this globality became possible only recently because of the technological infrastructure provided by improved telecommunication networks, information systems, including the Internet, microelectronics machinery, and computerised transportation systems. Today, as distinct from even a generation ago, capital, technology, management, information, and core markets are globalised.

Globalisation together with new information technology and the innovative processes they foment are driving a revolution in the organisation of work, the production of goods and services, relations among nations, and even local culture. No community is immune from the effects of this revolution. It is changing the very fundamentals of human relations and social life.

Information and innovation are two of the main bases of globalisation, and they, in turn, are highly knowledge intensive. Internationalised and fast-growing information industries produce knowledge goods and services. Today's massive movements of capital depend on information, communication, and knowledge in global markets. And because knowledge is highly portable, it lends itself easily to globalisation. If knowledge is fundamental to globalisation, globalisation should also have a profound impact on the transmission of knowledge.

Globalisation increases the demand for education, especially university education, and this increases pressure on the whole system for higher quality schooling, often producing perverse educational consequences, particularly from the standpoint of equity. An important question for democratic societies and societies transitioning to democracy is whether higher quality education for all is necessarily consistent with individual-centric democracy, particularly in societies marked by deeply rooted ethnic conflicts and weak states.

Globalisation also produces a reaction. This reaction takes many forms, but it seems in the current historical conjuncture to be increasingly focused on ethnic-religious nationalism/regionalism. The implications of the reaction for the transmission of knowledge are also important. Ethnic-religious nationalism represents a search for an identity that is often the antithesis of globalism/internationalism and even individualism. In some cases (religious-based nationalism) it confronts the concept of globalised knowledge as interpreted by the West with a different form of globalised (universal) knowledge, namely religious fundamentalism. In other cases, it confronts globalised knowledge with localised notions of knowledge/identity.

2.2. Globalisation and Educational Demands

Globalisation demands a certain quality in education. In economic point of view, the rising payoffs to higher education in a global, science based, knowledge intensive economy Make University training more of a "necessity" to get "good" jobs. This, in turn, changes the stakes at lower levels of schooling, and drastically changes the function of secondary school. In socio-political point of view, demographics (the changing family) and democratic ideals exchanged or communicated as it is produced.

In a global economy, governments need to stimulate investment, including, in most countries, foreign capital and increasingly knowledge intensive capital, which means providing a ready supply of skilled labour. This translates into pressure to increase the average level of education in the labour force. The payoff to higher levels of education is rising worldwide as a result of the shifts of economic production to knowledge-intensive products and processes, as well as because governments implement policies that increase income inequality. Rising relative incomes for higher educated labour increases the demand for university education, pushing governments to expand their higher education systems, and, correspondingly, to increase the number of secondary school graduates ready to attend post-secondary.

Globalisation also promoted education among women. In countries, such as those in North Africa and the Middle East, that were previously resistant to providing equal access to education for young women, increased competition in product markets and the need for more highly educated labour tends to expand women's educational opportunities.

Most countries have undergone rapid expansion of their primary and secondary education systems. This is not universally true. But thanks to a generalised ideology that basic education should be available to children as a right, even financial constraints in many debt-ridden countries, such as those in Latin

America, did not prevent them from increasing access to basic and even secondary education.

The Soviet Union and the nations it controlled, as well as China, Cuba, and Vietnam, all organised economically and politically under Communist regimes, made especially large investments in education and produced highly schooled populations even in previously illiterate regions, such as Central Asia. The Communists not only expanded educational systems, but also increased the quality of the education in terms of teaching math and language skills. Whatever the reasons for this educational expansion, when these societies opened up to establish market economies and, in some cases, became politically democratic, they entered the new era with relatively highly skilled labour forces and highly literate populations.

In most of the world's societies, university education has also expanded but, given the bias of global demand for the higher educated, the tendency is to push up rates of return to investment in higher education relative to the payoffs to investing in primary and secondary schooling. Rates of return to higher levels of education are also pushed up by structural adjustment policies. These tend to favour those with higher skill levels hooked into the export sector and the multinational companies. Estimated rates of return in countries such as Hong Kong, the Republic of Korea, and Argentina, as well as in a number of the OECD countries, show that rates of return to university education are often as high as or higher than to either secondary or primary. Furthermore, some of these same studies were able to measure rates of return for several different years in the 1970s, 1980s, and 1990s.

Rates of return to university have risen relative to primary and secondary rates. This is certainly the case in the former Communist countries, where university education was not highly rewarded before the 1990s, and now increasingly unequal incomes favour university graduates. Rising rates of return to higher education relative to lower levels of schooling also characterise many countries where measured rates to investment in university remain lower than to investment in primary and secondary.

Rates of return to higher levels of schooling increase not necessarily because the real incomes of university graduates are rising in absolute terms. Real incomes of university graduates could stay constant or even fall but, if the incomes of secondary and primary graduates fall more than those of workers with higher education, the rate of return to higher education rises and pressure on the higher education system increases.

Mark Blaug, Richard Layard and Maureen Woodhall studied the paradox of Indian universities many years ago. Graduates seemed to suffer high rates of unemployment, yet the demand for university education continued unabated. They found that although the rate of unemployment was, indeed, high among university graduates, it was even higher among secondary school graduates. This helped push secondary school graduates to go on to university.

Therefore, globalisation may benefit university graduates only in relative terms, but the implications for general educational investment strategies are the same as if university graduates' incomes were rising more rapidly than incomes of those young people with less schooling. By increasing the relative demand for university graduates more rapidly than universities can expand their supply, globalisation puts continuous pressure on the educational system to expand.

But, many people think that globalisation is reducing demand for unskilled and semi-skilled labour, that the new technology may be reducing demand for labour as a whole, and that countries have to compete for this shrinking demand by keeping wages low. These analysts claim that this is the reason that real wages are falling in most countries.

This is an incorrect analysis of both the effects of globalisation and of the new technology. New information technology displaces many workers, just as all new technologies have done in the past, and this may influence short-term education and training investments: But this aspect of labour markets does not negate the more important issue for educational strategies: globalisation and the new technology are knowledge intensive, and the new labour markets are increasingly information-intensive, flexible, and disaggregative, or individualising, of labour, separating workers from traditional communities. The increasing individualisation of workers and the increasing importance of education in defining individuals' social roles tend to make institutions that transmit and create knowledge, such as schools and universities, new centres of knowledge communities. Individualised families organise their activities around their children's and their own knowledge acquisition.

2.3. Globalisation and Educational Inequality

Quality education is the by product of globalisation. But at the same time, it widens the gap between haves and have-nots. Higher rates of return (both private and social) to higher education have important effects on the rest of the educational system and on income inequality. Rising rates to higher levels of schooling mean that those who get that education are benefited relatively more for their investment in education than those who stop at lower levels of schooling. In most countries, those who get to higher levels of schooling are also those from higher social class backgrounds. So not only do those families with higher social class background have more capital to start with, under these circumstances, they get a higher return to their investments. This is a sure formula for increased inequality in already highly unequal societies.

Higher socio-economic status (SES) students are those who get access to "better" schools in regions that are more likely to spend more per pupil for education, particularly in those schools attended by higher socio-economic class pupils. Competition for such higher-payoff education also increases as the payoff to higher education increases, because the stakes get higher. Higher SES parents become increasingly conscious of where their children attend school, what those schools are like, and whether they provide access to higher levels of education. The total result is therefore that schooling becomes more stratified at lower levels rather than less stratified, especially under conditions of scarce public resources. National economic competition on a global scale gets translated into sub-national competition in social class access to educational resources.

If globalisation pushes up the rates of return to university, intensifying the competition for access to higher education, higher-educated, higher income parents tend to step up the amount they spend on primary and secondary school to assure their children's university enrollment. This means that if promoting private education at the primary and secondary levels through vouchers is part of the strategy to expand access, parents who can afford it are likely to send their children to selective private schools. Even in the public system, wherever possible, parents with more motivation and resources will seek "selective" public schools that serve higher social class clientele. These same parents, willing to spend on the "best" (often private) primary and secondary schools for their children, then end up fighting for high quality, essentially free, public universities.

Likewise, the countries of the former Soviet Bloc, now democratic or transitioning to democracy, are also transitioning from purely state schooling and university systems that focused heavily on vocational education to a system with increasing numbers of private schools and a shift to general education. Further, under Communism, teachers and students were distributed among schools by a centralised state bureaucracy. Since the Soviet economic system was self-contained, the educational systems were insulated from the influence of international competition and increasingly unequal distribution of earning in the rest of the world. In the new democracies, the educational system is no longer insulated, and "quality" teachers and students are increasingly distributed among schools according to the social class of students.

Similarly, globally rising rates of return to university pressure on universities to accommodate more students. But financial constraints on increased public spending for education have pushed countries throughout the world to generate such higher education expansions by allowing for the rapid growth of private universities, often financed at least partly by Ministry subsidies to students.

These private universities compete for students but, in fact, the number of students wanting a degree is so great that competition hardly has to be fierce to attract students. Even so, private universities in some countries, such as Malaysia, "twin" with European and Australian universities to draw students. Most of these students are not "good enough" to get into the top public universities, so a private one, high fees and all, is their best hope for a professional career.

2.4. Globalisation and Women's Education

Globalisation also appears to have raised the rate of return to women's education. In many countries rates of return to education for women are higher than for men. The reasons for the increased participation of women in labour markets are complex, but two main factors have been the spread of feminist ideas and values and the increased demand for low-cost semi-skilled labour in developing countries' electronics manufacturing and other assembly industries. The world-wide movement for women's rights has had the effect of legitimising equal education for women, women's control over their fertility rates, women's increased participation in wage labour markets, and women's right to vote. The increased demand for low-cost labour and greater sense by women that they have the same rights as men has brought enormous numbers of married women into wage employment world-wide. This, in turn has created increased demand for education by women at higher and higher education levels. So, globalisation is accentuating an already growing trend by women to take as much or more education than men.

But, this does not mean that women receive wages equal to men's. That is hardly the case. Nor does it mean that women are taking higher education in fields that are most lucrative, such as engineering, business, or computer science. That is also far from true. Women are still vastly under-represented in the most lucrative professions even in the most "feminised" countries, such as Sweden or the United States. But globalisation seems gradually to be changing that, for both positive and negative reasons. The positive reasons are that flexible organisation in business enterprise requires flexible labour, and women are as or more flexible than men, and that information technology and telecommunications are spreading democratic ideas worldwide.

Women are paid much less than men almost everywhere in the world, and it is profitable for firms to hire women and pay them lower wages than men. Yet, both sets of reasons gradually seem to be driving both the education and the price of women's labour up relative to men's. For example, the percent of women in science and engineering university faculties is increasing worldwide. Although such increased "professionalisation" of women may contribute to the transformation of family life, it does serve to democratise societies and raise greatly the average level of schooling.

2.5. Demographic Changes and Education

Education has totally changed the life of women. Most of the educated women prefer to stand on their on foot and because of this they get marry in older age. Since they start bearing children when they are older, they end up having fewer children than less-educated women who marry at a younger age. In the developed countries, this appears to be the dominant pattern. In the developing countries, the pattern may be more complicated, especially because infant mortality rates may be considerably higher in low-income families.

Greater fertility among less-educated, lower-income families affects societies, especially in the current global environment. It means that most children may be growing up in families that cannot prepare them adequately for the ever-higher educational requirements needed to succeed in labour markets. This is not to say that higher educated men and women make better parents than those with less education. But being a parent in the global economy requires much more information than in the past, and the stakes in children's educational success are much higher. On average, less-educated parents are increasingly at a disadvantage in supplying what it takes for young children to be prepared to do well in school.

Children living in families with less-educated parents are significantly behind middle-class children when they enter school, and there is no evidence that they catch up as they move through the grades. This potential problem is accentuated by three other factors. First, income distribution in many countries has become more unequal in the past generation, with the real incomes of less-educated families stagnating or even declining. The second is that a high fraction of females heading households are not only poor because they are women, but are doubly poor because they have low levels of schooling. The third factor is public investment in the early care and education of children worldwide is low. Under these three conditions, the ability of children of less-educated families to escape poverty is the exception rather than the rule.

Since the family is still the entity responsible for child rearing, differences in access to information and networks extant among social groups are likely to be reproduced from this generation into the next. The State can and should play an important role in offsetting differences in access to resources and information. This may be the only way to raise achievement for lower income children.

Changing labour markets and demographics combine to create major changes in universities as well. In the past twenty years, "new" demand for higher education in both developed and developing countries have come mainly from two groups that traditionally did not attend universities: a "rising" lower-middle social class and women. These sources will continue to fuel higher educational expansion and will be fighting for more places in elite institutions. But a major source of growth in population in developed and developing countries is now and will continue to be very low-educated families, many of them disadvantaged majorities in the developing countries and disadvantaged minorities in the developed countries. The increasing proportion of such children in secondary school is already posing a serious dilemma for educational policy.

As secondary education becomes increasingly less valuable in labour markets, this growing part of the school population becomes the next "wave" of potential college graduates, yet in the traditional sense, they may not be "prepared" for college education. Poverty rates in developing countries are much higher, and this means that universities will face similar or even greater problems as they expand than those in developed countries. Even though most of the children raised in poor families today, especially in developing countries, are unlikely to get access to universities, as universities in developing countries expand more rapidly than incomes rise, they will take increasing numbers of young people from such "disadvantaged" backgrounds.

The AIDS virus could drastically reduce the number of children from lower income families who reach college age, as well as drastically reducing population growth over the next generation in many parts of Africa, including South Africa. In these countries, population growth rates may approach developed country levels not because of lower fertility rates, but higher death rates. Even so, the pressure for university expansion will be great and the students entering university will increasingly come from low-income, low-education families.

2.6. Impacts of Globalisation on Education

One of the major impacts of globalisation on education is increased pressure to improve the quality of schooling. This is the result of the increased pressure on economies to be more productive in the face of greater competition. Part of the formula for increasing educational quality pushed by international organisations has been the decentralisation of educational administration, including promoting competition in the educational sector from private education and through parent choice of schooling for their children. The notion of dismantling centralised educational bureaucracies in favour of school autonomy and school competition is based on the notion of greater efficiency associated with markets and local control.

There are important political reasons for local control of educational decision-making, but unless there exists an even distribution of capacity to manage and deliver education at the local level or among schools, there is a high probability that decentralisation would contribute to greater inequality in the quality of schooling. Parent choice and increased competition among schools is supposed to increase educational quality, but this also assumes that the management and teaching capacity exists across schools to respond to increased competition. Again, it is likely that in lower-income areas, there is less capacity to increase quality in response to competition, hence schools in those areas will tend to lose better students to schools with higher social class student bodies, and quality might decrease further.

There are other factors associated with democratisation of centralised, authoritarian societies that may also reduce the quality of schooling during this process. Centralised, authoritarian societies tend to be more economically equal and more socially ordered societies. Democratisation and marketisation is associated with increased income and social inequality, greater choice, and less order. This often means greater violence, more child labour, and greater spatial mobility, all factors that have a negative impact on student achievement, especially among lower-income students.

Unless there is a strong civil society (community) to replace central authoritarian institutions, state-driven social capital is not replaced by family and community social capital, and schools become less effective because it becomes more costly to produce student achievement than before the democratic transition. When school decentralisation is added to these other factors, we would expect not only a decline of student achievement, but much greater disparity of student achievement among social classes than under centralised authoritarianism.

This is one of the great contradictions of the transition to democracy in the formerly Communist societies. It is also one of the great contradictions of globalisation. On the one hand, globalisation represents the next stage of democratisation-this time on a world scale; on the other hand, globalisation threatens democratisation with increased social inequality and increased inequality in access to the high quality of education needed to develop democracy to that next level. Globalisation may also weaken the power of the national state or regional governments to control economic development and the demand for education to the degree that they could in the past. Globalisation may even pose a threat to decreasing the quality of education in many societies, or at least posing major barriers to increasing educational quality.

2.7. Globalisation and Social Development

More than to impart skills needed for work, education does much. Schools are transmitters of modern culture. The meaning of modern culture as interpreted by the state is a crucial issue for educators and is contested in every society. Globalisation redefines culture because it stretches boundaries of time and space and individuals' relationship to them. It reduces the legitimacy of national political institutions' to define modernity. So globalisation necessarily changes the conditions of identity formation. Individuals in any society have multiple identities. Today, their globalised identity is defined in terms of the way that global markets value individuals traits and behaviour.

Global markets value certain kinds of knowledge much more than others. As noted in the discussion of the changing market for skills, one major feature of global markets is that they place high value on scientific and technical knowledge and less on the kinds of local, artisan skills which serve more basic needs. The global market does not work well as a source of identity for everyone. Markets also increase material differences among individuals.

Even if the market creates a sense of community among those who share the same professional networks, it also continuously destroys communities, isolating individuals until they are able to find new networks and new sources of social worth. With the individualisation of workers and their separation from "permanent" jobs, even the identity individuals have with work places becomes more tenuous and subject to more frequent change.

Today's co-workers are not necessarily tomorrow's friends. Globalisation is not the only force changing modern culture. Important social movements have challenged globalisation in favour of cultural singularity and local control over people's lives and their environment. Caught in between are the traditional mainstays of culture: religion, nationalism, gender relations, and the power relations that have developed historically in local regions, for example because of landowning pattern.

Religious identity is another direction to which the less globally successful turn. Religious fundamentalism is on the rise worldwide. It rejects the market as authority, and although fundamentalist groups have targeted the nation-state as a power base, there is an inherent contradiction between religious fundamentalism and a territorially defined nation. The same contradiction does not exist when it comes to local communities or to globalised movements for religious identity. But religious localism necessarily means communities based on exclusion. Even ethnic movements move away from their inclusionary focus. Rather than centering on nation-state legislative and financial intervention that includes the particular ethnic or race group in the national project, they now focus on cultural identities independent from the national project or seek recognition in global terms, above nationality.

The appeal to fundamentalism is strongest for those who feel simultaneously threatened by the "inclusiveness" of a multiculturalist version of welfare democracy that offers a bureaucratic vision of nationality, and the "inclusiveness" of the global market that serves the power of money and complex information systems. Cultural identity, whether religious, ethnic, racial, or gender, and whether local, regional or more global, is an antidote to the complexity and harshness of the global market as the judge of a person's worth. For nationalists, cultural identity is also an antidote to the globalised bureaucratic state. But such a trend could mean increased social conflict.

If some localities/ethnicities/religious groupings feel increasingly excluded from the high end of the market, a weakened nation-state incapable of reincorporating them socially could mean less stability. Even though the political positions of various nationalist movements may differ considerably, they all tend to play to the sense for many of exclusion from participating in the fruits of globalising national economies. The market in itself has never been sufficiently inclusive. Strong undemocratic, non-egalitarian nation-states existed before the free market dominated economic systems, so many believe that states are no guarantee of inclusion. But the modern capitalist state developed into a successful market "softener."

The decline of that role in the face of powerful global marketisation of national economies pushes the "dispossessed" to seek refuge in new and more exclusive collectives. These collectives generally do not have the power or the funds to help the dispossessed financially nor to develop the skills and knowledge valued by global markets. They can help develop self-knowledge and therefore self-confidence. They can provide community and therefore a sense of belonging. They often do so by defining others as "outsiders" without the "true" self-knowledge or the "right" ancestors.

The communities are often highly undemocratic. If the nation-state does not have the financial capability or the political legitimacy to dissipate such movements by incorporating its members into much broader notions of community and values, societies unable to maintain market success may face serious, irresolvable divisions.

The conflicts in identity formation necessarily affect education. The distribution of access to schools and universities, as well as educational reforms aimed at improving its quality, are all headed toward forming labour for a market conditioned by globalisation.

Education can become more inequitable rather then more inclusive. Thus, in any strategy, central governments must still assume responsibility for levelling the playing field for all groups. This is particularly true because left-out groups see the educational system as both crucial to knowledge acquisition yet not serving the needs of their "community." Schools and the educational system become primary targets for social movements organised around "self-knowledge," such as religious or ethnic identity. The educational system has enormous resources devoted to knowledge formation for dominant groups.

Much of the struggle between religious fundamentalists and the secular, rational state, is over state education. The public sector has the funds to place children in an educational institution, but not the commitment to create a moral community. Instead, the state has succumbed to crass materialism on a global scale. Fundamentalists want to attract those who are not happy with their value in a world economy, and to educate them and their children in a way that will strengthen religious affiliation, not economic productivity. The more they succeed, the less the educational system will be able to develop global economy workers.

Schools and universities are the site of intense struggles over the definition of culture, they represent to those who are not included in the global economy the single most important route to access global culture. Minority groups may try to control the cultural norms purveyed by schools and universities, but they often engage in such battles believing that their children should have a chance to learn skills valued by the global economy.

Decentralisation of educational management to meet the goal of empowering regional and local social movements makes eminent sense when it is these movements that seek to gain control of the educational institutions that affect their children Educational democratisation movements have pushed for more power for parents and teachers at the educational site.

Decentralisation of control could promote greater educational productivity and greater sense of community when it is communities themselves that want that control. It might also effectively assuage groups seeking greater self-identity through influencing the production of knowledge in schools.

Besides, pro-active movements, such as feminism and environmentalism, post-modern in their outlook and in direct conflict with globalisation, are attempting to redefine the conception of "global" in the education system. For example, feminism is gradually shaping global culture to include gender equality and equity, first in education, then in labour markets. Environmentalism has had an enormous impact on global culture through environmental programmes in schools worldwide. These pro-active movements are having a major impact on how schools define new global culture, and in that sense, are most closely associated with challenges to the techno-economic definition of globalised culture.

In this struggle, education plays and will continue to play a fundamental role. The women's movement has made significant inroads into the educational system even in traditional Muslim countries. This reflects the movement's power over the past generation to shape knowledge institutions at the heart of the globalisation process.

2.7.1. Educational Policy in Modern Societies

In knowledge formation, globalisation is having significant impact because it revalues different types of knowledge, particularly the knowledge associated with higher levels of education. As it does so, it increases the pressure to expand higher education and it increases the competition at lower levels of schooling among families trying to "game" the education system for their children's social mobility. This increases the potential for greater inequality of access to quality education, even as globalisation brings new kinds of people into universities and other types of post-secondary schooling.

For societies in the transition to democracy from state socialism-those in Eastern Europe to those in Central Asia-the transition in the context of this economic globalisation poses great challenges for educational policies. The transition societies have generally inherited well-developed, high quality educational systems, in which teachers used to be paid wages little different from wages paid to other professionals. With the disintegration of their command economies and their insertion into global markets, these societies' social services, including education, have suffered severe budget constraints. Teaching has become a relatively low-paid profession, and private funding of schooling has increasingly supplemented public funding, with predictable increases in inequality of access to quality education and ensuing declines in average student academic performance. Correspondingly, increasing institutional diversity has also marked universities.

2.7.2. Ethnic and Class Competition

In some countries local ethnic groups are making access to higher education for Russian-origin young people more difficult. The opening of these societies has therefore not been able to overcome the prejudices and conflicts inherent in nineteenth and twentieth century history. Rather than being a path to resolving such prejudices and conflicts, the educational system in the new democracies is often at the forefront of the conflict. The difficulty of maintaining relatively high levels of K-12 schooling quality for young people in the opening societies is part of the overall problems created by increasing economic and social inequality. The increase in inequality poses a potential threat to the deepening of democratic institutions.

Educational privatisation, while an important source of new funding for resource-starved schools, simultaneously threatens conceptions of fairness and equity that are key to the deepening of civil society and democratic institutions.

Families cannot be faulted for trying to use private resources to give their children the best chance possible at social mobility in the new market economy. As a stopgap measure to assure that at least some fraction of the school-age population gets high quality schooling, greater inequality of access to quality education may a necessary, if not entirely satisfactory, way to provide social services. Similarly, in higher education, students and their families want to do what is necessary for the university to make them valuable in the global economic system.

Educational institutions, as the main sites of knowledge transmission in a knowledge economy, are the new loci of community formation. Higher education institutions are not only sites of community formation but, as in the past, also continue to act as centers of cultural leadership. Schools and universities are therefore under new kinds of pressures because global market culture is highly exclusive and destructive of local culture and, furthermore, also stresses individuality, competition, and unequal outcomes-factors that are not very consistent with building democratic institutions, particularly in societies that have long been accustomed to considerable emphasis on equity, at least in education, income, and employment. The new and contradictory pressures from greater competition and inequality will be played out in expanding educational systems over the next generation.

2.8. Multicultural Education

Schools and universities do not just serve to add market worth to students hoping for a place in the globalised economy. Universities are definers of culture for national and diverse regional and local communities. In many ways schools and universities are also cultural centers as such.

The school or university may represent for a community a center of particular culture in a multicultural society, or, may represent a new definition of multiculturalism. Thus, the school or university becomes an important site of conflict between global culture qua preparing students to be economically successful in a global economic environment (scientific, global, economically-valued knowledge) and local cultural forms that build self-identity (self-knowledge).

This self-identity is an antidote to a global identity that fails to include even many university graduates in the developing countries. It may be also be consistent with a new kind of globalism that creates incorporative multicultural forms. The newly open societies face additional problems of ethnic conflicts and increasing social class inequality. If states in the opening societies contribute to the cultural conflict by using education to exacerbate cultural divisions, new social identities consistent with democracy on a global environment will be impossible to achieve. All this complicates further the incorporation of all these groups equitably into the global knowledge society.

Today's more globalised notion of national identity in a period of declining state power makes it less logical to impose a narrow sense of national, regional or local culture. Since markets are increasingly global, an individual's economic value is determined by broader criteria than his or her local "acceptability."

Declining state capacity to impose norms creates political space for counter-dominant concepts of self-knowledge. In practice, groups that do not do assimilate well into the global market knowledge culture have greater political options today than even a generation ago of forming relatively autonomous cultural groups with their own knowledge institutions. This is true for fundamentalist religious groups as well as particular immigrant groups wanting to preserve language and native culture.

In terms of how school systems and universities may react to globalisation, these approaches to a self-knowledge community very different from those of the past. Two models come to mind. The first is one where the state allows any community group to create a knowledge institution with public funds as long as it met minimum legal criteria. Each community in a society could therefore socialise its children and transmit knowledge in the way it chose. This implies a vision of society where groups with widely different beliefs are held together by market relations but not necessarily other common bonds. Those who support educationai vouchers, charter schools, and ethnic or religious schools and universities catering toward very different groups tend toward this approach. The second model is one where the state uses a multi-cultural self-knowledge approach to socialise all young people in the public system. This multi-cultural approach differs from totally autonomous definitions of self-knowledge by each group. Neo-conservatives critique multi-culturalism in the form that could certainly occur under a voucher system or charter schools, educational alternatives pushed by neoconservatives. The state (national, regional, or local community) continues to impose an ideological perspective, but one that reflects the diversity of today's post-industrial societies.

The first model assumes that market relations (the profit motive) are enough to keep increasingly diverse societies working together successfully. To build social capital, diverse communities need to share common social experiences. In knowledge-based society, a common school and university experience with young people having at least some diversity in background and values serves this function.

Globalisation of education and schooling has four major dimensions. It began in medieval times, particularly from the eleventh century onward, with the revitalisation and bureaucratisation of the Western Church and the accompanying establishment of a decentralised European "system" of education for the production of clergy and secular officials. That dimension will be treated only briefly in favour of more recent developments. In the nineteenth century we find international comparisons and rivalries between countries involved in the initial construction of mass schooling, a process of mutual imitation that gave schooling a largely uniform structure among these competing countries.

In the twentieth century, educational globalisation intensified with the spread of the state as the dominant political form everywhere in the world, with the consequence that the construction of national educational systems became a ubiquitous endeavour, along with the establishment and growth of transnational or global organisations concerned with education. These organisations, especially UNESCO and the many non-governmental bodies associated with UNESCO, came to constitute a normatively authoritative "global center" for the discussion and implementation of educational ideas and organisational models.

2.9. Intellectualisation of Education

In the nineteenth century, most writing about education was moral-philosophical, concerned with prescriptions for the "proper" aims and methods of education rather than analyses of educational institutions' origins and actual operations. When analysis began to supplement prescription, internationally-oriented work quickly settled on the comparative study as the favoured model. Still common today, this model is usually a theoretical, concerned mainly with describing similarities and differences in the educational systems of two or a few countries and treating only speculatively such issues as the relative effectiveness of different systems or methods.

Economists began to incorporate education into their models via the concept of "human capital," first as a convenient residual category to account for economic growth not explained by conventional factors of production, later as a variable measured by school completion rates. On the sociological side, theories of the origins and effects of schooling received formal statement. Functionalist theory described schooling as a product of urbanisation and industrialisation in nineteenth-century Europe; for less developed countries, schooling was supposed to be an engine for modernisation, reversing the original causal relationship.

Schooling's effects were presumed to operate through the changes they wrought in individual students, and these changes were seen as beneficial both to the students themselves (empowering them as modern economic and political actors) and to the societies that schooled them. These were the ideas that came to dominate in transnational and intergovernmental educational organisations, particularly UNESCO and the host of non-governmental bodies associated with it.

The intellectualisation process crystallised into what can best be described as an unofficial but authoritative world ideology regarding education, a received wisdom that national schooling systems sought to implement as fully as possible. Consultants, advisers, and experts from global organisations became active agents of this ideology, teaching national school officials how to construct their systems in accordance with it.

Challenges to the received wisdom appeared in several guises from the late 1960s onward. Scholars reacting against the generally harmonious tone of functionalism emphasised the stratifying effects of schooling, developing theories of education as elite social control or as status competition among ethnic, religious, and class-based groups.

Careful historical studies overturned the presumed connection between modernisation and schooling, showing that schooling often preceded urbanisation and industrialisation and that education's effects on economic and political development were often small, sometimes negative, and at best ambiguous.

Education is better conceptualised as the symbolic transformation of individuals in line with idealised models of the good citizen than as a mechanism for the transmission of directly useful skills, attitudes, and self-concepts. So far, however, this and the other challenges to functionalist thinking on education have made little headway in the global education sector. The view that education is indispensable to economic growth, political modernisation, and individual development remains the bedrock of educational policy almost everywhere. Still only two decades old, global analysis has so far neglected several major issues in world educational development.

Traditional educational institutions in numerous societies have been ignored. Even though contemporary models of mass schooling derive mainly from the European experience, the interplay between traditional and contemporary models must enter the analysis. Much of the evidence regarding globalisation is purely formal. Researchers use readily available data on such matters as policy statements, official enrollments, and curricular plans for the allocation of teaching time, rather than the much less accessible information about actual administrator behaviour, student attendance, or teacher use of classroom time. The links between formal structure and everyday action must receive greater attention.

2.10. Conclusion

The development of a nation depends on the educated community. With the advent of globalisation the importance of education wide spread and it also raised the standard of education. The states also started giving primary importance to education because it needed intellectual people for the governance.

References

Arnove, Robert F., Philip G. Altbach, and Gail P. Kelly (eds.). *Emergent Issues in Education: Comparative Perspectives*. Albany: State University of New York Press, 1992.

Castells, M.*The Rise of the Network Society*. London: Blackwell. 1996.

Fuller, Bruce, and Richard Rubinson (eds.). *The Political Construction of Education: The State, School Expansion, and Economic Change*. New York: Praeger, 1992.

Meyer, John W., David Kamens, Aaron Benavot, Yun-Kyung Cha, and Suk-Ying Wong. *School Knowledge for the Masses: World Models and National Primary Curriculum Categories in the Twentieth Century*. London: Falmer, 1992.

Meyer, John W., Francisco Ramirez, Richard Rubinson, and John Boli[-Bennett]. "The World Educational Revolution, 1950-1970." *Sociology of Education* 50: 242-58. 1977.

3

ICTS AND SCHOOL REFORMS

3.1. Introduction

Schools are the nurturing ground for far-reaching changes. A variety of instructional reforms is under way, driven by a perceived need to reorient schooling from rote learning, shallow but wide coverage, and individualistic learning processes to higher level skills, problem solving, in-depth study, and collaborative learning. These reforms take different forms in different countries. Some are using curriculum standards and performance assessments to drive teachers and administrators to account for the success of all learners, especially the traditionally marginalised. Other countries are depending more on improved staff development and revised curricula, emphasising learning to learn as well as interactive, collaborative skills. Life-long learning is also a major concern although policies and programmes aimed at this broad area are often not visible in schooling.

Information and Communication Technologies (ICT) help to improve the quality of education and so, many countries around the world are investing in it by providing high quality education to their younger generations. Hardware and software industries continue their fast expansion and development, with new products for the educational system constantly emerging. As a consequence, many developing countries are facing a double challenge: First, they face a growing educational divide in terms of access to digital resources and services and of human capacity to take advantage of them; and second, when addressing the issues involved in defining ICT in education policy, decision-makers in these countries are experiencing increasingly complex scenarios.

Educational ICT revolution is going in parallel with educational reform. Every OECD country is working to install networks in schools, connect them to the Internet, and ensure a workable configuration of multimedia computers, educational software, technical support, and ICT-competent teachers. Building initially on the foundation of educational computing created in the 1980s, which centred on computer assisted instruction, this movement took a dramatic step forward in the 1990s by stressing professional development for teachers to use technology and focusing on the integration of ICT into a modern, teacher-taught curriculum. Computers moved to the classrooms as well as to the hallways, libraries, and laboratories and became productivity tools for students and teachers as well as communication hubs. This approach contrasted dramatically with the test-and-drill, learning games, and teacher-proof individual instructional programmes and integrated learning systems that dominated ICT use in many countries in the previous decades.

Defining an ICT policy is becoming increasingly difficult because of the many promises and differing alternatives that are presently available. Education has turned into a huge global market with aggressive players in place for countries willing to invest in e-learning, hardware, software, and networks. However, the growing evidence from large-scale programmes that has lasted for years and has documented their successes now offer ample opportunities for policy-makers to take advantage of these initiatives and thus avoid many mistakes, harbour more realistic expectations and eventually reduce costs on new programme implementations.

Well-trained and motivated teachers can improve the learning conditions with ICT, and can acquire ICT skills together with their students, thus preparing them more properly for the emerging knowledge society. Classroom, school and system-wide information management processes may also be enhanced through ICT, freeing teachers from clerical tasks, making information flow more efficient and transparent inside the educational system, and helping policy-makers with more timely and accurate decision-relevant data. ICT are also an equity issue in many developing countries where low income and isolated rural schools may use them to dramatically enhance their learning tools and resources and connect students with other realities, peoples and educational projects around the world.

Introducing ICT into the schools, without a proper staff development plan and without a pedagogical perspective, is a low-return investment. Technology is still expensive and requires constant support at the school level for hardware and network repairs and software configurations, updates and management. Relevant digital educational content, both from the Internet and from CDs is an important consideration that needs careful attention, especially in terms of addressing learning needs, teaching practices and models that may become critical factors inside the classroom.

A long-term commitment from various levels of government is needed for implementing an ICT policy in education. Therefore, this chapter offers a few guidelines for programme implementation in terms of management needs and programme enhancement. A sound evaluation strategy of the ICT programme, with achievement standards and performance indicators, will help in providing accountability. It will also be of great value for the program's management team once it gets into its implementation stages.

3.2. Importance of ICT in Education

Ever since the inception, Information and Communication Technologies (ICT) have been utilised by education, but they have been massively present in schools only since the early 1980s. Developed countries have applied them to K-12 education for a variety of reasons, most of which are still valid today, although in many cases they have remained unfulfilled expectations.

ICT are the pre-eminent tools for information processing, new generations need to become competent in their use, should acquire the necessary skills, and therefore must have access to computers and networks during their school life. There is an equity issue in this argument related to the need to prioritise access to ICT resources to the more underserved population, which is being left behind on a digital divide.

They are versatile and powerful tools that can help in this purpose and should therefore be present in every classroom, library and teacher room. It must be said, however, that so far ICT have not provided any large-scale breakthrough in learning improvements. They are still promises with great potential.

A technology-centred policy, i.e. one that focuses primarily on deploying machines, software and Internet connections, will not produce meaningful results or the expected impact on students learning. Although machines and networks are a fundamental component in any ICT policy, to achieve effective gains in student's learning, improved teaching practices and more efficient management at all levels (classroom, school, district and nation), the focus should reside on people and how to improve and develop their skills and practices with the help of ICT. In order to have long lasting effects, to be effectively infused into the schools' culture, and to be considered relevant by teachers and school administrators, an ICT policy should preferably not be designed in isolation. Rather, it should be part of a more comprehensive effort towards improving the equity and quality of an educational system.

Educational initiatives ought to be coordinated through all possible administrative and operational levels in order to effectively send coherent messages to teachers, parents and administrators.

3.3. Role of ICT in Education

Inside a school, ICT can and should play a variety of roles. Some of the more important ones are pedagogical, cultural, social, professional and administrative. ICT, if sensibly deployed and with carefully selected software, can positively affect many aspects of school life, from a healthy questioning of present teaching practices to a gradual improvement of the quality, scope and depth of the learning environment, as well as to provide a remarkable opportunity for teachers' development.

3.3.1. Pedagogical Role

Providing a new framework that can foster a revision and an improvement of teaching and learning practices is important role of ICT inside a school. Though many positive results have been reported on a small scale, there has been no breakthrough in learning improvements because of ICT on a large, replicable scale. Nevertheless, teachers and students can take advantage of the growing availability of educational resources as software packages and Web pages. Teachers will need curricula-related content and clear strategies and examples to effectively use these materials in the classroom.

Students can become highly motivated towards learning if technology makes up part of their classroom experience. Teachers can fruitfully use this positive attitude to explore new learning strategies in which students can be more actively involved in learning, as opposed to being simply passive information receivers. Collaborative, project-based and self-paced learning are just a few alternatives amply documented and particularly appropriate to use when ICT are present. Primary and secondary students with special talents (i.e. mathematics, music or literature) will find a vast amount of digital tools and resources as well as groups of similarly inclined youngsters all over the world with whom to share and develop their talents.

Students with special needs will also find resources and tools for remedial or self-paced learning. This can have a particularly high impact on more deprived and culturally isolated schools where primary students have fewer information resources and learning opportunities. However, it is important to emphasise that it is not the presence of technology in itself that will stimulate significant changes inside a school. Without teacher involvement, most students in primary levels in particular, but also in higher levels may not take advantage of all the available potential on their own. Teachers need to become active participants for effective ICT educational use, such as providing guidance, help and usage rules for the students. Teachers are needed to organise the learning spaces and to guide toward the achievement of significant learning objectives.

In developing countries, students often do not acquire sufficient mathematical skills, a basic understanding of scientific concepts or an adequate reading comprehension level during their school years.

ICT provides tools and content to exercise these abilities, which will be needed to take advantage of the vast amount of content present in today's networks. Information processing skills to transform data (i.e. searching, selecting, synthesising and communicating information) into knowledge is rapidly becoming a basic requirement for the emergent information society. If ICT policies are closely related to the curriculum, teachers will more likely use them for learning practices in classrooms.

Curriculum designers should consider the inclusion of ICT as transversal themes, i.e. in all curricular sectors, and in the curriculum-specification guidelines that will be used by teachers. It is not advisable to have ICT as separate, isolated technical subjects or sectors in the curriculum, because in this atmosphere, teachers will tend to regard ICT as special subjects and may not integrate them in their normal practice. Rather, ICT should be included as teaching and learning resources, along with examples of how to use them in classrooms, in all sectors, and in this way, turning them, explicitly, into a tool for all teachers in all grades and subject areas.

3.3.2. Cultural, Social, and Professional Roles

The cultural, social and professional roles of ICT are exercised primarily through an effective use of the vast amount of information sources and services available today via Internet and CD-based content for the entire educational community: students, teachers, administrators and parents. Also, nowadays new equipment and low-cost portable keyboards5 with text-handling capacities are helping teachers around the world with their professional routines. A school connected to the Internet can foster communication at local (i.e. inside a community), national and international levels. Educational projects that connect students and teachers from different countries might amplify the quality of the conversational spaces, may expand students' horizons by allowing them to know and interact with people from other cultures and can stimulate group work and social interaction.

Bandwidth and communication quality can become major constraints. A low bandwidth and/or poor quality communication infrastructure can restrict network usability to text-only e-mails, limited to a few times a week. This is a far cry from the potential benefits of e-learning and from participating in professional groups and learning circles using high bandwidth connections. This is particularly important for geographically and/or culturally isolated schools, which are common in rural and suburban areas. With up-to-date communications technology in place, students and teachers in these settings may experience a reduction in their cultural isolation and a significant improvement in their learning resources. Again, this will be highly dependent on the quality of the telecommunications infrastructure and its cost.

3.3.3. Administrative Roles

In making school administration less burdensome and more effectively integrated to the official information flow about students, curricula, teachers, budgets and activities through the educational system information pipelines, ICT have important roles to play. They are also a good means for informing community members (parents, politicians, and researchers) about educational news and policies.

Teachers can more easily keep student's marks and their personal and academic records permanently up-to-date, as well as produce all required data for school administration and for parents, using preformatted documents. Most importantly, teachers can maintain their subject content (lesson plans, exercises, evaluation) in digital format, making it easy to update, to share with other teachers and to enhance with time.

The many ways tools such as a computer, a handheld device or a portable keyboard (and a network) can help a teacher in administrative tasks is one of the more convincing arguments to make to inexperienced teachers so they will accept training eagerly. This should be carefully considered during teacher-training planning because before pedagogical use in the classroom, many teachers may prefer to become familiarised first with the technology outside the classroom. This can often be facilitated greatly by starting out with software applications or simple devices such as portable keyboards or handhelds that can be of immediate use. It is relatively easy to learn how to use these machines to store text in a portable keyboard, to construct spreadsheets, or to make use of word processing to record students' marks and records.

Policy-makers may consider the introduction of ICT at all three levels (classroom, school, system) as a great opportunity to acquire and to distribute information through the system and from the general public to the classroom teacher. A coordinated effort can achieve economies of scale and compatibility of information processes and flows at all levels.

There are a number of software packages for all these levels of usage, which should be carefully evaluated by the teachers and the school administration to assess their completeness, their adaptability to the school's reality and the level of support offered by the software vendors.

Educational systems are known as stable institutions, not prone to rapid changes and innovations. It is possible that a significant number of teachers and school administrators will resist the introduction of ICT in their schools. In this regard, a powerful modelling example is that of a Ministry of Education that introduces ICT to its management, gradually pressing all levels of administration—central, regional, district and school—to use technology for all their information processing needs, including information gathering and distribution. At the most important level—the school—the pressure to provide and receive information to and from the central system digitally is a powerful message and a driving force towards change.

Centralised systems normally have a well-consolidated circuit of information flow to and from all levels of the system. A change in a general rule or ordinance generally moves gradually through the circuit until it eventually reaches the classroom teacher or the parents if it is relevant to them. It is an administrator's responsibility at each level to decide when to move each piece of information and to whom. This reflects a power structure that imposes restrictions on the transparent and rapid flow of information. ICT can have a rapid and powerful impact on this structure by changing the rules of information flow.

3.3.4. Role in Evaluation

Evaluation is an important but complex issue when designing and implementing a national programme for introducing ICT in education. Probably because of such complexity, many programmes defer evaluation until sometime in the future or include it as a separate, understated and non-central task. But, if evaluation is not an integral part of each major decision, it will be difficult to reach sound and reliable conclusions about the effectiveness of the programme and to decide whether or not there is need for adjustments and change. Achieving a clear definition of what should be evaluated during the design of the programme brings about an additional important gain because it imposes a precise and measurable definition of goals and helps detect unrealistic expectations. It also proved to be important for political reasons because it will readily secure the programme at an eventual (and rightful) call for accountability.

A sound evaluation strategy that defines fundamental standards of achievement and performance indicators in advance, will be of great value for the programme's management team once it gets into its implementation stages.

The impact of ICT on students, teachers and parents considers a wide range of variables for each subject, such as: students' self-concept, creativity, reading comprehension and cognitive development; teachers' self-concept, teaching styles and perception of working conditions; and parents' perception of the school. Results of this evaluation showed that students increased their reading and comprehension capacity as well as their creativity and concentration ability. Results also indicated that ICT produced a high level of motivation among students, a more horizontal social organisation within the classroom and an increase in self-esteem. For the teachers, evaluations showed that a high number of them believed that the relation with the staff members was better and that they had better resources for teaching.

3.4. ICTs Educational Innovations

The application of ICT in education refers to an array of technologies that can be applied in a variety of ways, not to a single approach. The case study schools amply illustrate the variety of forms that ICT can take in schools. Some of the schools had developed sophisticated intranets providing access to course information, learning materials and other resources. Students could use the networks to store and submit assignments, access the web and display their own web pages.

Some of the innovations involved relatively modest technology. In one Mexican school a set of graphing calculators was used to encourage students to engage in critical reflection. One of the striking features of these schools taken as a whole is the diversity of ways in which ICT was used, which can be summarised under four general headings:

i) ICT as the focus of the innovation;

ii) Teaching and learning with ICT;

iii) Educational management with ICT;

iv) Extending the boundaries of the school.

3.4.1. ICT as the Focus of Innovation

In a number of the schools the innovation had begun with the need to develop ICT skills in the learners, itself driven by different factors. Development of a high quality ICT programme was seen as a key element in attracting new students. Although motivated by a desire to include the technology, the innovations in these schools often

extended beyond the technical. In the Hungarian case the entire town was mobilised in the effort to introduce ICT so fully into the school. Local administrative structures were involved in raising funds, all of the teachers received training, and many went on to complete degrees in related subjects.

Parents, even those with low incomes, began to buy computers for home use. As a consequence, the school established a national profile. Teachers have been invited to give papers at conferences, and to act as trainers in other schools. The students have been very enthusiastic, and have reached a high standard of ICT skill.

Teachers not involved in teaching ICT began to use it in their own subjects such as in Geography, Biology, Art and other subjects. Similar broad impact was reported in a Danish school, in which the innovation was the development of a school-wide ICT curriculum. This involved designing an ICT programme for each group of students, and developing methods to deliver that skill set in an integrated way. Not all of the teachers had sufficient ICT skills, and so the school began to experiment with team teaching. In the process the teachers began to engage in collaborative planning exercises and to work together in new ways. The staff feels the impact of this change.

3.4.2. Influence of ICT In Educational Change

The role of ICT in educational change, given its common association with new methods of teaching and learning and a student-centred approach is one of the central concerns of this study. Some expect ICT to promote increased collaboration between teachers, thus developing and sharing good practice. These case studies provide an opportunity to examine the relationship between the adoption of ICT and the educational reform in more detail. In doing so, a key question is the extent to which ICT acts as the change agent.

ICT had led to changes in pedagogy within the school. In Greece, a relatively affluent primary school introduced ICT as part of an effort to improve students' thinking skills. According to the deputy principal, technology use led to collaborative work among students, which then led to the teachers deciding to change their ways of teaching so that students now work more autonomously. In a secondary school in Finland, a very similar outcome was noted. The use of ICT led to more student-centred learning, and students became more active in collecting, processing and constructing information. Authenticity became an important component of learning content; students became more responsible for their own learning processes.

ICT is a support for making learning more fun, with communication still a major school focus. Over time teaching became more student centred and the classroom has become connected to the rest of the world. While the above examples support the idea of ICT as a catalyst for educational change, there were other cases where it did not appear to have acted in this catalytic role. In Luxembourg, the researchers dismissed the idea, saying "ICT is a resource like any other and not a catalyst". The Greek schools provide further cases where ICT did not trigger educational change. In one Greek secondary school, most teachers used ICT to complement their traditional lessons, either by providing ways to manipulate the information, or by making the presentation more attractive.

Adoption of ICT is a complex process of innovation. In most schools the teachers retained the freedom to adopt or reject ICT, even when its usage was encouraged by school management. Thus the integration of ICT into teaching involves its adoption by each individual teacher in the context of his/her own subject. The case studies highlighted a series of issues that appeared to be significant factors in encouraging this process. The differences appeared even within countries. An Italian school found that use of ICT correlated with teacher technical ability, a second stressed the infrastructure.

ICT adoption is a process dependent on the presence of a series of ingredients. These ingredients are present to different degrees in each school and hence different factors can serve as the limiting variable in the process of ICT adoption. Use of ICT is influenced by teacher beliefs about the appropriate role of the technology in education.

ICT is a flexible technology that can be used to support a variety of educational aims. In the absence of clear policies, schools adopting ICT may not all move in the same direction and policy may need to provide supports to encourage desirable school ICT use. ICT can facilitate student-centred approaches, and where this occurred it was tended to have led to significant reported benefits in motivation, understanding and, in some cases, performance in examinations. However beneficial progress on a small scale by individual teachers may be, a whole school approach is preferable. This may involve significant reorganisation of school schedules, working arrangements and staff roles. Innovation on this scale is more a process of educational change than one of technology adoption.

Where schools use ICT to support student-centred approaches, this often requires little more than standard office software. The web offers potential as a research resource, but its utility was often limited by the quality of connectivity. Once connectivity issues are overcome, schools will be faced with the question of managing large volumes of inappropriate material. This may be seen as a barrier, or as an opportunity to teach important information-handling skills.

3.4.3. ICT as a Catalyst For Educational Change

There will be less need for formal education to transmit a fixed corpus of knowledge, and much more need for the development of meta-cognitive skills; the skills of evaluation, analysis, problem-solving and learning to learn. It is anticipated that schools will move towards a more student-centred model of learning, involving more project work, with students taking more responsibility for their own learning and developing the kind of autonomous practices that will enable them to grow as lifelong learners.

ICT is often seen as playing an integral part in this change, and it has been suggested that it may act as a catalyst or stimulus for the change; a central question of this study was whether ICT had a catalytic effect. The studies revealed a varied pattern. Sometimes, ICT was clearly driving change; more frequently, it was facilitating pedagogical change which was already planned by teachers or management. In a third group of schools, mainly focused on teaching ICT skills, ICT was not associated with a pedagogical change at all. Overall, it could not be said that the introduction of ICT automatically resulted in educational change.

Besides, there were numerous cases where pedagogical change relied heavily on the technology. Where it did occur, this was usually associated with a strong belief in the methodology, by school leaders, by an ICT champion, or by innovative teachers. On this basis there were plenty of examples of ICT acting as a change agent—both by encouraging other teachers to get involved and by facilitating the practical application of the change. It is thus more realistic to characterise ICT as a lever, giving power to an existing movement, than as a catalyst or initiator of change.

The technology itself is value-neutral in this regard: it can be used to support strongly didactic traditional teaching or a student-centred model. But the technology implementation was not always value-neutral. Where school leadership consciously sought to encourage a shift in pedagogical practices, ICT was sometimes introduced to drive that change. In some schools, for example, teachers expressed surprise at the amount of educational discussion in ICT courses, and said that ICT had changed their teaching methods more than they had expected initially. In these cases, ICT was part of the process of educational change.

3.5. Conclusion

The teacher is central in the adoption and use of ICT. The impact of ICT on educational quality, on learning, and the differential benefits from these all flow from the way in which the technology is used. The same technology, in the hands of different teachers, produces different outcomes. The adoption of ICT is not a technical implementation but an ongoing process of educational change. It is about teacher beliefs and pedagogical practices as much as about infrastructure and bandwidth. As such, it may be a slow, often unpredictable process.

References

Aguti, Jessica N. and William J. Fraser. "Integration of Information Communication Technologies (ICTs) in The Distance Education Bachelor of Education Programme, Makerere University, Uganda". *Turkish Online Journal of Distance Education*-TOJDE. ISSN 1302-6488. 7(3) Article 7. July 2006.

Hativa, Nira, & Becker, Henry. J. "Problems and Potential Benefits." *International Journal of Educational Research.* 21 (1), 113-119. 1994.

Means, B. *Technology and education reform: the reality behind the promise.* San Francisco, CA: Jossey-Bass. 1994.

Mioduser, D.; Nachmias, R.; Lahav, O. &Oren, A. Web-Based Learning Environments (Wble): Current Pedagogical And Technological State. Tel-Aviv University, Science and Technology Education Center. Research Report No. 54, 1999.

Sagna, O. and S. D'Antoni, eds. "The Virtual University Models and messages". UNESCO (IIEP).2006.

Selwyn, Neil "Promoting Mr Chips: The construction of the teacher / computer relationship in educational advertising," *Teaching and Teacher Education.* Vol. 17, pp3-14. 2001.

World Bank. Improving educational quality through interactive radio instruction: A toolkit for policy makers and planners. Washington, DC. Africa Region Human Development Working Paper Series. 2004.

4

INTERNATIONAL STUDENT MOBILITY

4.1. Introduction

Mobility of students increasing day by day and it triggers the developments of higher education, which is one of the most undisputed positive goals. Mobility is perceived as a most suitable way of getting access to study provisions academically superior to those at home or in areas of specialisation hardly available at home; in those cases the term "vertical mobility" might be appropriate.

Mobility between countries and institutions of higher education of more or less the same level of academic quality, i.e. "horizontal mobility", is perceived as offering the opportunity to widen the horizon through experiencing contrasting academic environments and to enhance one's intercultural understanding.

Student mobility is expected to serve so various expectations that this might be a case of unrealistic over-expansion and over-stretching of functions. Second, student mobility is recently more frequently assessed controversially: "brain drain", "commercialisation of trans-national higher education", "flooding by foreign students", risks for quality of higher education and other skeptical judgements are put forward in this context. Both, the high expectations and the increasing skepticism with respect to student mobility call for a closer look at the actual trends of student mobility, the factors stimulating and discouraging student mobility, the outcomes of student mobility, and the controversial issues recently debated in this area.

Today, education has the prominent place in all societies. All wants to get high quality education. So, the international student market is changing. An increasing number of higher education opportunities for study at home and abroad is contributing to rising competition in the international student market. In an attempt to attract the growing number of prospective students seeking higher education, individual institutions and national governments are looking to differentiate themselves from their competitors. In an attempt to do so, they are developing and implementing targeted recruitment strategies to grow new markets or expand in already established ones. Motivational factors in the decision-making process for student application to an overseas destination include employment and residency opportunities, the quality of the 'student experience', including accommodation and social activities, and the costs associated with an international education.

International student mobility has become an increasingly important part of the global higher education landscape over the past 10-15 years. Significant changes in the infrastructures and capacity of higher education systems across the world partially explain why there has been such growth in such a short time. The large majority of national governments have been allocating more funds to higher education to improve the quantity and quality of tertiary education being offered within their borders. Even so, capacity is insufficient to meet demand in the major source countries. At the same time, with higher household levels of wealth and rising GDP per capita, more students from across the world are able to participate in higher education abroad, especially those from countries with rapidly growing economies.

Traditionally, more than 90 per cent of international students have enrolled in institutions in countries belonging to the Organisation for Economic Co-operation and Development (OECD) with the main destinations (the US, the UK, Germany, France and Australia) recruiting over 70 per cent of them.

However, developments over the past five to six years demonstrate that international student demand might not continue to focus on what have been the main destinations in the past. The US, the UK and Australia have all experienced either a decline in enrolments or a 'slump' in the growth experienced in previous years. Many European countries, which traditionally have maintained significant and stable recruitment numbers from a range of nations with which they a share historical or linguistic connection have stepped up their marketing efforts.

In the meantime, new players in Asia and the Middle East have entered the market with declared ambitions to become regional education centres by attracting as many as several hundred thousand international students to their countries. Importantly, Western economies are increasingly seeking to both recruit international students and retain them after graduation because in an era of globalisation, international students hold several short- and long-term gains for institutions and countries. In the first instance, with public per student funding for higher education decreasing in many countries, universities and colleges are looking to diversify their generated income and the revenue earned from overseas student tuition has become one important way of doing so. In the long term, and in the wider socio-economic context, developed countries are looking to attract foreign skilled labour to supplement their rapidly decreasing and ageing populations.

4.2. Patterns of Student Mobility

The definitions of 'international' or 'foreign' students in education systems across the world challenge the analysis of comparative mobility between countries. Terminology used in one country often has little or no equivalent in another, and for this reason, countries report enrolment statistics in different capacities as they relate to their own national contexts. To address existing discrepancies, in its most recent Global Education Digest (2006) UNESCO introduced the concept of 'internationally mobile students', individuals who leave their country or territory of origin and travel to another for the purpose of studying there. According to UNESCO, statistics about 'internationally mobile students' more accurately represent inbound and outbound student flows, as they consider more than the singular criterion of citizenship, which has traditionally been the defining indicator of 'foreign students'.

The concept of the 'internationally mobile student' eliminates potential misunderstandings resulting from different definitions between countries and facilitates a more comprehensive understanding of trends in worldwide mobility.

Citizenship, whilst a practical indicator for students who are not citizens of the country in which they study, conceivably distorts the number of non-citizens who are nonetheless permanent residents studying in what is effectively their home country.

All of these English-speaking countries source significant amounts of students from a wide variety of countries throughout the world, and have consistently done so for many years. By successfully attracting tens of thousands of students from several different countries, each has managed to establish a diversified market with strong growth potential. Over time, certain markets have performed less well than others, but each of these host countries has maintained relatively steady numbers in a core stock of source countries. All three have extremely high numbers of students from India and China, the world's two most prominent source countries.

However, the US, the UK and Australia have successfully managed to supply a massive demand for international education for students coming from both countries, especially in recent years. Moreover, each country could potentially record even higher numbers because the percentage of Indian and Chinese citizens seeking higher education provision is only predicted to grow in the coming years.

Education organisations in the US, the UK and Australia have developed impressive marketing strategies to target potential students. Not only can these three countries provide foreign students with the opportunity to study in English at internationally renowned facilities with 'world-class facilities', but the US and Australia often offer substantial financial incentives to do so. Quite significantly, they thus have the capacity to give considerably more to students than can other competitor countries, and this is a major reason why they manage to recruit more international students.

The US, the UK and Australia are the leaders in the international student market not just because they annually record the highest number of foreign students but also because they strategically target students in potentially high-yield countries. With a sound awareness of the contribution that foreign students make to host nation economies, both culturally and financially, these three countries seem to recognise how advantageous international higher education can be as an export service. Having already taking considerable steps towards internationalising their higher education systems, especially in recent years, each is currently implementing further initiatives to facilitate the arrival and integration of overseas students, including substantial amendments to immigration requirements and procedures. For these reasons, they are likely to remain the top host nations in an increasingly competitive market for the foreseeable future.

Malaysia, Singapore and China have set ambitious targets to attract thousands more foreign students in the coming years, with each having declared ambitions to become major exporters of higher education. Within the past decade, all three countries have allocated substantial financial and human resources towards the development of 'world-class' higher education, and this is one of the main reasons why they are becoming contenders in the global student market. Indeed, the decision to invest in their national higher education systems is a crucial development in their competitiveness, and changing mobility patterns suggest that they might well succeed in establishing a broader portfolio of source countries and students.

The increasing use of English as a language of instruction is contributing to their growing popularity as an overseas student destination. In the past, language may have acted as a 'mobility barrier' to Asian countries but the adoption of English as a language of instruction in a range of programmes seems to be enabling Malaysia and China to substantially widen, and Singapore to strengthen, their recruitment pools so as to compete on more equal terms with other destinations, and especially with English-speaking ones.

Tuition fees and living costs are considerably lower than those in the US, the UK and Australia, and the comparatively low cost of higher education is an attractive feature. By investing substantial resources in the development and implementation of international higher education initiatives, including recruitment, Malaysia, Singapore and China are rapidly emerging as contenders in the global student market. Certainly, they face certain challenges before increasing their market share, not least regarding infrastructural capacity and immigration procedures.

Yet because they appear interested in welcoming overseas students from an increasingly diverse range of countries, they may eventually succeed in their ambitions to become centres of higher education excellence for students beyond Asia.

Neither Malaysia nor Singapore, nor even China can seriously compete with the established English-language destinations, as the cost of higher education becomes increasingly significant, it is likely only a matter of time before they start to challenge at least the non-elite institutions in the competitor countries.

Given increasing competition in the market and changes in mobility patterns, many countries have started to consider how they might implement or strengthen their strategic approaches to international recruitment.

The most important reason Indian students chose to come to study in Australia was not the academic reputation of the universities but the opportunity to gain permanent residency visas. In light of this realisation, institutions and countries appear to be increasingly cognisant of the importance of satisfied international graduates, and are thus looking to ensure that recruitment is not only as 'user-friendly' a procedure as possible, but that foreign students receive the education and overall student experience they were promised during the recruitment process. From this perspective, especially since 'word of mouth' and information widely disseminated via the internet have become efficient marketing tools, the little 'perks and privileges' afforded students, in addition to employment and residency rights, could go a long way in today's competitive market.

Moreover, cost is increasingly likely to motivate students to apply for study to particular destinations, and to deter them from applying to others, not least because it can be a determining factor in the quality of the overall 'student experience'. The usually high value of certain currencies, the UK pound (£) and US dollar ($) most prominent amongst them, could arguably dissuade students even further from going to high-cost nations, since unfavourable exchange rates exacerbate the already considerable financial concerns of foreign students, especially those from Africa and Southeast Asia.

4.3. Objectives of Student Mobility

The mobility of students is not a recent phenomenon. Historians suggest that about one tenth of students in the medieval universities had come from other countries.

Five different objectives of international student mobility are emphasised most frequently at present, some already for more than a century and some quite recently.

- First, highly reputed universities and scholars attract students from other countries who aim to benefit from study provisions on a higher level of quality than those at home or in an area of specialisation not available at home. This type of mobility played already a role in the 19th century and remained important until now.
- Second, we noted in the past or note today a colonial or post-colonial flow of students from colonies and developing countries to more advanced higher education systems in economically advanced countries where political ties often played a substantial role in determining the flows between country of origin and country of study. Often, student mobility is intended to and possibly turns out to be the first step towards migration.
- Third, some students spend their period of study in a neighbouring country—a less risky option, whereby the motives might vary. This type of mobility has a long tradition, and it can be observed in various regions within Europe today. Certainly, efforts to promote and facilitate intra-European mobility are also viewed by some political actors as means of creating a similar understanding of neighbour relationships across Europe or even as steps towards European integration.
- Fourth, short-term study in other countries in order to learn from academically and culturally somewhat but possibly not too much contrasting countries and institutions and in order to increase mutual understanding got momentum after World War II when the United States promoted short-term student exchange between the U.S. and Europe. Activities by the Council of Europe already in the 1950s to facilitate recognition of study achievements and degrees

acquired in other European countries were based on similar objectives. Obviously, short-term mobility of this kind works best if the mobility is "horizontal", i.e. if the quality of study programmes and level of competences between the students of the home and host country are similar. Last but not least these objectives played a major role when ERASMUS support for short-term mobility within Europe was inaugurated in 1987.

Mobility might serve quite divergent purposes for the mobile students. Also, the actors involved—governments, institutions of higher education, teachers and students—might have divergent intentions in mind. Obviously, the mix of objectives and actual activities of student mobility have changed over time. In recent years, the public discourse in Europe about the virtue of short-term student mobility, about structural convergence for increasing student mobility and about mobility under conditions of increasing competition between universities, among others the impact of tuition fees on the universities' mobility policies and the increasing trans-national trade of higher education provisions, might lead observers to believe that views and activities as regards student mobility developed similarly across Europe. A recent comparative study, however, shows that internationalisation policies vary substantially between the various European countries and within the European countries between the individual institutions of higher education.

4.4. Growth of Student Mobility

Short-term intra-European student mobility spread substantially as a consequence of the establishment of ERAMUS programme in 1987. The number of students annually supported increased from about 30,000 around 1990 to almost 150,000 in 2004. Precise information on short-term student mobility not supported by ERASMUS does not exist, but available information suggests that it grew as well substantially and that it remained until today more frequent than mobility supported by ERASMUS.

The ERASMUS scheme for the mobility of students is generally viewed as a "success story". Even though bureaucratic procedures of the programme were often criticised as excessive and even though the stipends provided for students as a rule cover only part of the additional costs for study abroad, ERASMUS became quite popular. Short-term study in another European country is stimulated for the purpose of academic enhancement, cultural enrichment and improvement of foreign language proficiency and fostering the "European dimension" of higher education. The individual cooperating institutions of higher education and departments are free to set more specific targets, as long as they take care to facilitate life and study of the mobile students and take measure to ensure recognition upon return of the study achievements abroad.

Almost all participating students are highly satisfied with the ERASMUS experience in another European country. On average, they believe that their study progress abroad was higher than during a corresponding period at home, and many students report a substantial enhancement of proficiency in the host country language. About 70-80 percent of their study achievements abroad are recognised upon return. About 20 percent of the students experienced financial, administrative and accommodation problems, while academic problems are less frequently stated.

As students of the 2nd, 4th and 12th cohorts of EARSMUS students were sent similar questionnaires, the evaluation studies could examine change over time.

The results of the various surveys were strikingly similar. Obviously, neither the expansion of the number of students supported undermined the outcomes nor did the continuity of the programme lead to progress through experience. Only the extent of recognition increased moderately with the spread of the credit system ECTS.

Studies addressing the professional impact on short-term mobile students in Europe show that the study period abroad turned out to be helpful in the job search process.

With respect of income and status, formerly mobile students do not perceive any clear advantage to formerly non-mobile students. Two professional effects of short-term student mobility are most striking: Almost 20 percent are professionally active abroad a few years after graduation as compared to only about 3 percent of formerly non-mobile students, and formerly mobile students not employed abroad take over clearly more visible international work assignments such as communicating with foreigners, using foreign languages, travelling abroad for professional purposes, using knowledge on other countries etc.

The impact of short-term study in another European country of leading more frequently to visible international work assignment has diminished over time. The authors discuss two possible causes for this phenomenon. First, short-term student mobility might have expanded more rapidly than the demand for competences fostered. Second, international experiences and learning might spread so much as a consequence of a general internationalisation and globalisation of European society that the comparative advantage of short-term study abroad for enhancing international competences is bound to decline. The latter interpretation clearly argues that a persistent programme supporting student mobility with stable quality such as notably ERASMUS is not likely to yield the same level of results, because student mobility is increasingly loosing its exclusivity in enhancing international competences.

The European Union has decided to extend and to expand its support for student mobility. ERASMUS will continue as sub-programme while the name of the umbrella educational support programme will be Life Long Learning programme from late 2007 onwards instead of SOCRATES. The number of European students awarded ERASMUS support might double in the next few years.

National policies in the various European countries continue to play an enormous role regarding the extent to which mobility is encouraged, whether efforts are made to reach a balance of incoming and outgoing students or not, what sub-groups of students are encouraged to be mobile etc. Altogether, one should not overlook that student mobility is only one mode of international learning. Student mobility is likely to grow in the future, but many experts predict that "trans-national" or "border-crossing" mobility of study programmes as well as "internationalisation at home" will increase in the future at a more rapid pace than physical mobility of students.

4.5. Conclusion

Student mobility is changing the global higher education landscape, with an increasing number of students going abroad for tertiary studies. Importantly, because nations understand and account for student mobility differently, this area is still characterised by a lack of comparable data, and for this reason, definitive statistical analyses of reported figures are challenging to produce. The growing number and diversification of players in the international student market partly explains why countries are seeking innovative strategies to attract higher numbers of students. Yet because the current generation of 'savvy student customers' are more knowledgeable about the opportunities available in certain countries, prospective hosts arguably have little choice but to offer targeted advantages.

Visa schemes and immigration procedures will play an increasingly important role in the decision-making process, with students not only seeking employment upon graduation, but perhaps (at least temporary) residency in their country of choice. Countries which facilitate the arrival and integration of overseas students through employment and immigration initiatives are likely to be more competitive in the market. Institutions and countries are furthermore striving to meet, if not exceed, the expectations of prospective overseas students, because the 'student experience' and the costs associated with an overseas education, including tuition fees and accommodation are becoming significant motivational factors for application to one country over another. Given the rising fees of study abroad, the comparative cost of higher education in particular is likely to give certain countries a competitive edge in the coming years.

Trends in international student mobility, however, institutional and national recruitment strategies will almost certainly consider a growing number of indicators to compete in a rapidly changing industry.

References

Alesi, B. et al. *Bachelor and Master Courses in Selected Countries Compared with Germany*. Bonn and Berlin: Federal Ministry of Education and Research. 2005.

Bracht, O. et al. *Professional Value of ERASMUS Mobility*. Brussels: European Commission. 2006.

Bürger, S. et al. "International Study on Transnational Mobility in Bachelor and Master Programmes". In: German Academic

Exchange Service (ed.). *Transnational Mobility in Bachelor and Master Programmes*. Bonn: DAAD, pp. 1-98. 2006

Huisman, J. and van der Wende, M. (eds.) *On Cooperation and Competition: National and European Policies for the Internationalisation of Higher Education*. Bonn: Lemmens.2004.

Kehm, B.M. and Teichler, U. "Which Direction for Bachelor and Master Programmes? A Stocktaking of the Bologna Process". *Tertiary Education and Management*. Vol. 12, No. 4, 269-282. 2006.

Kehm, B.M. and Teichler, U. "Research on Internationalisation in Higher Education". *Journal of Studies in International Education*. Vol. 11. 2007.

Kelo, M., Teichler, U. and Wächter, B. (eds.) *EURODATA: Student Mobility in European Higher Education*. Bonn: Lemmens. 2006.

Knight, J. "Internationalisation: Concepts, Complexities and Challenges". In: Forest, J.J. and Altbach, P.G. (eds.). *International Handbook of Higher Education*. Dordrecht: Springer, pp. 207-227.2006.

5

CHANGING PATTERNS OF EDUCATIONAL PARTICIPATION

5.1. Introduction

In order to educate all, new and revitalised partnerships at all levels" should be built. The call for more involvement of parents, communities, NGO's, and teachers in the implementation of educational programmes is at the heart of the expanded vision of basic education and constitutes a great challenge for educational planners and administrators.

The purpose of the IIEP research and training programme on 'Collaborating for educational change', launched in 1990, was to go beyond the usual rhetoric about participation and to focus on specific things which planners and managers at different levels can do in order to encourage participatory approaches to educational development. This focus was achieved through the detailed, comparative analysis of generally successful cases in different parts of the world in terms of what seems to work and what makes it work.

Like decentralisation, a major lesson of the exercise is that participation simply does not happen by itself. It requires systematic analysis of what kinds of participatory mechanisms and of what facilitating conditions and constraints to participation already exist in a given society. It also requires both clear divisions of responsibility at various levels of the system and between agencies inside and outside the system and high-level commitment to the idea of greater participation. It generally implies that the Ministry brings together across its various units and levels a combination of supportive instruments—legislation, policies, programmes, mechanisms, training activities, resources—in a planned and systematic way.

The basic learning needs are very complex and diverse. To meet these needs requires multi-sectoral strategies and actions which are integral to overall development efforts. Many partners must join with the education authorities, teachers, and other educational personnel in developing basic education if it is to be seen, once again, as the responsibility of the entire society. This implies the active involvement of a wide range of partners—families, teachers, communities, private enterprises, government and non-governmental organisations, institutions, etc.—in planning, managing and evaluating the many forms of basic education.

The persistence of poverty in many parts of the world after decades of so-called 'development' and the sea changes occurring more generally today in political, social, and cultural life have once again made education an issue of critical importance. The transformation of the macro-political landscape, the promise of expanded democratisation, the threat of narrow nationalism and fundamentalism, the increasing risks of environmental degradation and endemic disease—all of these challenges call for the more effective development of human resources and thus for a greater demand for, and supply of, education of better quality.

But just as so much hope is being placed on education, doubts about the general vision of education systems, the actual availability of schooling, and the quality of education of education have increased. In much of the world, especially the least developed, education is becoming less, rather than more, available. In many countries, the growth of primary school enrolments is declining while the absolute numbers of illiterate adults and of school-age children not in school are increasing.

Declining individual demand for an education seen as being irrelevant to a family's current welfare and a student's future success, and declining public investment in education measured both as a percentage of the national budget and as per pupil expenditures are the reasons behind a sizeable percentage of children and adults often remains unreached by primary schooling and literacy programmes even in countries where enrolment rates have continued to grow. The disturbing trends are not only quantitative in nature. In many countries, both research data and more anecdotal observation indicate an erosion in the general quality of education provided to learners as defined in traditional terms of inputs (teachers, facilities, books, and supplies), outputs (literacy and completion rates, achievement scores), and processes (the nature of the teaching-learning act).

Good education must now be defined not only in relation to the extent to which a school is well-housed and well-supplied; teaches literacy, job skills, and 'facts for life'; and facilitates an effective teaching-learning process. Education of good quality must also encourage a more integrated view of how the world operates and how development does (or does not) occur, make students more critically aware of how their actions, individually and collectively, will hinder or help the world to meet future challenges; and help to mobilise and empower people with the knowledge and skills to participate more actively, more democratically, and more collectively in the development process.

Increasing the availability and the quality of education more traditionally defined, most education systems of the world would need to be considerably reformed. Given the history of educational reform, however, it is not easy to be optimistic about the possibility of altering a given system in significant ways.

5.2. Need For Encouraging Education

In the past, many traditional, large-scale reforms designed by central governments—both conventional reforms and alternative, more non-formal innovations—have proven very difficult to implement, disseminate, and sustain. Debt and recession, the isolation of marginal populations, and the interruptions of war and natural disaster share much of the blame for this persistent inability of many governments both to supply an increasing (or even a constant) number of educational places and to improve, on a day-to-day basis, the quality of education occurring in their schools—let alone re-define the very nature of education itself.

The character of centralised bureaucracies and of their technocratic planning techniques also plays an important role in this regard. The central level is too 'specialised' and imagines itself on a pedestal too high to 'descend' and to 'lower itself' to the level of the classroom. Despite such limitations, and in the face of the economic, social, political, and educational issues discussed above, planners and managers have no choice but to make further attempts to re-organise and reform education systems and processes. In doing so, they face several challenges.

5.3. Participation for Educational Change

Social, cultural, and political contexts affect participatory and collaborative approaches. What is practicable in one country may not work in another. These approaches therefore cannot be treated as recipes able to be implemented in the same way in all regions of the world. Rather, they should be seen as items on a menu of mechanisms, procedures, and administrative actions which can lead to a higher degree of participation in education, at both local and national levels. The choice of the items on the menu will vary by context and may very well change over time. The specific nature of the items on the menu and of the suggested steps in their implementation will need to be adapted to the particular political, economic, educational and cultural context of each country.

5.3.1. Participatory Development

Popular participation consists of restoring the power of local people to take the initiative and the decision of formulating and implementing activities and programmes concerning their own future. Promoting popular participation means instituting a partnership, a contractual relationship among the various agents of development, in particular between the people concerned and those intervening from the outside. Whether the programmes are initiated from outside or in support of previously existing local initiatives, those intervening from outside should start off where the needs and aspirations of the people begin and accept to negotiate on that basis. If, as in many cases, such a partnership is initially held back by such factors as poor organisation and improper formulation of requests for assistance, the conditions for the partnerships must be created."

The assumption, sustainable development ultimately depends on enhancing people's capacities as individuals and groups to improve their own lives and to take greater control over their own destinies, is the beginning of a more participatory approach to development. This assumption may seem self-evident, but, in fact, it is really quite radical in implication. A participatory approach to development represents a considerable change in the process of governance, in social and political relationships, and in who participates in, controls, and is empowered by the development process.

A government bureaucracy, a community cooperative, a parent-teacher association do not suddenly, by fiat, become more participatory in nature, leaping from the first degree of participation to the last—or even to the middle. Rather, their willingness and ability to participate—and the feasibility of their doing so—evolve over time, faster or slower (perhaps with some backward steps), depending on a number of complex factors and conditions.

Underlying all of the more participatory approaches to development are several important implications and issues that planners and managers as well as the political leadership of a government must understand. These all relate to the general process of the 'restructuring' of educational systems. This process represents a "significant change in the pattern of school governance, where governance refers to the norms and practices of decision-making regarding three critical areas of school life: (1) instructional methodology and curriculum; (2) administrative management and organisation; and (3) the generation, allocation, and use of resources". Such restructuring generally includes issues related to decentralisation, accountability, autonomy, and empowerment.

5.3.1.1. Decentralisation

It is a process often particularly crucial in any attempt to facilitate the participation of a broader range of actors in development. Decentralisation is another concept, however, fraught with multiple and often contradictory variations. The diversity and complexity of the services and policies which often result from decentralisation make necessary more systematic and sophisticated monitoring and training of people working in such a system. And given the newly defined functions of powers of different levels of the system, decentralisation might require careful planning and extensive training and more staff, resources, and equipment, rather than less. Thus, "decentralisation will not prove a cheaper form of management; its justification must be that it is better.

Decentralisation is often more rhetorical than real; that, as "compensatory legitimation", it is designed to manage and diffuse conflict and fragment reform movements rather than bring about real change; and that if it involves only administrative aspects of a system, it "can result in more rather than less central control as the administrative function becomes more efficient at the local level". Thus, "decentralisation of government in itself does not necessarily involve a devolution of power. Far from it, the extension of the state outwards and downwards can just as well serve the objective of consolidating the power of the central state as it can serve the objective of devolving power away from the centre. It can extend the state's control over the people just as it can aid the people's control over the state and its activities.

5.3.1.2. *Accountability*

Accountability continues to span a very wide variety of concepts and policies, making it an elusive concept to grasp. It relates to who is required to report to whom about—and therefore can ultimately be held responsible for—the determination and implementation of policies and procedures, the achievement of goals, the performance of institutions, and compliance with standards and regulations.

In regard to participation and decentralisation, it relates to the extent to which various levels of the administrative hierarchy are responsible to other levels both above and below it and to other 'partners'. In systems both decentralised and participatory, higher levels of the bureaucracy are to some extent accountable to lower levels (rather than only the other way around), and local government agents are to some extent accountable to their 'clients' (e.g. children, parents, the community) as well as to the local government office and the bureaucratic levels above. The question, answered differently according to the context, is how such accountability is put in place.

5.3.1.3. *Autonomy*

Societies where multi-directional accountability occurs guarantee some degree of autonomy or 'self-government' to lower levels of the system. This includes both autonomy for organisations to make and implement decisions regarding their own operations, and for individuals, to make decisions regarding matters pertaining to their own concerns. Such autonomy, within a context of accountability to other actors above and to clients below, can help to encourage better management, higher professional competence, and more effective services. One important premise of such a process of providing greater autonomy is that the various actors in the autonomous institutions (e.g. a school) are professionals and able to make informed decision and conscious of self-responsibility for consequences arising from the decisions.

5.3.1.4. *Empowerment*

It is a very important concept in attempts to move the concept of participatory development from rhetoric to concrete practice. This concept is perhaps best defined as "a group process where people who lack an equal share of valued resources gain greater access to, and control over, those resources". As a result, "poor communities come more explicitly to assert rights and responsibilities in determining the direction of their own development". This power must be real, formal, and legitimate, including both the ability to make use of formal structures and regulations and control over decision-making processes, knowledge, and techniques. People who are empowered "have the power to find direct solutions to their problems—they propose solutions, they do not beg for them.

A great part of the impact of participation and empowerment is said to lie at the level of the individual, in the process of "human resource development". Some of this impact is cognitive. Through greater involvement in a variety of development activities, people can gain more knowledge, learn better practice, and end with a greater awareness of the development problems that exist, the causes behind these problems, and, in some cases, their possible solutions.

Some of the impact is also psychological; people feel greater self-confidence and self-reliance, less dependence on external inputs and 'wisdom', greater pride in the significance and validity of local knowledge and experience, a greater sense of accountability and responsibility for their own actions, less of a feeling of marginalisation and powerlessness. The combination of such impacts can lead to greater demand on the political and social system: people gain a better idea of the kind of life they want to lead, a greater understanding of what prevents them from achieving such a life, and a greater willingness to make their needs known and, when necessary, to play a larger role in fulfilling these needs themselves.

5.3.2. Difficulty Involves in Participation

Participation—and any accompanying devolution of authority and "empowerment of the masses"—should not be seen as a new panacea for underdevelopment. It is a difficult, frustrating process, sometimes risky and often unsustainable; both skeptics and advocates of participatory development recognise that it is a process fraught with disappointments, dangers, and unkept promises.

Many communities—perhaps especially those most disadvantaged—are not at all homogeneous in nature. Social stratification, divisions along caste, religious, and ethnic lines, personal rivalries and social factionalism, and the incompatibility of interests are all factors which make it difficult to talk of 'community' mobilisation through participation.

A community seen as 'natural' in some ways may not necessarily be the community most appropriate to mobilise towards a particular outcome, and a community defined by geography, perhaps most appropriate for improving a particular social service, may be too riven with social discord to permit mobilisation. In such a context, participation may bring unresolved and unresolvable conflicts out into the open, exacerbating rivalries of class, caste, and ethnicity by making potential differences in goals and tactics explicit, rather than keeping them constrained and hidden through the operation of traditional roles and responsibilities.

Even where community members may want to work together, a major obstacle may be the sheer lack of experience and skill in participatory and collaborative activities. Participation by the community in development and the collaboration of the community with other partners imply certain knowledge and skills: setting goals and priorities, running meetings, planning budgets, accounting for resources.

Potential participants, especially those economically and socially weakest, may lack a sense of self-confidence and political efficacy—the feeling that "individual political action does have, and can have, an impact upon the policy process". They may also feel, or may have been encouraged to feel, that, given the overriding authority of the government, they have little political power, few obligations beyond receiving government services, and little ability to affect government policy.

Marginal communities cannot bear the added expense of participatory processes—especially in terms of financial resources and of the time and energy required of participating community organisations, government agencies, and individuals.

Overworked village leaders and community members struggling for survival, particularly if affected by the inherent passivity and illiteracy of many communities, do not find it easy to participate in labour-intensive, collaborative activities, and participation in the management of meagre resources is often seen as not worth the effort. And because sometimes "there are so many development agencies each dealing with problems in each sector, people can get only more and more confused because they do not have the training necessary to understand how all those activities which are being proposed willy-nilly to them tie into one another. The tendency is to set up village groups, associations, and committees each time a new operation commences. This has the double inconvenience of multiplying, at times needlessly, people's organisations and marginalising existing forms of organisation with the result, in [some] cases, of creating social tension.

Participation is often in conflict with a political culture where initiatives toward reform may require clear sanction from above and where, for example, both parental participation in designing school policies and flexible, non-standardised responses to a variety of development contexts are difficult to imagine.

Similarly, many institutions and individuals have a pro—found inability or resistance to change. The inertia of inflexible systems, bureaucratic delays, the lack of teamwork and coordinating mechanisms, the absence of clear rules as to who should do what and when, poor technical support from those meant to provide it, and the fear of losing control to other agencies, to lower levels of the system, or to outsiders—all make it difficult, at least early in various reforms, to encourage new initiatives. Thus, for example, reforms involving the participation of the community and of other sectors in education require flexible, multi-sectoral approaches and are often seen as interfering with the academic, examination-oriented aspects of the curriculum or as being intrusive, unprofessional, and working against the accepted wisdom that quality necessarily (and solely) depends on higher teacher salaries, better facilities, and the competence of a better teaching staff.

Such problems are compounded by more concrete administrative obstacles. Logistical problems and staff turnover are notable in this regard; when staff trained in a more participatory approach and method are transferred or resign, much time and effort are wasted. Administrative procedures may also discourage collaboration. In some countries, for example, ministry regulations forbid parent associations from involvement in 'academic' matters, and in a number of countries more than one ministry may have responsibility for primary education. This can make any innovation, let alone that based on greater popular participation, difficult to implement.

5.4. Risks Involve In Participatory Development

5.4.1. Risks of Participation

Participatory approaches to development can also carry risks. These approaches can raise expectations, and then frustrations, and lead to greater political and social instability. Participation can also threaten the political order of things.

The lack of technical expertise, supervisory skills, and animators and of a participatory grassroots tradition in many societies can lead to failed projects and a decline in the quality of services provided.

The participatory process may place greater power in the hands of the 'wrong' people—factionalists, demagogues, racists, reactionaries. It can also be taken over by those parts of any community—i.e., often corrupt and inefficient local elites and party cadres—most able to 'participate'. These groups may use their increased authority to manipulate the 'participants' and extract further resources from them. Attempt to encourage community involvement in development may therefore lead instead to the promotion of people who speak only for given segments of the population. It is they, rather than the "poorest of the poor", who benefit. The result may be an unequal distribution of participation itself and of its benefits either of the direct benefits meant to be derived from the new service or of the more generalised benefits of involvement in the development process..

A further risk of participatory processes may be the domination, at the local level, of narrow community self-interest, which may be based on short-sighted perspectives and aim at short-term benefits. Such self-interest may ignore longer-term political or economic implications for the community or the larger society and contradict more general goals of national integration, the dissemination of scientific truth, and the modernisation of society.

Popular traditions and customs in areas such as health, nutrition, productivity, or social justice may, in fact, represent "developmentally inadequate practices and behaviour" which should not be reinforced in development programmes or reflected in local social services.

Another problem lies in the risk of tokenism—only marginal change, wrapped in new packaging, leading not to an alternative model of development but rather to the reinforcement of central power, and the reproduction of central values. Participation, in other words, may end up being 'system-maintaining', designed to "transform disadvantaged and disaffected groups into 'responsive citizens' implementing policies outlined by some higher authority", rather than 'system-transforming', designed to "effectively transfer political and economic power to hitherto disadvantaged groups and thus to introduce more radical social change". Attention paid and energy spent by the general population on such token achievements are then lost to attempts to change more fundamentally the basic political and administrative patterns of a society. The process of change therefore becomes de politicised.

The very public efforts to wrap the new package in an attractive cover of 'participation' can lead to a fifth risk—the opting out of government from its responsibilities for delivering basic social services and for the better management, or more equitable allocation, of resources. In some countries, rather than maintaining their monopoly on the education system as omnipotent planner and funder, governments are moving in the opposite direction—surrendering their (expensive) responsibility for basic education to the family and the community. This may end up with the government co-opting NGOs and other community-based associations into State mechanisms and bureaucratic processes. Governments may even be able to blame poor results and poor quality on the other 'partners'; the more actors involved, in other words, the more blame can be distributed and the less the government itself can be held accountable.

5.4.2. Uncertainties of Participation

Besides the difficulties and risks of more participatory processes in development, there are also considerable uncertainties about it. First is the sheer inability to know, and to show to others, when a participatory process has succeeded. Participation is a process and its products are often psychological, procedural, or organisational in nature rather than concrete in terms of money saved or services delivered.

The inability to standardise or generalise the implementation of participatory development due to the different configurations of participation in various regions of the world and even in different parts of a country is the next problem. To the extent that participation is not an 'intervention' per se, that culture, history, and government policy affect its success, and that it is a dynamic process which requires flexibility, it is very much situation-specific. In other words, there cannot be a standard recipe for achieving participatory development; what makes it 'work' varies tremendously across different economic, political, and cultural contexts. There are many reasons for such variety: different histories of development, different social relationships and cultural traditions related to participation, and different political constraints or freedoms. Thus, schools and communities may respond in quite different ways to regulations concerning collaboration, and the nature of such collaboration and the kinds of structures which might encourage it differ across urban, suburban, and rural contexts. Attempts to develop manuals, guidelines, and training materials related to participatory approaches must therefore be tempered by their extensive adaptation to local conditions.

However, participatory approaches to development have proven instrumental, in particular contexts and under particular conditions, in expanding the supply and increasing the relevance of basic social services and in enhancing people's capacities as individuals and as groups to improve their own lives and to take greater control over their own development.

5.5. Participants in Education

The development of more participatory approaches in education the broader and more active partnerships both inside the system at the central level and in the school and the greater collaboration of educational personnel and the external community in planning, managing, and implementing educational programmes. The potential partners are many: teachers, headteachers, and local educational officials; parents and members and leaders of the local community; community associations and non-government organisations (NGOs); private enterprises and universities. For the purposes of this analysis, we will focus on four major partners: two 'internal' and two external.

5.5.1. Government and Officials

It is important to differentiate between the political and the administrative sides of government in order to find out the general characteristics of 'government' and its officials which affect their usual reaction to more participatory approaches to development. The political side is critical for any discussion of participation. Depending on the government's philosophy, legitimacy, and strength, it may either ignore, resist, or actively prohibit greater participation in society—or permit, encourage, and actively facilitate it.

Parental and community participation is essential for the maintenance of local schools. And in countries which accept some level of ethnic and/or religious diversity in public institutions, it may also promote local participation in the delivery of locally-determined curricula in areas such as language, culture, and religious instruction. But even if the politics of a nation tend to encourage participation, the administrative side of government may also do the opposite. Although bureaucracies—in education ministries as well as in other sectors—may be effective managers of top-down development projects and programmes and may have a range of human and material resources, an extensive infrastructure, and administrators and experts who bring to their work considerable knowledge, skills, and experience, they also may possess several characteristics which work against more participatory approaches to development.

Older educational administrators often may have started their careers as teachers but then worked many years in various parts and at various levels of the ministry structure, far from the everyday reality of schools and communities. While some younger ones may have teaching experience, many may have moved directly into ministry positions following university or college training. Their experience has largely been gained, therefore, in academic or office settings rather than in the field. The experience of both kinds of administrators, only reinforced by their position within the central bureaucracy, may produce a particular view of development.

With limited financial and human resources, governments may be hard-pressed to implement the standardised policies they often seek to promote, let alone react flexibly to the particular needs of diverse communities. These limitations may be particularly acute in increasingly expensive and complex educational systems where central governments attempt with great difficulty to control the daily life of literally thousands of schools.

A huge variety of conditions in schools within and across countries of the developing world, there are certain common characteristics of schools of poorer countries and for marginal and disadvantaged populations. Teachers go in and out between classes, but it is clearly not easy to teach and learn in these conditions. Some children erase the first pages in their notebooks in order to write on them again. Some children go around the class trying urgently to borrow a pencil to do an assignment.

Many teachers must work with insufficient and irregularly paid salaries, poor promotion opportunities and living conditions, the burden of excess subject content, reduced prestige, and either low enrolment and often absent pupils or overcrowded classrooms. Heads of schools, as well as supervisors and inspectors, are often chosen more for seniority of tenure (and nearness to retirement) than for expertise and thus may have neither the knowledge nor the status to assist their colleagues professionally. Mechanisms of teacher support, let alone of administrative or pedagogical consultation, are therefore often weak.

5.5.2. Perfect Partnership

The hybrid would recognise the right of school personnel, local authorities, and the popular sectors to adapt and implement the national framework and fill it with local content. It would encourage a distribution of power in which each side has an equal opportunity to influence the other, and it would respect the traditional wisdom of local communities, the experience of teachers and principals, and the legitimacy of non-government organisations. It would also encourage the exchange of experiences, information, techniques, approaches, and resources among government offices, NGOs, and community groups.

Perhaps, this ideal partnership would see the usual 'controllers' of development—governments and the donors which support them—rather as the 'enablers' of development. They would be charged with permitting other actors, from the bottom up, to assume both the rights and the risks of being partners in educational development and with "preserving, protecting, opening or creating necessary 'spaces'—political, legal, social, economic, and cultural—for participation to emerge and thrive". An ideal partnership would also help facilitate participation by these actors (e.g., through parent training programmes), in order not only to share responsibility with them for the failure of projects and programmes, but also to build the capacity of otherwise marginal groups in assessing needs, designing and managing programmes, and making decisions.

It would reduce the "constraints to local initiatives imposed by absolute and unresponsive administrative forms"; guarantee enough autonomy at the local level to encourage school and community partnerships in formulating, implementing, and evaluating school improvement programmes; and search for the optimal, if ever-changing, mix of centralised and decentralised structures and procedures. Such a mix might see central governments retaining responsibility for establishing:

- a core curriculum;
- standards of financial accountability;
- minimum levels of teacher qualification and compensation;
- a minium number of schools days per year; and
- minimum levels of centrally-provided school financing.

The publishing and/or procurement of textbooks, and the production of locally-relevant teaching and learning materials; the collection and management of local resources; adjustments to the school calendar; inspection and supervision; and the hiring, training, and promoting of teachers. The case of the State of Victoria in Australia illustrates one such mix of powers.

Community participation in significant areas of decision-making relating to the operation of schools has been enshrined in legislation. Schools have become responsible through their councils to the community, establishing their own evaluation procedures, with programme budgeting being gradually introduced across the state. New attitudes and roles must be learned by many persons throughout the system.

This hybrid of responsibility requires a greater emphasis on school-based management, where individual schools have considerable autonomy in decision-making. In such management, "the school becomes the principal entity of any change in the educational system. It is the epicenter for the implementation of educational reforms". This, in turn, requires "the sharing of responsibilities among all those who participate in the life of the school".

5.6. Potential Collaboration Areas

The educational system should be a subsystem highly interactive with all other parts of the social whole and it should not be regarded as a branch of the bureaucracy. The point is to give pupils, parents and teachers responsibility over their own affairs, to the point of enabling them to administer the educational system on their own within the context of natural or contractual communities. This assumption of responsibility must necessarily embrace three indispensable areas: participation in design and decision-making processes; regular, structured involvement in the processes of management and evaluation; and finally financial accountability with regard to both income and contributions".

Participation in education can be analysed in terms both of the degree of participation and the areas of education in which greater participation can occur. The first can be examined in relation to the earlier analysis of the 'ladder' of participation in development. It posits a range of involvement in education by various actors from both inside and outside the school. For those from outside the school (parents, community members, NGOs), the range goes from:

— Complete non-participation and exclusion from school affairs, except in the provision of resources; through
— Involvement (at home) with motivating children and helping them with homework; to
— Involvement as an 'audience' and passive supporters at school-run meetings or assemblies; and to
— Participation as 'consultants' on school issues;
— As 'partners' in teaching or training;
— As implementers of delegated powers; and, ultimately,
— As citizens or a community in control of the school

The range can be quite similar for those already inside the school. Teachers themselves may be kept ignorant of non-classroom school programmes and policies; may be involved merely as an 'audience' to activities and as passive supporters of decisions arranged by others; or may be more active participants in providing input to school policies, planning and implementing school curricula and programmes, and controlling more directly the management of the school.

The first few levels of such a range of participation are limited to 'involvement', defined as "implicating, including, and entangling or wrapping up in"—where parents generally help in activities organised by the school—and thus are "of a rather formal nature and school—rather than parent-oriented.

Participation is defined as "having a share in, having a part in, being part of. It is achieved farther along the range, where parents take a more active part in the activities of associations, perhaps help in the classroom, and assist in other work. "In this way, the focus of their relationship with the school widens from that of the parent concerned with his/her child's education per se, to a more global concern with the school as a whole". For teachers, as well, such expanded participation can widen the focus of concern from his/her classroom and pupils to a broader interest in the quality of the entire school and of its relationship to the surrounding community.

5.7. School Governance

Schools are unique educational entities. So, a more decentralised governance structure is needed so that it can offer their local communities the services, programmes, and activities which they desire. If adults are going to develop this ownership and commitment to their local schools, the governance of education must be decentralised so they can participate in decision-making activities, at the local school level, which directly influence the quality and quantity of education offered to children. The school committees, school councils or parent-teacher groups established to facilitate participatory decision-making must be based on a collaborative management philosophy of governance.

Policy-making and governance is the second area where greater participation is possible. The term 'governance' can cover a wide range of activities. The most effective policies are those that either have originated on site or use the input from and participation by teachers, administrators, and the community to support teachers and the school. Policies implemented or adapted by the school community to respond to teachers' needs in context have proven more effective in the long run than those implemented by other entities. The participation of teachers and school staff in their own process of change has been proven to have a positive effect on the development and implementation of policies directed at teachers.

Schools may have neither the autonomy nor the capacity to address locally important issues, being expected instead to focus on the implementation of centrally-determined reforms and programmes such as student-based active learning or the adoption of a new curriculum on family life education. And they may receive all of their funds from school fees and/or from the central ministry, based on a standard, predetermined method, and be required to disburse them according to predetermined categories, with little authority or ability to seek funds from other sources or allocate them to areas of particular need.

Even if mechanisms for more autonomous school governance do exist, they may be centred largely in the hands of headteachers, local education officers, a small group of senior teachers, or a hand-picked executive committee of the local PTA. Teachers, parents, and the community surrounding the school may have little role to play in these processes.

However, because greater participation in school management by a variety of interested partners can increase the demand for, and 'ownership' of, the education which occurs in the school, governments should move towards a policy of strengthening school-based partnerships. This is especially important in the area of school improvement activities. Educational innovations are difficult to implement in any event. Greater teacher involvement in their design and management may help to ensure their implementation. By the same token, greater involvement by parents and community members in school governance can increase their demand and support for education school.

Teachers, parent groups, and school committees can play a more active role in school governance. A variety of mechanisms exists which can be used to enhance their participation. Some of these are restricted to actors within the school—i.e, the greater involvement of teachers—while others include the participation of partners from outside the school: parents, community organisations, NGOs, private enterprise, and other local actors.

Financial management participation is often defined as extraction; that is, parents, the community at large, and even teachers are seen as sources of financial and material support and of physical labour. This can include land, labour, and materials for the building; the repair and maintenance of facilities; the donation of equipment and learning materials; and the raising of money.

The communities in which the schools were located provided the housing for the schools, community Boards of Education, and candidates to be trained as combination teachers/community leaders. The Government provided its moral support and, as the project progressed, it provided on an increasing annual basis, funding towards the payment of the teachers' salaries. A technical committee was set up to supervise the progress of the pre-school programme.

Teachers perform different roles. They are teachers, public educators, community mobilisers and executive managers of the programmes all at once. The choice of girls from the communities is generally based on their interest in the job, the regard with which they are held in the community and their own inherent abilities. Most of them, as a result, have been good' choices from the point of view of an in-built community support and a reciprocal unwillingness to let the community that chose them down. Communities vary in the extent of their responsiveness, but the vital back-up that the teachers get from the field officers keeps them motivated and encourages them to keep on trying to overcome difficulties as they arise.

Various management mechanisms inside or outside of school exist or can be established and strengthened in order to promote more participatory approaches to school governance. But the choice about what kind of mechanisms to establish and what powers to invest it with is not necessarily an easy one. A variety of issues must be explored and decisions made before these mechanisms have any real impact on how schools are run and financed.

The 'basic school' is defined as a school created and managed by a village or a group of villages, a neighbourhood or a group of neighbourhoods, or a group of parents—thus, by local communities. Such a definition is possible within a system where some authority is deconcentrated to the level of the village or neighbourhood. The basic school is the initiative and the fruit of labour of a community—rural, urban, even corporate—which becomes its sponsor.

The teachers use the official curriculum of the first cycle of basic education and teach the pupils until their graduation into the second cycle. In one such school, neither of the two teachers had received any special training one was a catechism teacher, the other a former secondary school student, but they obtained such good results that the public authorities especially the school administration, became interested in their experiences.

5.7.1. Process of Instruction

Community consists of a group of citizens bound up in a social system with common identity for survival. Some school administrators believe that the local people are not knowledgeable enough to take part in curriculum building at the local level. This is an erroneous impression. Community citizens have bona fide interest in the local school. They have invested their money, time, and effort in the building of the school. Besides, their children attend the local school. They deserve to know what is taught at the school and also should take part in the building of the curriculum. They should be directly or indirectly involved in the teaching and learning process as resource persons.

Instructional process comprised both educational content and teaching and training. It is in this area—the determination of what should be taught, using what materials, and in what ways where greatest collaboration can often occurs.

Unlike the area of school governance, where centralised systems may severely limit the autonomy of schools in setting individually their goals, planning new programmes, and even managing budgets, many schools may have considerable freedom to alter and adapt the nature of their instructional processes. Schools may be given national curricula, syllabi, and textbooks; their teachers may be provided common pre-service and in-service training in 'proper' methods and required content; and there may be standard criteria and processes for evaluating issues of quality such as school facilities and pupil achievement.

However schools—partly because of their 'loosely-coupled' nature—may also have considerable autonomy, with or without central ministry encouragement, to insert local material into the curricula, develop site-specific teaching materials, upgrade and monitor the performance of their teachers, and improve both their own physical plant and, ultimately, their academic results. If individual schools find it difficult to implement such changes, collaboration across schools, in school clusters or teacher clubs, may make such grass-roots improvement feasible.

One issue in looking at the current nature of participation in the instructional process is the extent to which individual schools or groups of schools can, through the greater involvement of their own personnel, try to improve the quality of this process. Another, of course, is the extent to which others outside of the school—especially parents but also other community members, agents of other development sectors (e.g., health and agriculture), private enterprises, NGOs, etc.—participate in this process. There is a variety of mechanisms available to make greater collaboration in various aspects of the instructional process possible. Some of these (school clusters, teacher clubs) are limited to members of the school community; others involve individuals or groups from among parents or from the larger community. Some involve the 'partners' as observers and listeners; others as more active consultants, managers, and even teachers.

5.8. Benefits of Educational Participation

It is not always easy to demonstrate the effectiveness of participatory approaches to development. Clear, concrete results in regard to enrolment and achievement gains or increases in resources provided to education—measurable in quantitative terms—are less often available than more impressionistic evidence of changes in processes and procedures, attitudes and values. Anecdotal information of programme 'success' abounds in the literature, but much of this is brief and lacking in detail. And evidence of such success is not necessarily proof of generalizability or replicability, since achievement may depend greatly on the particular context of participation.

The participatory approaches adopted during training provide opportunities for trainees to contribute to their own training, thus encouraging greater commitment, creativity, initiative, confidence, and independence among them. The knowledge and skills they acquire help them to interact better with, and to mobilise, parents and communities to participate in the provision of quality services in pre-schools and in curriculum development. This has led to the adapting of curriculum to specific community requirements through the development of locally designed play and learning materials and through the collection of local stories, poems, riddles, songs, and games.

Through dialogue and awareness meetings, people have come to see that there are numerous roles in education for various partners and are more aware of what those roles are. As a result, there is greater involvement in school life by primary headteachers and school inspectors and a warmer interaction between teachers and pupils. There is also collaboration with nutritionists and officers from the Ministry of Health, and NGOs and local authorities are beginning to accept responsibility for the payment of teachers' salaries, one of the most serious problems facing the programme. For such effective collaboration to take place, the government must allow for and respect the decisions made by other partners. It must recognise that other partners, when tapped and motivated, may play important roles in improving the quality of pre-school education.

There is evidence of more skilled teachers and development agents—more confident, flexible, interactive, facilitating, and responsive to people's conditions and needs, and able to be trained in these skills through systematic programmes which focus on practical work, participatory approaches to training, and community involvement.

The studies speak of greater pupil creativity and pride in their work and more enjoyment in their learning. The results of the PROPEL project appear particularly interesting in this regard. Graduates of the non-formal education centres are said to be able to succeed in formal system examinations and to read to their parents and siblings, write letters, and keep accounts—all skills which, according to the project's rules, must be demonstrated in their homes every day. Pupils are also encouraged to speak in village meetings, and do so with a certain 'social etiquette'; for girls, especially, who are often shown to be learning more rapidly than their brothers who are usefully put in government schools, this has led to greater respect in their communities and greater demand for further education.

5.9. Conclusion

The pattern of education has to be changed in order to provide education to all. Today, the number of illiterate people is increasing even in the highly developed states. Illiteracy hinders development and it has to be eradicated. Active participation from the side of government is necessary to give education to all.

References

Aungles, P., Karmel, T., & Wu, T. *Demographic and Social Change: Implications for Education Funding*. Department of Education, Training and Youth Affairs, Canberra. 2000.

Anderson, D.S. & Vervoorn. A.E. *Access to Privilege: Patterns of participation in Australian postsecondary education*. ANU Press, Canberra. 1983.

Andrews, L., Aungles, P., Baker, S., & Sarris, A. *The characteristics and Performance of Higher Education Institutions*. Department of Education Training and Youth Affairs, Canberra. 1998.

Cooper, T. & Meyenn, B. *A school based project and educational change. Research and Educational Futures: Technology, development and educational futures,* collected papers, Australian Association for Research in Education, National Conference, Education Department of Western Australia, Perth. 1984.

Department of Employment, Education and Training. *Young People's Attitudes to Post-compulsory Education and Training Young People's Attitudes to Post-compulsory Education and Training*. AGPS, Canberra. 1994.

James, R., Wyn, J., Baldwin, G., Hepworth, G., McInnis, C., & Stephanou, A. *Rural and isolated school students and their higher education choices*, AGPS, Canberra. 1999.

Sprague, T. "Explanation of a new formula for interpolation." *Journal of the Institute of Actuaries*, Vol. 22. 1881.

Stevenson, S., Maclachlan, M. & Karmel, T. 'Regional Participation in Higher Education', *Higher Education Division Occasional Paper Series*, AGPS, Canberra. 1999

UNESCO. Education for All Global Monitoring Report 2002. Is the World on Track? Paris: UNESCO. 2002.

6

ACCOUNTABILITY IN SCHOOL EDUCATION

6.1. Introduction

Solving critical educational problems throughout the world, and providing better communication among policy makers, researchers, and practitioners is inevitable to foster scholarly excellence in all fields of education. As the economies of nations compete for strong positions within a competitive global market place, many governments have become increasingly interested in the performance of all aspects of their education systems. This trend, coupled with the enormous expenditures that are devoted to education, has also precipitated widespread public requests for higher levels of scrutiny concerning the quality of education. These demands for information about school system performance can only be addressed through the implementation of systematic accountability systems.

The education profession has conformed to the requirements of regulatory or compliance accountability systems (usually based on government statutes), and has also subscribed to professional norms established by associations of educators. However, at the beginning of the 21st Century, accountability systems have also been required to respond to demands that professional performance be judged by the results that have been achieved.

6.2. Types of Accountability Systems

Compliance with regulations, adherence to professional norms, and results driven are three main types of accountability system in the field of education. In the Education Policy Booklet Series, these principles and strategies are described, with particular attention given to the political and technical aspects of accountability. Accc untability systems are not new. The differences between current systems and those employed previously are matters of "for what" and "to whom." Educators have worked mostly within three accountability systems, often simultaneously. The first system demands compliance with statutes and regulations such as those embodied in the British Office for Standards in Education. Anchored in an industrial model of education, compliance systems view the school as the embodiment of constant processes and allow for variation in results, generally attributed to the varying characteristics of students.

Educators were accountable for adherence to rules and accountable to the bureaucracy. The second system is based upon adherence to professional norms. Although neither mandated nor required, the impact of widespread agreement on certain principles and practices has done much to elevate education as a profession.

The curriculum and evaluation, the standards for educational and psychological testing, and the programme evaluation standards exemplify the professional norm approach to accountability. Within this system, educators are accountable for adherence to standards and accountable to their peers.

Results, the third accountability system, are defined in terms of student learning. This system has emerged from increasing political involvement in education. The "No Child Left Behind" requirements in the United States and the Australian National Education, Performance Monitoring Task Force are examples of results-based systems. In these systems educators are accountable for student learning and accountable to the general public. Educators often find themselves responding to all three systems, attempting to balance the requirements of each. Professional norms complement both compliance and results systems.

However, compliance and results systems often conflict. Part of this conflict stems from the fact that the emergence of results systems has been fostered by dissatisfaction with historic results;

that is, those achieved under compliance systems. At present, accountability systems focus less on compliance and more on results.

The system defines educators' responsibility for all students, regardless of the advantages or disadvantages they bring to school. It must be built upon aligned components-objectives, assessments, instruction, resources, and rewards or sanctions. The technical aspects of the system must meet high standards. Furthermore, the system must provide the vehicle for positive change. The relationship between the educational attainment of citizens and the quality of their life has grown from a point of research interest to a call for action.

Governments in a number of Western nations experienced low relative performance of their students on academic assessments when compared with students from certain Asian nations; and a loss of historic industries (and jobs) to these nations in the second half of the 20th century. Within the United States, the insistence on comprehensive accountability systems was intensified by two events: widespread publication in the popular press of results from the 1995 Third International Math and Science Study (TIMSS) and the 1996 National Governors Association Education Summit. The TIMSS results suggested that United States students in Grade 3 were slightly behind their peers in other developed countries and, importantly from a policy perspective, this difference increased the longer they remained in school.

Accountability is an international issue. England has a national curriculum accompanied by assessments and measures for rating schools. France, Hong Kong, China, Japan, and others use national assessments to measure student and school progress and to make decisions about each. Many European systems use examinations to determine student access to the next level of education. All these systems are based on explicit definitions of what students are expected to learn and to what level they are expected to perform.

Furthermore, examinations are used to monitor student learning, with the data providing the basis for changes within the system. Educational opportunity, an extension of civil rights and economic inclusion, has been redefined: concerns for equal access and treatment have been replaced with an emphasis on equal attainment. To have equal attainment, however, variations in access and, particularly, treatment must be available to meet the needs of increasingly diverse populations of students.

Although, schools have been expected to teach students, there has been general acceptance that only those students who bring advantages to the school are likely to benefit from the exposure to this teaching. Minority students, economically disadvantaged students, disabled students, and other groups simply have not been expected to learn at the level of their advantaged peers. Current research findings counter the premise that some students cannot benefit from schooling.

Ron Edmonds' work on effective schools identified principles that should underlie school practices almost a quarter century ago. Subsequently, teaching practices have been identified and instructional models developed that promote high levels of learning for large numbers of students, regardless of the disadvantages they bring into the classroom. The combination of national aspiration, cultural support, and individual effort overcomes both real and perceived barriers.

Assuming responsibility for the learning of all students transforms the school and the classroom environment and, to some degree, the way that teachers view their profession and themselves. The popular literature is replete with heroic educators who, despite overwhelming odds, are able to change and improve a school through their zeal. A challenge of accountability systems is to make the heroic, customary. In results-based systems, students' learning failures are attributed to weaknesses in educational programmes and practices rather than to students' characteristics and backgrounds.

Schools that are accomplishing the goal of all students achieving success are most likely to have strong and stable teachers and administrators. Strength comes from factors such as greater content knowledge and visionary instructional leadership. Stability, in terms of commitment to the school over time, is needed to shape the school culture and climate. Stability enables the development of relationships with parents and the community that are anchored in mutual trust and focused upon students' present and future needs.

Educators may find themselves overwhelmed by the disadvantages that students bring to the learning environment over which they have no control. Educators also have little control over the resources available to them to achieve the goals. Administrators must build consensus around the goals and cultivate a professional dialogue that encourages the definition of solvable problems. This dialogue must be extended to the broader community so that the disadvantages students bring to the school can be ameliorated over time. Workable, defensible accountability systems are built upon aligned components-objectives, assessments, instruction, resources, and rewards or sanctions.

6.3. Components of Accountability Systems

Education systems emphasise literacy, mathematical reasoning, scientific inquiry, and historical and social understanding to support civic participation. Within developing nations, literacy is the most often defined learning expectation. Within developed nations, the emphasis is on increasing mathematical and scientific competence. In general, curricula mirror the economic focus of nations.

The establishment of content standards impacts on the nature and structure of the curriculum. Teachers must exhibit an understanding of the structure of the curriculum both horizontally (within levels) and vertically (across levels). Access to a variety of learning resources (including supplementary materials) and extended or enriched informal learning opportunities are important.

The introduction of content standards has proceeded at a much faster pace than have the learning resources and supportive opportunities that must be aligned with the standards if the intended learning is to occur. The use of assessments to inform decisions about students, schools, and personnel has been accelerated by the rise of results-based accountability systems. Aligned with the content standards, assessments are used to make decisions about student eligibility for and progress to the next level of school; for administrator and teacher employment and rewards; and for resource allocation. When these assessments are used in this way, they are referred to as "high stake" assessments. These "high stakes" decisions generate demands that information from assessments can be used to improve the teaching-learning process.

Accountability assessments generally do not offer sufficient diagnostic information for teacher planning and in-class work with individual students. Some assessment programmes release items and/or parallel assessments so that teachers are comfortable with both the content to be tested and the manner in which each standard is assessed. Changes in expectations about students should lead to changes in instruction. The rapid change of the curriculum, particularly in mathematics and science, has left many teachers responsible for teaching content they may not have learned in a formal setting. Teachers also are expected to adapt their teaching for students from diverse backgrounds, exhibiting a range of motivations and prior experiences. Instead of a consistent methodology yielding differentiated results, teachers are expected to differentiate their methodologies to yield consistent results for diverse student populations.

Accountability systems, based on results, utilise public reporting to a greater degree than do the compliance or professional norms systems. In the latter two systems information about student performance is held within the profession. Results-based systems rely upon widespread communication of results to parents and the general public. Many results-based systems generate school report cards or school profiles for distribution to general audiences. These reports include summaries of the performance of students or subgroups of students as well as information about resources, programmes, and behaviour.

Providing this information to the public has required that teachers and administrators become comfortable discussing strengths and weaknesses, explaining a variety of statistical data, and facilitating positive change. This new communications role for educators can be intimidating as educators struggle both to understand underperformance and to inspire confidence that they can lead the change process needed to improve performance.

In most results-based accountability systems performance is publicly acknowledged and rewards, sometimes financial, are provided to those schools or individuals exhibiting high and/or improving performance. Schools not succeeding are provided encouragement and often technical assistance. Technical assistance is most effective when the local school assumes ownership of the results-based change process. Schools needing to improve dramatically benefit from increased attention and resources. Yet these schools also may be overwhelmed by the infusion of new practices and greater expectations for simultaneous rapid and long-lasting change.

Another layer of educational governance may assume management of the school in extreme circumstances. The continuum from providing technical assistance to taking control often is ill defined. Technical assistance should provide immediate and temporary support whereas assumption of responsibility extends to governance and data management. All schools are most vulnerable when the public demands quick change, rather than exercising the patience to implement sustainable changes. Long-lasting change requires integration of remedies across community agencies and responsibilities.

Content standards and the accompanying assessments are the components with which the other components, most importantly, instructional materials and teaching-learning strategies, must be aligned. When content standards, assessments, materials, and strategies are aligned, students have the maximum opportunity to learn. Also, when the public understands data derived from an "aligned" accountability system, they are more likely to respond to the performance of schools in a thoughtful and supportive way.

Textbooks formed the basis for instructional planning throughout much of the 20th century. Although the structure and content of textbooks changed in response to discipline-based organisations, the presumption was that textbooks incorporated all that was needed to facilitate the desired student learning. Thus, alignment was part and parcel of buying into the textbook "package". As access to multi-media and a wider range of materials increased, reliance on a primary textbook for the design of an instructional plan began to fade. Currently, the specification of content standards presumes independence from a primary text and the use of diverse materials and teaching-learning strategies.

6.4. Results-based Accountability Systems

Accountability systems emphasise student mastery of specified content and rely more on criterion referenced assessments than on norm-referenced ones to determine how well students are learning. If these measures are misaligned with content standards, the information they yield is irrelevant to determining school effectiveness.

Assessments in results-based accountability systems must be of sufficient technical quality to support the decisions that are based on the results.

Assessment systems can "lower the stakes" when educators and others have sufficient documentation that the assessments have met technical standards and there is clear understanding of how the assessment data are to be used. The stakes also are lowered when assessment data are used for positive purposes such as providing technical assistance to schools, initiating supplemental services to students, and amending policies and practices that interfere with goal attainment. When the stakes are consistently negative, the assessment data are viewed skeptically; when the stakes lead to improvements, assessment data can become accepted as an integral and necessary part of the decision-making process that leads to educational improvement.

The quality of school is not only evident in assessment results, but also in the diversity of programmes offered, the preparation and performance of educational professionals, student behaviour and attitudes, and the relationship between the school and the community. School reports should publish contextual and programmatic information along with assessment results. This additional information provides a more complete description of the school and enhances the public's understanding of its overall performance. The information also offers a point of comparison among schools as patterns of inputs, processes, and outputs are related to levels of school performance.

Fiscal and other resources, teacher quality, students' backgrounds, and parent/community norms, etc are included in inputs. Processes include the organisation of schools, the curriculum and pedagogy, and opportunities for student participation in non-academic activities. Outputs include student achievement, participation, attitudes, and aspirations. Other potentially useful information includes attendance (both teacher and student), student behaviour (or misbehaviour), teacher professional development, and parents' and students' perceptions of the school. As school reports gain public attention, programme advocates view publication of data as a way of ensuring much needed attention to their programmes.

6.4.1. Quality Information

Schools establish and maintain data bases that can be manipulated in response to a variety of inquiries. The most extensive system includes different security levels and permits inquiries on a school, classroom, or student basis. Data systems, however simple or complex, require administrative time and attention to accuracy. When the data are meaningful to those reporting them, use of the data is more likely to impact the quality of reporting. As data are used in decision-making at the school level, attention to accuracy should increase. Users of the data should not forget that while standardised collections offer uniformity and consistency, the unique aspects of a school or programme may be sacrificed to standardisation.

6.4.2. Quality of Performance

Accountability systems, oriented on results, are based on student performance. There are three general ways in which student performance can be interpreted and reported: status of a cohort of students against a criterion; change in status of a cohort of students over time; and longitudinal change in the performance of individual students. Status against a criterion is the simplest to collect, report, and explain. Cohorts of students are used as the unit of analysis. The report might state that "68 percent of our students in grades three through five met the standard." Extensions of this type of reporting include the percentage of students scoring at various performance levels or the achievement patterns of various subgroups.

6.4.3. Finding Useful Information

Results-based accountability systems should provide information that is understood and can be used by a variety of audiences. Systems fail when they yield only a single level of analysis and fall prey to the assumption that one report satisfies the needs of all audiences. Each audience should have sufficient information to carry out its particular responsibilities. For educators, the information must enable them to identify needed services and resources and evaluate the impact. Stewardship of resources such as time, teacher quality, and positive working relationships with parents and the community stimulates higher levels of student performance. School personnel generally focus their energies on those elements over which they can exercise control.

High levels of teacher attendance are desirable, but not at the cost of denying teachers opportunities to participate in meaningful professional development. Missing two days of face-to-face teaching to learn an effective instructional strategy could lead to higher results than perfect teacher attendance. Some systems employ a data warehouse with varying access to levels of analysis. Parents may have access to information about their individual child but are precluded from data on other children or teacher performance. Decisions about warehousing data should consider retrieval strategies and security.

6.4.4. Participation of Parent and Community

To carry out its responsibility, each audience should have sufficient information within the overall accountability framework. Parents have a responsibility to make decisions for their children, to advocate for their children, and to support positive changes in the educational system (both locally and elsewhere). Useful reports for parents are those that help them understand what is in the best interest of their children. Consequently, these reports should be private, but allow for interpretation of the child's progress against explicit standards, against grade level expectations, and in comparison to peers. School reports should be provided in formats that are easy-to-read and at reading levels appropriate to the general population.

Graphic representations should be used and ancillary materials provided to parents who wish to go beyond the published summary. Parents are expected to use the information to encourage and motivate their children and as a basis for interacting with school personnel. Ultimately parents also are expected to portray the school factually to the community and to advocate citizen responsibility for creating a culture of high expectations and performance. Policymakers range from local officials through members of state and national governing bodies.

Those who make the rules require information to help them understand what progress is being made, to inform their resource allocation decisions, and to enable them to ensure that the system meets not only the present requirements and needs but those of the future. Public polices provide the framework for the actions of those who work in and benefit from results-based accountability systems. Those policies serve as both the foundation and the subject of the system.

Accountability systems embody the values and aspirations of a society. Societies communicate their values through their policies and practices. Policymakers need to know that the measures used to assess student performance and evaluate school performance provide valid descriptions of the quality of education. They need to understand the meaning of the assessment results. They also need to know the populations of students to whom the results do (and do not) apply. Because no society has unlimited resources, those charged with policy development must examine the available information to determine how resource allocations promote or hinder achievement of the primary goals. Allocation patterns and usage that slow progress must be redirected.

Policymakers need information to ensure that the system continues to improve. As substantive and technical challenges arise, accountability systems can be modified to focus more intently on desired learning, to assess that learning more accurately and precisely, and to communicate assessment results in proper forms to a variety of audiences. Sound and defensible policies provide for these changes, enabling growth over time.

6.5. Accountability and School Leadership

In almost all organisational circumstances, some leadership practices are for practices associated with transformational leadership. Evidence from many schools varying in size, location and level provides support for this claim in the context of educational organisations. Such practices, however, ought to be considered a 'necessary but not sufficient' part of an effective school leader's repertoire.

The practices of school leaders need to acknowledge important features of the context in which they find themselves.

The framework used for identifying leadership implications is a four-fold classification of approaches to accountability developed as part of a recent study conducted in seven countries.

6.5.1. Leader as Salesperson

This approach to accountability increases the competition for students faced by schools. It is an especially prominent approach currently, versions of it evident in several European countries, Canada, the United States, New Zealand, Australia and parts of Asia, for example. Competition is also increased by altering the basis for school funding so that money follows students, and by publicly ranking schools based on aggregated student achievement scores. These tools are often used in combination. The common thread binding together these different tools for increasing competition is a belief that schools are unresponsive, bureaucratic and monopolistic.

By advocates of this approach, to have little need to be responsive to pressure from their clients because they are not likely to lose them. In relation to schools, this means that they will come to view their major task as offering programmes that they believe are good for their clients. Such organisations, it is argued, seek efficiency on their own terms and are prone to view clients as objects to be treated rather than customers to be served.

Advocates of this approach to educational accountability hold a series of assumptions about how such competition is likely to result in greater student achievement.

Increased competition allows parents and students to select schools with which they are more satisfied and which better meet their educational needs. Second, parents who are more satisfied with their child's school provide greater support to that school and to their child's learning. Third, students are likely to be more engaged when their own learning styles are matched to a particular school. Fourth, when teachers have chosen their work settings, and have been active in designing their own schools' programmes, they will be more committed to implementing those programmes effectively.

All of these outcomes will combine to increase student achievement, attendance and educational attainment. Market approaches to accountability assume an ideal set of responses from school leaders suggested by the label 'salesperson' or 'entrepreneur'.

The first order of business is having a good product to sell. These leaders market their schools effectively, develop good customer/client relations, and monitor 'customer' satisfaction. To prosper in such contexts, school leaders continuously redesign their organisations in response to fast-changing market conditions. They collect data about competitors' services and prices, and find niches for their schools. They have exceptional levels of clarity about their missions because these missions are viewed as a central criterion in parent and student choices. Evidence about how school leaders actually respond to increased market competition, while still relatively modest, suggests a more complicated reality.

Choice arrangements vary considerably in the autonomy awarded principals: as an explanation for the few differences found in the practices of US principals of magnet and nonmagnet schools, Hausman pointed to the wide array of district policies regulating all principals in the district.

Evidence demonstrates that some school choice settings actually put very little pressure on leaders and schools to compete. This is the case when a school is oversubscribed, or when it serves parents and students who, for economic and other reasons, feel unable to travel to a school outside their own neighbourhood.

School leaders facing the same competitive conditions may respond quite differently for reasons associated with their individual abilities, values, beliefs and motivations. Grace interpreted his evidence as capturing three quite different responses by individual school leaders. One group of leaders welcomed the more managerial role they believed was implied in policy changes. A second group was preoccupied with the loss of a professional orientation to schools, and concerned about managerialist values encroaching on their work. The third group of school leaders actively opposed those features of market approaches to school reform which they believed were unlikely to lead to school improvement.

Competition has unpredictable effects on the propensity of heads to engage in instructional leadership, some finding little time for it while others increase their attention to it.

6.5.2. Leader As Teacher

When decentralisation or devolution of decision making is used for purposes of increasing accountability (the 'voice option'), one of its central aims is often to increase the voice of those who are not heard, or at least not sufficiently listened to, in the context of typical school governance structures. When this is the goal, a community controls form of site-based management is, typically, the instrument used for its achievement. The basic assumption giving rise to this form of site-based management is that the curriculum of the school ought to directly reflect the values and preferences of parents and the local community.

It is claimed that school professionals are typically not as responsive to such local values and preferences as they ought to be. Their responsiveness is greatly increased, however, when the power to make decisions about curriculum, budget and personnel is in the hands of the parent/community constituents of the school. School councils in which parent/community constituents have a majority of the membership are the primary vehicle through which to exercise such power.

However, devolution of decision making is sometimes rooted in a broader reform strategy for public institutions generally, which Peters has referred to as "new managerialism". While there are variants on this approach to accountability among countries, they share in common a shift in emphasis (a) from policy formulation to management and institutional design, (b) from process to output controls, (c) from organisational integration to differentiation and (d) from "statism to subsidiarity ".

This goal is pursued through the implementation of an administrative control form of site-based management which increases school-site administrators' accountability to the central district or board office for the efficient expenditure of resources. These efficiencies are to be realised by giving local school administrators authority over such key decision areas as budget, physical plant, personnel and curriculum. Advocates of this form of site-based management reason that such authority, in combination with the incentive to make the best use of resources, ought to get more of the resources of the school into the direct service of students. To assist in accomplishing that objective, the principal may consult informally with teachers, parents, students or community representatives. Site councils are typically established to advise the principal, with membership at the discretion of the principal.

Decentralisation approaches to accountability assume a role for school leaders as teachers to those with newly-found voices, usually parents and/or teachers. This approach to accountability assumes that the school leader's role is to empower these people and to actively encourage the sharing of power formerly exercised by the principal. School leaders, it is assumed, will act as members of teams rather than sole decision makers. This role entails teaching others how to make defensible decisions and clarifying their decision responsibilities. School leaders will embrace, as well, the belief that, through participation in decision making, teachers and parents will not only be more committed to the results of such decision making, but that the decisions themselves will be better. The school leader becomes the keeper of the process, not the outcome of the process.

Evidence of the effects on school leaders of decentralisation or school-based management in its various forms is quite extensive. These data indicate that assumptions about the role of school leaders in decentralised settings sometimes describe what actually happens in practice. But it is not the whole story. Decentralisation is associated, as well, with a radically increased emphasis on budgetary considerations and less attention to providing leadership about curriculum and instruction. Decentralisation greatly increases the time demands on school leaders (and the need for more attention to time management), intensifies their role and, under competitive conditions, may isolate them from other administrative colleagues outside their own organisation. When parent-dominated school councils are part of decentralisation, principals often provide leadership in respect to both internal and external processes associated with councils.

Principals often find themselves setting the agenda, providing information to other council members, assisting council decision making, and developing a close working relationship with the council chair. Externally, principals often act as strong, active supporters of their school councils, communicating with all stakeholders about council activities, and promoting the value of councils for the work of school staffs.

6.5.3. Leader as Chairperson

The two radically different accountability strategies that have a professional orientation are: One of these approaches manifests itself most obviously in the implementation of professional control models of site-based management. The other approach encompasses the standards movement as it applies to the practices of teachers, administrators and occasionally others. What both strategies share in common is a belief in the central contribution of professional practice in schools to their outcomes. They differ most obviously on which practices they choose for their direct focus: in the case of professional control site-based management, the focus is on school-level decision making, whereas teachers' classroom instructional and curricular practices are the focus of the standards movement. Professional control site-based management increases the power of teachers in school decision making while also holding teachers more directly accountable for the school's effects on students.

The goal of this form of site-based management is to make better use of teachers' knowledge in such key decision areas as budget, curriculum and occasionally personnel. Basic to this form of site-based management is the assumption that professionals closest to the student have the most relevant knowledge for making such decisions, and that full participation in the decision-making process will increase their commitment to implementing whatever decisions are made. Participatory democracy, allowing employees greater decision-making power, is also presumed to lead to greater efficiency and effectiveness, and to better outcomes.

A standards approach to accountability in the traditional professions emphasises heavy control of entry to the profession by government, with responsibility for subsequent monitoring of accountability turned over to members of the profession itself. Such an approach requires clear standards of professional knowledge, skill and performance, something the professional standards movement in education set out to define—beginning in the US, for example, in the early 1980's. Different products of the standards movement are available by now as the basis for the licensure of entry-level teachers and school administrators as well as for recognising advanced levels of teaching and school administrator performance.

Professional approaches to accountability assume a role for school leaders suggested by the label chairperson. Leaders, it is implied, have an increased need to stay abreast of best professional practices and to assist staff in the identification of professional standards for their work. In the context of professional approaches to accountability, leaders need to both set expectations and create conditions for professional growth. It seems likely, as well, that these leaders will find it productive to monitor progress of staff towards the achievement of professional standards, buffer staff from external distractions, and assist parents to understand and appreciate such standards.

School leaders will need to mobilise resources to meet not just higher but more sophisticated, standards. They will need to be vigilant about such unintended side effects of standards as the narrowing of curricula. Maintaining teacher morale in schools identified as low-achieving, and helping ensure equitable treatments for needs of students, also seem likely challenges for school leaders responding to this form of accountability. But there is a dearth of systematic evidence about the extent to which these implications for school leaders come close to describing reality.

6.5.4. Leader as Strategic Manager

This approach includes systematic efforts to create more goal-oriented, efficient and effective schools by introducing more rational procedures. The main assumption underlying this approach is that there is nothing fundamentally wrong with current school structures. Nevertheless, the effectiveness and efficiency of schools will be improved as they become more strategic in their choices of goals, and more planful and data driven about the means used to accomplish those goals. This approach encompasses a variety of procedures for strategic planning, especially at the LEA level, as well as multiple procedures for school improvement planning, school development planning, and monitoring progress.

Management approaches to accountability assume that effective school leadership conforms to what is sometimes labelled strategic management. Heads exercising this form of leadership are skilled in collecting and interpreting systematically collected data. They develop, with their staffs, clear manageable goals and priorities for school improvement. Progress in accomplishing such goals is carefully monitored and plans refined accordingly. Because LEA resources and cooperation are often needed to accomplish school priorities, school leaders find it productive to develop especially good working relations with their LEA colleagues.

These assumptions about effective leadership for school improvement have considerable real-world validity but that they are only part of the picture. In the context of two projects carried out by the University of Cambridge Institute of Education, successful school improvement appeared to depend on establishing and sustaining a culture of enquiry and reflection, a commitment to collaborative planning and to staff development, high levels of stakeholder involvement, and effective coordination strategies. Strategic management in these projects also entailed developing school improvement plans from the results of enquiry and reflection, and carefully monitoring and evaluating the implementation of those plans.

6.6. Conclusion

Most approaches to increasing accountability in schools make one of four quite different sets of sassumptions about the status of schools and what is required to improve them. Because of these assumptions, each approach places unique demands on school leaders that require at least partly distinctive responses to be effective. Putting aside, for the moment, possible disagreements with the assumptions themselves, leading school reform premised on any one of the four approaches to accountability is likely to be a manageable task. But almost no one uses the term manageable in reference to the job of principal or head these days. Manageable headship (like airplane food) has become an oxymoron.

Most reform initiatives are eclectic. They bundle together into a single reform platform elements of all, or most, of our four approaches to accountability, in the process creating significant leadership dilemmas. So school leaders attempting to respond to their governments' demands for change can be excused for feeling that they are being pulled in many different directions simultaneously: they are being pulled in many different directions simultaneously.

Much of the variation in the extent to which externally initiated reforms actually result in school improvement can be explained by the ability of potential implementers to make sense of the reforms—to find them meaningful. So, in the face of policy eclecticism and the resulting sense of confusion and uncertainty, school leaders, with their staffs, parents and other stakeholders, need to locate and adopt elements of external initiatives that cohere with their schools' directions that make sense in light of the schools' goals and priorities. No matter the particular nature of the eclectic mix of policies and assumptions faced by a school, effective leadership will always include, for example, buffering staffs from their conscientious tendency to feel they must respond comprehensively to demands for policy implementation from governments.

References

Adams, J E & Kirst, M. "New demands and concepts for educational accountability: striving for results in an era of excellence". In J Murphy & K Louis (eds). *Handbook of research on educational administration* (2nd edition). San Francisco. Jossey-Bass. 1999.

Bass, B. "Does the transactional/transformational leadership transcend organisational and national boundaries?" *American Psychologist.* 52. pp 130-39. 1997.

Bullock, A & Thomas, H. *Schools at the centre? a study of decentralisation,* London. Routledge. 1997.

Clune, W H & Witte, P. *School-based management: Institutional variation, implementation, and issues for further research.* New Brunswick, NJ, Eagleton Institute of Politics. Center for Policy Research in Education. 1997.

Fullan, M. *The new meaning of educational change.* Toronto, OISE Press. 1991.

Giles, C. *School development planning: a practical guide to the strategic management process.* Plymouth. UK. Northcote House Publishers. 1997.

Grace, G. *School leadership: beyond education management.* London. Falmer Press. 1995.

Hausman, C S. "Principal role in magnet schools: Transformed or entrenched?". *Journal of Educational Administration.* 38(1), pp 25-46. 2000.

Hess, G A Jr. *School restructuring Chicago style.* Newbury Park. CA, Corwin Press. 1991.

Kerchner, C T. "Bureaucratic entrepreneurship: the implications of choice for school administration". *Educational Administration Quarterly*. 24(4). pp 381-92. 1988.

Lauder, H & Hughes, D. *Trading in futures*. Buckingham. UK. Open University Press. 1999.

Lee, V. "Educational choice: The stratifying effects of selecting schools and courses". *Educational Policy*. 7(2). pp 125-48. 1993.

Leithwood, K, Jantzi, D & Steinbach, R. *Changing leadership for changing times*. Buckingham. UK. Open University Press. 1999.

Murphy, J & Beck, L. *School-based management as school reform*. Thousand Oaks. CA. Corwin Press. 1995.

Ornstein, A C. "Administrative decentralisation and community policy: Review and outlook". *Urban Review*. 15(1). pp 3-10. 1983.

Brown, R. S. "Creating school accountability reports". *The School Administrator*, 56 (10), 12-17. 1999.

Linn, R. L. "Assessments and accountability". *Educational Researcher*. 29 (2). 4-16. 2000.

MacPherson, R. J. S. "Struggling for the soul of education: Towards accountability policy research". *International Journal of Educational Research*. 23. 561-566. 1995.

7

QUALITY LEADERSHIP IN SCHOOLS

7.1. Introduction

The quality of a school and its children depends on the quality of leaders. The leaders should be highly qualified to nurture new generations. So, the recruitment, retention, and development of school principals are matters of great importance for all school systems because effective educational leadership is absolutely vital to bringing about improvements and advances in all those activities, institutions, and processes that foster the provision of education and student learning. Governments, school system authorities, school-based personnel, universities, leadership institutes, and professional associations are therefore increasingly turning their attention to the development of policies and strategies to address concerns in this area.

Historical, political, cultural, and organisational contexts will all impact significantly on the role of the principal and the relative success of policies and practices designed to improve principal recruitment, retention, and development. In addition, there is a need to recognise that policy makers, system officials, school-based personnel, and those involved in the provision of leadership training, need to take account of a number of possible tensions between key factors such as: political, bureaucratic, and professionally-based approaches to recruitment, retention, and development; the conception of the principal as pedagogical, administrative, and community leader; the authority of the principal and the autonomy and professionalism of teaching staff; the values and culture of the school; and the social and cultural environment within which the school is located.

7.2. Recruitment of Good Principals

Educational leadership and questions concerning the optimum approaches for effective recruitment, retention, and development of principals have become matters to which increasing concern has been devoted in education systems internationally. In some countries national inquiries have been set up to analyse the dimensions of what is seen as a problem in the provision of educational leadership. National leadership institutes have been established to identify new initiatives in educational leadership and to provide overall coherence and direction in the provision of quality leadership for schools and effective lifelong professional learning for school leaders. Resources have been allocated to support new leadership programmes.

National approaches to setting standards, determining certification requirements and evaluating impacts have come under consideration and review. Individual professionals are increasingly recognising that the need to ensure lifelong professional learning, career planning, and the provision of quality schooling is a responsibility that has to be accepted by them, as well as being shared with and between all educational institutions and agencies.

Although there is no shortage of potential principals, there is both concern about the quality of leadership and about the question of whether the structures and cultures within which leaders work, and through which they are trained, are adequate. Politics, formal and informal structures, enduring cultural values, and norms have all been variously identified and defined as impacting on the success of any new policies or strategies to improve principal recruitment, retention, and development.

There is increasing emphasis on the need for coherent, integrated, consequential, and systematic approaches to leadership recruitment, retention, and development. Underpinning such approaches must be the co-operative support, direction, and commitment of all interested constituencies, requiring negotiations among school principals, representatives of professional associations, employing authorities, government, universities, and members of the broader community. Of particular importance is the need to contextualise approaches to ensure relevance and to customise approaches to ensure responsiveness to particular needs.

A cadre of qualified and experienced educators is required for schools and school systems to provide them with a number of suitably qualified and trained aspirants to apply for and assume positions of leadership in schools. Unfortunately, in many countries the numbers of applicants for principals' positions have been declining and there has been a high turnover among incumbent principals. Both of these factors have been identified as constituting problems for the provision and delivery of effective schooling. These problems are costly for schools and school systems in monetary terms.

The loss of leadership experience, expertise, knowledge, and wisdom has the potential to impact adversely on school quality and student learning. Of particular concern in some settings is the difficulty of attracting and retaining women and members of particular ethnic and minority groups, and the difficulty of filling positions in rural, remote, and disadvantaged areas. For these reasons many are claiming that the education profession needs to move towards an approach to career planning, that is systematic, integrated, and interrelated.

7.2.1. Role of a Principal

Strategic approach needs to be a co-ordinated within school systems and schools for attracting and retaining principals and for succession planning for educational leadership in the future. Responsibility rests at many levels. Consideration of principal recruitment and retention can only be well thought-out in the broader context of recruitment, retention, and development in the teaching service as a whole. Policies and strategies designed to address the demand for and supply of an adequate cadre of principals must guard against the negative effects of dysfunctional factors affecting the number of applicants to leadership positions, and instead promote those incentives that add value to leaders' professional experiences, work conditions and personal concerns.

It is very important to give importance to strategies such as: reconceptualising the role of the principal; reviewing workplace conditions; and providing frameworks of mentoring and support.

The process of principal selection and certification must be such that able candidates are confident about the process and not discouraged by aspects of the process itself. Developmental programmes and activities for professional renewal need to be part of a lifelong professional learning programme and contribute to the development of a portfolio of leadership skills and competencies. Approaches to leadership learning need to blend a number of approaches and experiences and acknowledge that some of the most effective mentors and facilitators of leadership learning are principals themselves, sharing good practice and experience based wisdom.

The role of the principal has tended to focus on the interpretation of national/state rules and regulations, and the exercise of delegated responsibility in functional areas such as administration, planning, finance, student welfare, and reporting. In these contexts less emphasis has been placed on the principal's role as decision-maker and as educational leader in the enhancement of school improvement and quality learning. In centralised systems, bureaucratic and hierarchical approaches to principal recruitment, retention and development have tended to prevail as part of a system-wide approach to educational planning and management.

The trend towards the implementation of changed arrangements along the centralisation decentralisation continuum and the effect on schools of more market-orientated approaches to educational provision has had an impact on the role of the principal.

The movement towards greater decentralisation, school site management, and privatisation has shifted responsibility for policy making and decision-making to state, municipal, and local authorities; to parent, church, and community groups; and to education professionals at the school site. This has resulted in an intensification of the role and responsibilities of principals, a diversification of decision making, and an expansion in the range of community-based agencies with the responsibility for educational provision and the management and organisation of schooling.

The role of a principal is increasingly complex and multifaceted. Recent educational reforms have added to the complexity of the principalship and have demanded that principals need new kinds of knowledge, skills, and attitudes. The change and intensification of the principal's role has not always been accompanied by provision of the necessary training and support. This has impacted on the work satisfaction of principals and had an effect on recruitment, retention, and development.

Studies of principal turnover have found that there is a need to adopt new approaches to conceptualising the role of principal and alternative strategies for redesigning and restructuring positions of leadership across the school. A number of possible models for conceptualising the role of principals have been identified: the co-principal model; the principal/business manager model; the multi-principal model; the principal/associate principal model; the principal teacher/principal administrator model; and the principal/educational specialist model.

Moreover, attention needs to be paid to the diverse virtues and values of the various models of the principalship, attention should be paid to the job design requirements of other leadership roles in the school, especially those of assistant and deputy principals. Many assistant and deputy principals are moving into the principalship after serving a relatively short time in these roles. There is therefore, a need to be more deliberate in designing these positions to serve as preparatory ground or apprenticeships for principalship.

7.2.2. Policy and Practice

The principal's role and of leadership positions across the school is required to be restructured realistically. To achieve this goal there is a need to review the ways in which the conceptualisation of leadership roles and the allocation of responsibilities and tasks meet both the needs of the school and the various personal and professional stages of individual's careers and lives. Consideration should also be given to features of leadership roles in order that we might be able to identify ways in which the principalship might be reconceived and redesigned to attract the interest of and applications from members of under-represented groups.

There is a need to expand, support, recognise, and reward leadership exercised by all members of staff at all levels of the schools' operation. In particular, it is time to look anew at the leadership team, especially the roles of assistant and deputy principals and the ways in which their roles could be redesigned to promote a sense of enthusiasm and satisfaction for career advancement in school leadership. Most importantly the time has come to consider the various models of the principalship and accept that it is no longer a case of "one size fits all".

7.2.3. Setting Educational Leadership Standard

The most controversial area associated with principal recruitment, retention, and development is that concerned with the setting of standards for educational leadership, the selection of candidates for leadership programmes, and the licensure/certification of leaders. Only a few countries have made significant advances in the identification of a set of commonly agreed national standards for educational leadership. Even fewer countries have used national leadership standards as a basis for the design and accreditation of leadership programmes for school leaders and for the development and implementation of assessment tools for the licensure/certification of beginning principals and the re-licensure of practicing principals. Differences in approach reflect deeply held differences in philosophy regarding professional learning and career planning.

The presence of standards and mandatory requirements may create hurdles that function as disincentives for people who might otherwise consider applying for leadership positions. Others argue that the determination and assessment of standards and certification is necessary in order to enhance professionalism and ensure quality.

In a number of countries attention is being focussed on the development of leadership standards. The most successful attempts involve the engagement of a wide range of constituencies in consultations and surveys to arrive at shared understandings and agreement.

The work of school leaders should be learner centred, focused on leadership, and professionally oriented. These principles underpin the knowledge requirements, personal qualities, and actions of leaders in six areas: creating the future; leading, learning, and teaching; developing self and working with others;

managing the organisation; securing accountability; and strengthening community through collaboration. These standards offer a framework to guide professional learning and a basis for the development of leadership programmes. The concern for quality leadership has also drawn attention to selection and admission practices for entry to leadership programmes.

Standards for admission to leadership programmes need to be reviewed and alternatives to traditional selection criteria and procedures need to be put in place. Alternative approaches to admission to leadership programmes have been identified.

Another area under review in response to the concern for standards and quality assurance is certification and licensure. In the past many countries have not required certification of its leaders but are now seriously considering its introduction. It should be pointed out however that in some settings where certification and licensure have been in place for many years, the assumptions that underpin traditional approaches to certification and licensure are currently being contested.

There are others who argue that there is a need not only for certification and licensure at the beginning of a person's career but also for advanced certification beyond the requirements of licensure, claiming that, if standards and targets were set to guide the development of principals, the status of the profession would be elevated.

The concern regarding standards and the assurance of quality in all aspects of schooling has implications for the recruitment, retention, and development of school leaders. In the climate of accountability that characterises educational provision in many countries there is increasing support for the position that an indispensable condition of quality assurance is the continuing engagement of all constituents of the education community in the ongoing determination and evaluation of leadership standards.

Leadership standards provide a more informed and accountable basis for the selection of principals, the development of leadership programmes, and the implementation of assessment tools for licensure of beginning principals and the re-licensure of practicing principals.

7.3. Learning for Leadership

Changes in the principalship have been occurring from the general determination to ensure the provision of quality schooling. Changes in approaches to leadership learning have been slower to change. There is widespread agreement that there is a need for a fundamental rethinking of the content, structure, delivery, and assessment of leadership learning. This involves the development of a framework for leadership learning to ensure that formal university based programmes, employer sponsored programmes, and programmes offered by leadership institutes and other providers of leadership development, are complementary. There is a need for political will and the existence of incentives and rewards to bring about this cooperation and collaboration.

Learning should be part of a continuous process involving both formal study and field based learning. The important connections between the self-identity and career goals of individuals need to be taken into consideration when planners are designing leadership learning opportunities. Each of the partners with a stake in leadership learning has a part to play in its development.

7.4. Making Tomorrow's Leaders

Inculcating positive values in leaders is essential for making them good leaders. The recruitment of potential educational leaders and the process of leadership learning must be regarded as continuous and progressive. The process begins with the identification and development of individuals with leadership capacity. Recruitment and development are all the more important in an environment where there is a shortage of principals and in rural or disadvantaged areas where it is often difficult to attract good candidates to apply for principal positions. There are significant differences among countries in regard to approaches to the identification of people with leadership capacity and the provision of pre-service development.

Incoming principals require the completion of a university course in leadership and administration and certification and licensure to become practicing principals. In many other countries people believe that pre-service training programmes at university are not necessary and that adequate preparation for leadership is on-the-job experience. There are a variety of approaches to identifying and developing leadership capacity. They are:

7.4.1. Evaluation Centres

It is a diagnostic tool for determining the presence and strength of leadership skills. Participants engage in an integrated system of realistic school-based simulations designed to generate responses to problem situations and behaviours similar to those required for success in principal positions. Assessors are selected from a pool of talented individuals who have school leadership experience and training in the assessment process. It has been found that the assessment centre is a valuable tool for identifying leadership potential.

7.4.2. Profiling Instruments

These instruments have been used to identify leadership talent and potential in mid-career teachers with a view to helping them fast track their route to the principalship and accelerate their participation in national leadership programmes. Research has shown that this can be an effective approach to developing an accelerated route to headship and that the "potential" group are likely to function effectively as headteachers once relevant contextual experience and specific job-related competencies complement their profile of talent.

7.4.3. Principal Scouts

Principals themselves can serve as "Scouts" for identifying and encouraging leadership potential. One successful approach saw the principal: host sessions that explain the details of school leadership positions; offer half-day or all-day substitutes so that interested candidates can shadow the current principal or assistant principal; set aside time each month to meet with interested teachers and share anecdotes and discussion based on real problems; and start assigning pairs or small groups of aspirants to special assignments and targeted learning experiences.

7.4.4. Internship

Internships, often up to a year in duration, have been found to be among the most effective strategies for developing leadership capacity. Steps in the design of an effective internship have been found to include:

- Effective integration of the intern into the school and the leadership team,
- The development of a shared vision for the internship experience,
- Gradually increasing the responsibilities of the intern,
- Providing time for continuous evaluation, and
- Availability of an external supervisor when problems arise.

The past education systems have been heavily reliant on a process of self selection in the identification of future leaders. Now a more systematic and collaborative approach, involving employing authorities, schools, universities, leadership centres, and individuals is required. Strategies might include the use of generic calls for those interested in leadership, the use of more personal and direct approaches from people in more senior positions, and the use of Profiling Instruments and Assessment Centres to identify those with interest and capacity.

Principals in future will also be more easily recruited when they have had positive experiences of opportunities to lead and a satisfactory experience of working collaboratively with others. A range of practices is available for the development of those with future leadership capacity. These include: mentoring and coaching; internship; shadowing; education platform development; special assignments and targeted learning experiences; formal university award bearing study; and engagement in programmes organised by learning institutes and academies. A carefully conceived and comprehensive programme of leadership learning would involve the incorporation of many of these strategies in a portfolio of leadership experiences shaped in accordance with a personal learning development plan.

7.5. Improving the Efficiencies of New Leaders

Newly appointed principals in some countries receive little

induction or in-service training. A one or two-day induction programme at the beginning of the school year, with some in-servicing regarding the employing authorities' agenda for the year, is considered sufficient. In other settings new principals have a formal, structured programme available to them as one component of a multi-faceted approach to enhancing their leadership capabilities and building leadership capacity in schools. Entry year programmes might include the development of mentoring relationships by joining early career principals with experienced principals; on line discussions; collaborative inquiry, participation in networked learning communities; coaching; inter-visitations; and engagement in seminars and other learning activities relevant to their own needs and the needs of their school and employing authority. There are a variety of approaches to enhancing the leadership capabilities of newly appointed leaders. These include:

7.5.1. Induction Programmes

The induction programmes are needed to help put into practice the knowledge, skills, and understanding gained from prior experience; assist in forming a strategic view of the development needs of the school; provide support in developing constructive relationships with all stakeholders in school; and to provide access to different kinds of learning opportunities.

7.5.2. Mentoring Programmes

This is the most valuable strategy for providing newly appointed school leaders with support. Although mentoring is a most effective process for professional development, the personal dimension makes it very resource-intensive. This problem has been addressed by the National Association of Secondary School Principals (NASSP) which has launched an online Virtual Mentor Programme. The programme is designed to provide principals with direct access to recognised school leader practitioners for advice, guidance, or ideas.

7.5.3. Leadership Coaching

In leadership coaching, a coach brings a different perspective to the relationship between the "coachee" and his/her context. The coach moves between instructional and facilitative coaching strategies based upon assessment of the coachee's needs and in pursuit of agreed goals. The coach's fundamental commitment is to student success. The programme specifically addresses principals' needs, designed around the challenges that principals face.

Leading the school assumes an approach in which leaders model: a preparedness to face and manage the challenges of change, a capacity to exercise critical and creative intelligence in the solving of problems, and a belief in the complex, shared, and incremental process of learning to learn—and to lead. Newly appointed principals are in special need of assistance when taking on responsibility for a school. Integrated and articuiated strategies of professional support, guidance, and development must be available to new principals. These might include mentoring; inter-school and district visitations; peer pairings; network interactions; face to face and online sharing of good practice; and access to modular programmes to address specific skills in areas of leadership responsibility relevant to the particular setting in which principals are located.

7.6. Professional Development of Experienced Principals

Leaders are subject to the effects of a complex array of factors that have the potential to impact negatively on their performance and continuing survival in the role. Principals must be given support to face the challenges of their responsibilities and to renew and reinvigorate their professional performance. Experienced leaders should be able to look to system support, professional networks, and leadership institutes for the provision of renewal experiences and activities. These will include: sabbatical leaves; job sharing; professionally expanding work engagements; and the utilisation and affirmation of their wisdom and competencies in the mentoring and coaching of the next generation of leaders.

7.6.1. Retaining Experienced Principals

The reason behind principals leave their jobs might be effective in retaining people in the principalship. These included: job sharing for principals; reinvention of the role of principal; and improving and increasing opportunities for professional development. Employing authorities can assist in these processes by: offering financial support for sabbaticals; creating a family-friendly environment to accommodate principals' personal lives; reviewing the salary schedule in order to find a way to reward principals; determining flexible attendance requirements, and expectations at school functions; and redesigning the organisational structure of the job.

7.6.2. Programmes for Professional Development

The professional development needs of experienced principals attention has been drawn to the need for experienced principals to have available to them a range of learning opportunities from which selection can be made in accordance with specific needs. These learning experiences may usefully involve: study groups; advanced seminars; reading and discussion groups; presentations by current thinkers or expert practitioners; attendance at national academies or conferences; and opportunities to become coaches, facilitators, or trainers themselves. Their learning should not however be haphazard or fragmented.

Instead, the curriculum should be: carefully designed with attention to prior learning; coordinated and aligned across all learning providers and activities; provide core skills and knowledge that will enhance leadership, but also knowledge and skills related to the specific administrative procedures, contractual requirements, and community characteristics of the environment in which they are working.

7.6.3. Learning Networks

Learning networks and networked learning communities approach has been based on the concept of nested learning communities. In 'nested learning communities' the school is viewed as a learning organisation that, under its principal's leadership, is continually improving its capacity to teach children. The principal must lead by creating a culture of learning, and by providing the right kinds of specialised professional development opportunities for all members of the school community. Another variation has been based on the concept of "communities of practice" involving activities such as intervisitations and buddying.

The continuing professional renewal of experienced principals is an important part of what is essentially a process of lifelong learning. At the same time as programmes of professional development should be made available to principals seeking to enhance their own professional growth and development, principals themselves can play an important part in the professional advancement of aspiring principals and others who have been newly appointed to the position of principal, and indeed to other positions of leadership in schools and educational institutions more generally.

There is a professional obligation about this kind of mutuality. Those coming to take principal and leadership positions for the first time are looking for informed and supportive sources of help and advice from those who have acquired rich funds of experience, practical wisdom, and professional intelligence during their own exercise of the principalship, and who are willing to offer these as resources to their successors.

Experienced principals know they can benefit enormously from the rich resources of new ideas, thinking and adventurousness which new appointees to principal positions can bring with them. Such exchanges benefit both parties immeasurably. They furnish principals and school leaders with that firm foundation on which future developments in the nature, roles, responsibilities, and values of school leaders may be more soundly and securely based and hence lay a strong, professional base for the recruitment, retention, and development of principals into the future.

7.7. Recruiting Quality Teachers

Recruiting quality teachers is essential for the overall development of students. The preparation, recruitment, and retention of teachers can be viewed as a pipeline that springs leaks over time. In many developing countries, the number of new teachers cannot keep up with population growth. In Western countries, where sufficient numbers of teachers are prepared, many newly prepared teachers either choose not to teach at all or leave teaching within a few years.

Policy efforts directed toward meeting the need for teachers have focused primarily on supply issues, such as instituting and encouraging alternative licensure routes into teaching, establishing scholarships and loans for prospective teachers, and increasing salaries to make teaching more attractive. Much less effort has been directed toward improving working conditions in schools, one of the primary causes of teacher attrition. What seems to be lacking is a framework for policy that creates a "coherent infrastructure of recruitment, preparation, and support programmes that connect all aspects of the teacher's career continuum into a teacher development system that is linked to national and local educational goals".

Congruence and commonality of effort are difficult to achieve in a decentralised system of education. Without a set of common understandings, these education systems will implement teaching policies on an ad hoc basis, with gaps, conflicts, and inefficiencies being inevitable outcomes. Countries with a national system of education find it easier to develop a coherent framework of policies that reinforce and support one another because education policy is under the control of the central government.

Even though the challenges of implementing a policy framework that links teacher preparation, teacher recruitment, and teacher retention are great, they must be met. To create and maintain an effective policy framework aimed at teacher quality, governments must develop and use a system for collecting data to inform policymakers of the results of various policy initiatives. Policy coherence is difficult enough when policymakers are dispersed among separate jurisdictions. However, without effective data gathering and analysis, policy coherence is virtually impossible.

Pupil enrolment, pupil-teacher ratios, and turnover are three major components of teacher demand. The supply of teachers depends on several factors, including the number of students graduating from teacher preparation programmes, the proportion of these students who choose to enter teaching, the number of teachers licensed through alternative programmes, and the number of returnees from the reserve pool of teachers, including retired teachers. Other factors influencing the supply of teachers include salaries and benefits, working conditions, difficulty of licensure standards, presence or absence of incentives to attract teachers, and public perception of teaching as a profession.

On the other hand, just having enough teachers is a major problem. In an attempt to increase access to schooling, the growth in the number of school-aged children has outpaced the growth in the number of teachers in most of these countries. In many Western countries, there is a shortage of minority teachers. Although an increasing number of students are members of minority groups, teaching staff tend to come from the majority group. This disparity in the cultural backgrounds of teachers and those of the children they teach often results in low teacher expectations and the use of inappropriate teaching strategies.

Therefore, recruiting quality minority teachers is very important. When faced with difficulties in finding sufficient numbers of quality teachers, school administrators traditionally do one of three things. They either hire less-qualified teachers, assign teachers trained in one area to teach in the shortage area, or make extensive use of substitute teachers. As a consequence, many students, particularly at-risk students, are being taught by teachers who lack the knowledge and skills necessary to produce desired student learning. The effects of teacher quality are long lasting and cumulative, especially for these at-risk students.

There are various strategies used to deal with the problem caused by the gap between the supply of high quality teachers and the demand for them. They include strengthening teacher preparation programmes by emphasising standards and accountability, creating alternative pathways into teaching, attracting mid-career professionals, luring retired teachers back into the classroom, establishing scholarships and forgivable loans for prospective teachers in high need areas, raising teacher salaries and benefits, and creating signing bonuses, housing assistance, and other incentives to attract teachers.

Additional strategies are being implemented in terms of hard-to-staff schools. These include bonuses for teachers of mathematics, special education, and other shortage fields, bonuses for teachers who teach in high-poverty schools, financial support for graduate study, and partnerships between local education areas and colleges to help such areas "grow their own" teachers. Unfortunately, evidence of the effectiveness of these various efforts is scant.

There is little systematic research on the effects of different kinds of alternative licensure programmes on teachers, teaching, or student learning. What research there is suggests that successful alternative licensure programmes possess many of the same characteristics as successful traditional teacher education programmes. In addition, however, alternative licensure programmes do attract a more diverse pool of potential teachers, in terms of ethnicity and age, than do traditional programmes.

For attracting high calibre teachers, the governments should continue to experiment with various strategies. Increasing teacher salaries is not likely to attract people into teaching who don't have the "calling." However, adequate salaries to support a family and to save money for children's education are likely to keep teachers who do heed the calling. All new teachers, whether graduates of traditional or alternative programmes, should be held to high academic and performance standards. It makes no sense to strengthen the requirements for college-based teacher education programmes, while at the same time ignoring standards for those coming through alternative licensure programmes.

7.7.1. Preparation of Teachers

Depending in large part on the economic, political, and social contexts that exist within each country, there is great diversity in teacher preparation programmes. In many countries, preparation standards are different for teachers preparing to teach in elementary and in secondary schools. Elementary teachers for primary school are often trained in special institutes or teacher training colleges. Secondary teachers are more often trained at universities, increasingly in "consecutive" programmes in which a degree in a subject area is earned prior to undertaking pedagogical training. These differences in preparation requirements between elementary and secondary teachers do not so much reflect a philosophy that elementary teachers need less schooling as much as a concession to issues of supply, demand, and compensation.

Teacher preparation programmes consist of four components that contribute to their effectiveness. The first is the existence of high standards for entry. Over the past two decades, there have been increases in the entry-level qualifications of students enrolling in teacher education programmes, both in terms of undergraduate grade point average and standardised test scores. The second and third components of effective teacher education programmes are strong content (subject matter) preparation and substantial pedagogical training.

Most researchers believe in the importance of solid subject matter knowledge in terms of content preparation,. However, the idea that more content is better is not always necessarily true. Rather, there may be a point after which additional content courses produce minimal value. What seems to be needed is not necessarily more content preparation but rather having sufficient knowledge of content to teach it well. In addition, teachers need to know how to organise and present the content in a way that makes it accessible for increasingly diverse groups of learners.

The final component of an effective teacher education programme is supervised clinical experiences that are integrated with more formal coursework. Although most pre-service teachers describe their practicum experiences as the most valuable component of their teacher preparation programme, many practicum experiences are narrowly focused and disconnected from students' previous coursework. Clinical experiences are most effective when they are carefully planned, interwoven with coursework, undertaken with highly effective classroom teachers, and carefully supervised. The importance of well-prepared teachers for student learning is unquestionable.

Teachers who prepared better are more academically able, are rated as more effective by principals, supervisors, and colleagues, and enter and remain in teaching in greater numbers. In contrast, less well prepared teachers have more classroom difficulties, are rated less effective by evaluators and colleagues, and leave at much higher rates at earlier points in their careers. Whether prepared in traditional or alternative teacher education programmes, well prepared teachers are the foundation for ensuring that high quality teachers are working in all classrooms.

The ultimate determiner of whether a teacher is "high quality" is student achievement. If the teacher is consistently successful in helping students to achieve at or above expected levels of academic performance, then he or she can be considered effective and of high quality. Research shows that having a sequence of quality teachers can help students overcome the deficits of their home environments.

High standards of quality for teacher preparation programmes are the key to preparing high quality teachers for our schools. Although teacher shortages require implementation of a variety of recruiting strategies, it is essential that all teacher preparation programmes contain high entry standards, a combination of subject matter preparation and pedagogical training, and a longterm, supervised clinical practicum.

7.7.2. Retention of Teachers

Teaching is important work and contributes significantly to society. The most academically able new teachers are most likely to leave. Although salaries can make a difference in terms of teacher recruitment, teachers generally report the importance of good working conditions in making a decision to stay in teaching. A number of school organisational factors play a crucial role in teacher turnover, including inadequate support from school administration, student motivation, and discipline problems, and limited teacher input into and influence over school policies. These factors also affect the motivation and commitment of those teachers who stay at the school.

Migration and attrition are two kinds of teacher turnover. Migration refers to teachers leaving one school to take a job at another school, which does not result in an overall permanent loss of teachers. Attrition refers to leaving teaching altogether, either to take another job outside of teaching, for personal reasons as child rearing, health problems, family moves, and retirement. Whether through migration or attrition, teacher turnover is expensive. There is the hidden cost of public investment that goes into tuition and tax support for preparing new teachers, many of whom leave teaching within a few years.

Local areas bear the costs of recruiting, inducting, and mentoring new teachers, only to lose many of them through the revolving door of teaching. Also, with so many teachers leaving, there are opportunity costs related to disruption of coherence, continuity, and community that are critical to effective schools, particularly those serving large numbers of atrisk students. The most serious long-term consequences of high teacher turnover are loss of teaching quality and lower levels of student achievement.

Teachers who switch schools or school districts tend to move to schools where student achievement is higher. While policy efforts are often directed to the supply side of the equation, school staffing problems are primarily the result of the demand created by teachers leaving for reasons other than retirement. Since the primary cause of teacher turnover seems to be due to poor or difficult working conditions, changing the culture of schools should be the primary target of policy efforts. This cultural change would involve the creation of learning communities—schools that are learner-centered, assessment-centered, knowledge-centered, and community-centered. Cultural change would "contribute to lower rates of turnover, thus diminish school staffing problems, and ultimately aid the performance of schools."

7.7.3. Programmes for Correction and Induction

Induction support is important in their development as teachers, there is a great deal of disparity in terms of both the quality and accessibility of induction programmes found in schools. Rather than focus on "fix-it" approaches to specific problems (for example, classroom management), effective induction programmes should focus on the subject-specific pedagogical strategies needed by novice teachers to promote and foster student learning. Improving instruction and student learning often proactively addresses the classroom management issues experienced by many new teachers. To focus on such pedagogical issues with novice teachers, mentoring programmes need to be structured to accommodate professional discourse.

Mentors need to be selected based on high quality standards and trained to analyse and evaluate instruction effectively and conduct discussions about their findings with novices. Effective mentor programmes also include common planning time for mentors and novices as well as release time available to both teachers so that each can observe in the other's classroom.

Incentives should be provided to mentors in an effort to encourage high quality teachers to participate in the programme. Mentor programmes that provide incentives for attracting mentors and for quality mentor training tend to be more effective. High quality induction programmes are effective in providing the support needed by novice teachers during their first years of teaching. Novice teachers indicate that where such programmes are supported and financed, the guidance offered them has increased the likelihood that they will remain in teaching.

Support for teachers that enables them to move along the developmental continuum is also important. The second is funding the development of effective mentor/induction programmes and quality assessments of these programmes. Because student learning is the ultimate goal of classroom instruction, the assessment of mentoring programmes must include the monitoring of student learning. When funding for induction programmes is on a par with that provided for recruitment of new teachers, both teachers and the educational system benefit. The time, effort, and money necessary to mentor novice teachers are substantial. Fortunately, the rewards in terms of teacher retention are also substantial. Investing in the short term yields long-term payoffs in terms of higher quality teachers who remain in the profession longer.

7.8. Conclusion

School authorities must possess certain qualities to bringing up students with high motivation and clear objectives. The teachers and principals must be highly qualified and efficient. Otherwise it leads to the degeneration of a generation.

References

Ben-Peretz, M. "Curriculum of teacher education programmes". In L.W. Anderson (Ed.). *The international encyclopedia of teaching and teacher education*. New York: Elsevier Science. 1995.

Bolam, R. "Teacher recruitment and induction". In L.W. Anderson (Ed.), *The international encyclopedia of teaching and teacher education*. New York: Elsevier Science. 1995.

Bristor, V.J., Kinzer, S., Lapp, S., & Ridener, B. "The teacher education alliance (TEA): A model teacher preparation programme for the twenty-fi rst century". *Education,* 122 (4), 688-699.1995.

Cobb, V. L. *An international comparison of teacher education*. Washington, DC:ERICClearinghouse on Teaching and Teacher Education.1999.

Coleman, D. & DeBey, M. "Weaving teacher education into the fabric of a liberal arts education". *Kappa Delta Pi Record,* 36 (3), 116-120.2000.

Darling-Hammond, L. *Doing what matters most*. New York: National Commission on Teaching and America's Future. 1997.

Darling-Hammond, L. "Keeping good teachers: Why it matters, what leaders can do". *Educational Leadership*. 60 (8), 6-13.2003.

Delpit, L. *Other peoples' children: Cultural conflict in the classroom*. New York: The New Press.1995.

Farkas, S., Johnson, J., & Foleno, T. *A sense of calling: Who teaches and why*. New York: Public Agenda. 2000.

Feiman-Nemser, S. "What new teachers need to learn". Educational Leadership. 60 (8). 25-29.2003.

Galluzzo, G. & Arends, R. "The RATE project: A profile of teacher education institutions". *Journal of Teacher Education*. 41, 56-58.1989.

Genzuk, M. & Baca, R. "The paraeducator-to-teacher pipeline: A 5-year retrospective on an innovative teacher preparation programme for Latina(os)". *Education and Urban Society*. 31(1), 73-88. 1998.

8

SCHOOL-BASED MANAGEMENT

8.1. Introduction

School-based management is not a "silver bullet" that is capable of solving all problems in the management of school systems. However, when implemented under the appropriate capacity building conditions, and in the context of an allocation of responsibilities among school-system levels that is sensitive to local contexts, it does offer one of several strategies that appear to have a positive and measurable impact upon student learning outcomes.

The governments of every nation want to see the transformation of schools. Transformation has been achieved when significant, systematic, and sustained change has occurred, resulting in improved outcomes for all students in all settings, thus making a contribution to the social and economic well-being of a nation.

Schoolbased management is invariably proposed as one strategy to achieve the transformation of schools. School-based management has been institutionalised in places like England, where more than 25,000 schools have had experience with the practice for more than a decade; or like New Zealand or Victoria, Australia or in several large school systems in Canada and the United States, where there has been experience for similar lengths of time. The practice seems irreversible in these settings.

School-based management has many shades of meaning. It has been implemented in different ways and for different reasons and at different rates in different settings. Even the more fundamental concepts of "school" and "management" are different, as are the cultures and values that underpin the efforts of policy makers and practitioners.

However, the common ground in all places where schoolbased management has been implemented is that there has been an increase in authority and responsibility at the school level, but within a centrally-determined framework that ensures that a sense of system is sustained. An important implication is that school leaders should have the capacity to make decisions on significant matters related to school operations and acknowledge and take account of the elements in a centrally-determined framework that applies to all schools in the system.

8.2. Reforms in SBM

School-based management has been evident in policy and practice for more than three decades to the point that there are now few nations that have not moved down this track. Indeed, by the start of the 21st century, there seemed to be three major tracks for change in systems of education: the building of systems of self-managing schools (school-based management), an unrelenting focus on learning outcomes, and the creation of schools for a knowledge society and global economy.

Nevertheless, no system of education seems to remain at the same point along these tracks for very long. An important implication is that school leaders should have the capacity to adjust to the changing scope of school-based management and must be ready to respond to central initiatives as these may be determined from time to time at the national, state / province, or district levels.

It is challenging to achieve a balance of centralisation and decentralisation, depending on what values are preferred or are required and the capacities of people at different levels to carry out their respective functions. Some practices are similar, but conceptually different to decentralisation. Notable among these are déconcentration or dispersion that involve moving people who previously worked at a central location, such as a capital city, to another location, such as a region or a province or a city, closer to the action. Under these arrangements, power, authority, responsibility, and influence can remain just as centralised as before. The advantages of déconcentration may lie in control in the gathering of intelligence about conditions in the field and efficiency in direction and support to schools.

Forces driving the move to school-based management include demand for less control and uniformity and an associated demand for greater freedom and differentiation, interest in reducing the size and therefore the cost of maintaining a large central bureaucracy, commitment to empowerment of the community, and desire to achieve higher levels of professionalism at the school level.

8.3. Centralisation vs. Decentralisation

Schools leaders should be comfortable in operating in a political climate that invariably accompanies the shifting balance of centralisation and decentralisation and the values that underpin such a shift, but acknowledge and draw on the capacity of central units, however dispersed, to provide support. School-based management that has been driven by concern for empowerment of the community and enhancement of the profession has often been associated with governments of the left. School-based management that has been driven by an interest in greater freedom or more differentiation has often been associated with governments of the right, with school-based management sometimes seen as a manifestation of efforts to create a market among schools in systems of public education.

Management based on school is often contentious in the early stages of adoption, but it invariably gains acceptance after a period of time to the point that few stakeholders seek a return to a more centralised approach in school operations. The aims of the government's decentralisation reform were to strengthen control and to ensure educational quality through management techniques. That is, "quality" was defined in terms of an efficient use of resources, output assessment, performance indicators, and external evaluation. Neither a distribution of authority nor an empowerment of the stakeholders was its main goal".

A critical criterion for judging the effectiveness of reform that includes school-based management is the extent to which it leads to or is associated with the achievement of improved educational outcomes, including higher levels of student achievement, however measured. In recent times, there has been an alignment of views that a primary purpose for school-based management is the improvement of educational outcomes and, for this reason, most governments have included it in their policies for educational reform.

School leaders should ensure that the attention of the school community (including staff) is focused unrelentingly on learning outcomes for students and that this must remain of central concern even though the notion of school-based management is often highly contentious.

There have been three generations of studies and it is only in the third that evidence of impact on outcomes has emerged, and then only when certain conditions are fulfilled. The first generation was in times when impact on outcomes was not a primary or even secondary purpose. The second generation was when such purposes may have been to the fore but the database was weak. The third, emerging in the late 1990s and gathering momentum in the early 2000s, coincides with a pre-eminent concern for learning outcomes and the development of a strong database.

School leaders should be aware that self-management does not necessarily have an impact on the learning outcomes of students and they should make every effort to ensure that mechanisms for making the connection are in place in different areas of school operations.

They should focus on the core business of the school in their efforts to bring about improved learning outcomes for students, and this includes curriculum, pedagogy, professional development, and building the support of the community. Local decision-making being pre-eminently concerned with learning and teaching and the support of learning and teaching, especially in building the capacity of staff to design and deliver a curriculum and pedagogy that meets the needs of students, taking account of priorities in the local setting, including a capacity to identify needs and monitor outcomes. Also evident is the importance of building the capacity of the community to support the efforts of schools. Expressed another way, the introduction of school-based management may have no impact on learning unless these measures, broadly described as capacity building and capacity utilisation, have been successful.

Decentralisation, with a relatively high level of school-based management being one element of decentralisation, including local decision-making on matters concerned with personnel, professionalism, monitoring of outcomes, and the building of community support. These reflect the importance of intellectual capital and social capital in building a system of self-managing schools. The building of intellectual capital is an instance of capacity building. Social capital refers to the building of mutually supportive relationships among school, home, community, church, business, and industry, and other agencies in the public and private sectors.

It will take many years for a shift in the balance of centralisation and decentralisation in favour of the latter to have impact on outcomes. It is one thing to pass legislation shifting power, authority, responsibility, and influence from one level to another—such a shift is a change in structure. It is another thing to build capacity to have the desired impact on learning and to change the culture at all levels.

School leaders should ensure that they and their colleagues are up-to-date with their knowledge of good practice in school improvement, and that the building of social and intellectual capital lies at the heart of the work of senior leaders in the school.

8.3.1. Assessing Learning Outcomes

Greater attention to the measurement of outcomes is invariably an aspect of school-based management in recent times. The heightened attention to the measure of outcomes is a feature of school reform in every nation, regardless of the extent to which there has been a focus on school-based management. On the other hand, however, a focus on outcomes is an aspect of accountability that invariably accompanies the introduction of the practice.

In return for gaining greater authority to manage its own affairs, a school should be expected to show how well it is doing in addressing the goals of the school system. The case for school-based management in recent times is invariably cast in terms of impact on learning, especially in the face of evidence of how the link to learning can be made. If there is to be success for all students in all settings, then schools must have a capacity to measure how well students are doing at any point in time, determine what learning experiences are necessary to ensure success, and then measure and report on the outcomes.

Benchmarking the performance of schools in similar socio-economic circumstances is common practice in systems where school-based management has been introduced. Teachers are becoming skilful in the analysis of data about student performance, within their own schools, and across different schools in systems where benchmarking has been introduced. In this respect, the professional in education is developing the same capacity as the professional in health in an outcomes-oriented data-driven approach to their work.

The implication for leaders in schools and school systems is that building a capacity for measurement of outcomes is important if the links between school-based management and learning are to be made.

8.3.2. Making Changes in Schools

While an initiative in school-based management is usually an initiative of government and the most senior leaders in a school system, personnel at the centre frequently resist the change, for they perceive and indeed experience a loss of power, authority, responsibility, and influence. Forces that may drive a return to centralisation may soon appear. This need not occur if there is appreciation that the change may call for an increase in power, authority, responsibility, and influence in matters related to the centrally-determined framework of goals, policies, curriculum, standards, and accountabilities. There remains a need to provide strong support for schools, and this is often best done at the regional or district level through déconcentration and dispersion of non-school based personnel. Building capacity at the centre to do these things well is just as important as building capacity at the school level.

Leaders at the central level should have a deep understanding of the nature of school-based management and of the links to learning that are required for school improvement to occur, acknowledging that this means the building of different capacities for direction and support rather than a loss of status.

8.3.3. Expense for Decentralisation

There is a unique mix of student learning needs in the school and that calls for a unique mix of resources of all kinds. It is no longer possible for such a mix to be determined at the centre, whether it be for the standard allocation of staff or the determination of how money should be spent on supplies, equipment, and services. Some school systems have decentralised to the school level decisions related to the allocation of more than 90 per cent of the state budget for public school education. The challenge under these circumstances is to design an appropriate resource allocation model that will distribute resources in a fair and transparent way, ensuring that schools have a "global budget" that enables them to resource efforts to meet the unique mix of local learning needs.

Years may take this task, with continual refinement based on experience and changes in policy. A resource allocation model usually takes account of the number of students, level of schooling, special education needs, and the location of the school. There is considerable experience in several nations in doing this work. An important implication is that leaders at the central level should develop the capacity to determine an allocation mechanism that delivers resources to schools in a manner that reflects the unique mix of needs that may be found in different schools. School leaders will develop the capacity for plan-driven budgeting that ensures high priority learning needs are supported and centrally determined priorities are addressed.

8.4. Capacity Building

Capacity building, for teachers, have taken the form of professional development that deals with such topics as needs assessment, curriculum design, research-based pedagogy, and continuous monitoring. For principals and other leaders at the school level, these topics are also relevant, but others are essential, including strategic leadership, human resource management, policy making, planning, resource allocation, community building, and boundary spanning—between schools and other organisations in the private and public sectors that can support the work of schools including those in health. Building these capacities is important for creating what some have called a "new professionalism" in education that is research-based, data-oriented, team-focused, and outcomes-driven.

The education profession, in these respects, is taking on the characteristics of the medical profession, where continuous lifelong learning is an expectation and a pre-condition for accreditation and re-accreditation. These needs give rise to the new field of knowledge management in schools. This refers to building the intellectual capital of the school, and involves the creation, dissemination and utilisation of professional knowledge that takes account of a rapidly expanding knowledge base, and the need for access to that base in a timely and easily understandable manner. Extensive use of information and communications technology and the design of an intranet at the school level will aid the effort. Postgraduate programmes in knowledge management are now emerging to take their place with programmes in human resource development, financial management, curriculum, and pedagogy. Universities have an important role in building capacity and undertaking research on the processes and outcomes of school-based management. These are best conceived as partnerships with schools and school systems.

School leaders should devote a major part of their work to capacity building in the school and will place a high priority on knowledge management to build the intellectual capital of the school. The introduction of school-based management has been criticised on the grounds that a sense of system is lost, with schools tending to operate in isolation if not in competition. This need not be the case. To state it more positively, when schools in a system where school-based management has been implemented are working together in powerful networks, the opportunity for impact on learning across the system is enhanced.

8.4.1. Capability of School-based Management

School-based management allows schools more autonomy in decisions about their management; that is, in the use of their human, material and financial resources. The popularity of this trend is clear for all to see through the diversity of agencies showing interest or manifestly promoting it, the amount of articles discussing its merits and demerits and, most crucially, the growing number of countries that have adopted aspects of this policy. Concern with educational quality has seldom been at the heart of this policy—the reason for its introduction being related more to financial and managerial arguments.

However, its impact on quality is undoubtedly a core and contentious issue, with some authors claiming that SBM is the panacea for quality improvement, while others argue that its introduction has led to deterioration especially in the weakest schools.

SBM is the transfer of decision-making power on management issues to the school level. When responsibilities are transferred to professionals within the school, generally the principal with senior teachers, and school based governance, which implies giving authority to an elected school board, which represents parents and the community.

School-based governance is one in which a school is put in the hands of a group of private managers because the school's public management has failed to obtain good results. The American "charter schools" are one such a group: the school managers sign a charter, which identifies the results they promise to obtain and are given great freedom in the management of the school.

However, the autonomy is counterbalanced as well as limited by the development of a strong accountability framework. In some cases, that framework consists of curriculum guidelines, regular national examinations and the publication of school results; and it is so restrictive that schools are now arguably less autonomous than before these reforms. Debate about how far SBM has led to more or less school autonomy is popular and at times heated. It is clear that SBM is not the same as giving schools a blank cheque: more autonomy equals more accountability. It is almost impossible to list all countries that have adopted, under one form or another, SBM policies. The diversity of policies that this term encompasses coupled with the fact that there is at times a wide disparity between policy and reality would make such an inventory vague.

As schools receive too few resources from the Ministry to survive, they feel forced to collect additional resources from the community. As a result, the school principals manage some funds autonomously. When these funds are used to recruit extra staff, they also manage that staff. At the same time, international agencies are proposing to send block grants to schools, which can be spent how they wish. Through these different aspects, school principals are playing a bigger role. It is therefore correct to say that there is greater school autonomy, but this is not the result of national policy and neither is it reflected in it. This poses a problem, as, for instance, there is little control over school funds and little support to school boards and principals.

8.5. Pros and Cons of SBM

There are a number of solid arguments to defend the introduction of SBM; the five most recurrent ones are:

- *More democratic:* Allowing teachers and parents to take decisions about an issue of such importance as education is certainly more democratic than to keep this decisions in the hands of a select group of central-level officials.
- *More relevant:* Locating the decision-making power closer to where problems are being experienced will lead to more relevant policies as local staff generally know their own situation better.
- *Less bureaucratic:* Decisions will be taken much quicker if they do not need to go through a long bureaucratic process (from school through several intermediary offices to the central level), but can be made at a level close to the school.
- *Stronger accountability:* Allowing schools and teachers greater say implies that they can be held accountable for their results towards parents and the close community directly. Such accountability is expected to act as a tool for greater effectiveness.
- *Greater resource mobilisation:* Teachers and especially parents will be more eager to contribute to the funding of their school if they have a say in the organisation and management it.

There is also some general research evidence to support the introduction of SBM. Indeed it has been demonstrated that the quality of education depends primarily on the way schools are managed, more than on the availability of resources. It has also been shown that the capacity of schools to improve teaching and learning is strongly mediated by the quality of the leadership provided by the headteacher. Both factors could be used to argue for stronger control over management within the school.

However, there are a long series of preoccupations around the introduction and implementation of the SBM policy. The following highlight what appear to be the crucial ones, particularly with regard to developing countries. In many, if not most developing countries, the trend towards SBM, and the wider decentralisation of public services, including education, has not been the result of an internal debate. The conviction might have existed that such a policy will lead to higher quality, but that argument was more of an afterthought. Pressure by the local authorities or communities demanding a more participatory decision-making process, has generally been absent.

Weak governments cannot be expected to develop accountability frameworks to counterbalance school autonomy or to offer support to schools. The absence of an efficient and supportive State is risky not only for the individual schools, but also for the system as a whole, being threatened by disintegration and disparity. Two groups are expected to be the main beneficiaries of SBM as well as the main guarantors of its successful implementation: the senior teachers, specially the school's principal and the parents, and at times the wider community. In both cases, the transfer of responsibilities will encounter preoccupying challenges. In developing countries, few headteachers can be considered strong and well-trained professionals. Quite a few are simply teachers benefiting from end-of-career promotion, which is hardly their fault. If blame needs to be assigned, it lies with central policy-makers whose policy declarations have been accompanied by insufficient measures to strengthen the position of headteachers.

In most countries, selection and recruitment practices have not changed; capacity-building initiatives cover few staff; professional development opportunities, if they exist, remain scarce. Headteachers, especially in the more remote schools, are isolated and receive little or no support from the administration. In many countries, the incentives to become or remain a headteacher are decreasing rather than increasing. The overall result of the feebleness of reforms is a wide discrepancy between the present profile of the headteacher, which has undergone very little change, and the ideal profile of an innovative pedagogical leader and a proactive manager. SBM has in several cases made life harder for school principals by increasing their administrative and managerial workload, to the detriment of their role as a pedagogical leader.

However, school staff and, especially, principals are not always ready and willing to undertake reform. There is already much demand on their time and, as a result, only a "relatively small proportion of a school staff's total energies are available for improvement purposesThis factor is at least as important in developing as in developed countries.

Besides, many management-related decisions, especially financing and staffing issues, are intricate and complex. Studies covering four OECD countries found that "principals were troubled by ethical dilemmas in all four countries and some reported an increase in the frequency with which they were confronted with difficult decisions in recent years". This combination of heavier workload and increased stress has led to a drought of candidate principals in places such as the UK. This brings up the issue of gender. Keeping in mind that the teaching profession is increasingly becoming feminised, while headteaching remains male-dominated in many countries, the question can be asked as to what impact SBM will have on the prevalence of women among headteachers and on their position in schools. It is an area that has received little attention so far, particularly in developing countries. Little empirical information is thus available, but two contrasting hypotheses can be proposed.

In other words, a successful leader in a school with SBM will need to be supportive and collegial, with a willingness to negotiate, so as to bring all teachers along on the road to reform. This may come closer to the type of leadership women will be more comfortable with. On the other hand, the increased pressure, especially in terms of time, may render it more difficult for women to occupy such posts. With regard to the community, it is evident that it occupies a central place in SBM through its involvement in the school board or council.

Schools need to have a minimum of resources and competent teachers. Schools in which the principal has no management training whatsoever, where the teachers have few resources, and the surrounding community is extremely poor with little expertise in education, can hardly be expected to engage in strategic planning and self-evaluation with enthusiasm. Where teachers are recognised professionals, benefiting from the accompanying status, privileges and working conditions, decentralisation, especially to the school level, makes much more sense. Even a well functioning school cannot go it alone immediately.

It is a big mistake to take out the old structure of support too early. This is even more the case with "weaker" schools, which probably need support more than autonomy. The lack of policy changes in line with the more important role and increased workload of the school leadership has already been underlined. Indeed, there is an urgent need to develop an integrated policy at central level, which is explicitly aimed at improving school management and at strengthening the headteachers. Such a policy should, among other things:

— Clarify the areas of autonomy and the levels of accountability so that headteachers feel strengthened rather than overburdened;
— Accompany such autonomy and accountability with a strong and consistent support system, especially for beginning and/or isolated headteachers;
— Improve recruitment and selection procedures, for instance, by early identification of potential headteachers and a system of mentoring by selected innovative practising headteachers;
— Develop a motivating career path, by offering professional development opportunities and strengthening in-service training;
— Set up a mutual support system and discussion forum for headteachers.

Schools will need information on their performance through a series of indicators that allow them to compare their own evolution and progress or lack of it with that of other schools, the district or the nation as a whole. That will help them to identify their strengths, weaknesses and priorities as well as to prepare a school development plan. Providing such information may not be sufficient though. In some cases, informing schools that they are doing poorly has only had a further de-motivation effect on the staff. Such information needs to be accompanied by capacity-building on data analysis in addition to support on improvement strategies. The role of the local and district office is also crucial. For broadening school autonomy does not imply at all that the local level offices do not have any role to play anymore. The opposite is in many cases true.

Educational institutions will need more support, which demands changes within the local offices. They will need quality information on schools, so as to know who needs help most and what type of support will be useful. Their role will be transformed: from control over the respect of official rules and regulation to supporter of innovation and initiative-taking—or in other words, from a supervisor to a colleague.

Raising performance levels therefore critically relies on effective support systems, either located at individual school levels or in specialised support institutions, which provide professional advice and assistance to teachers and school management. Various models are used by different countries or projects in this regard.

It is difficult to find the correct balance between support and control and between offering advice and exercising accountability. A system which is overly focussed on accountability, will have a detrimental impact on poorly performing schools, who will no doubt be told that they are doing a poor job, but perhaps not given advise on how to improve. No external formal accountability system can have an impact in the long run unless it has a capacity-building philosophy. While this is the foremost primary goal, the external accountability system must also have the responsibility to intervene in persistently failing situations. Balancing accountability support and accountability intervention is obviously a tough call, but this is precisely how sophisticated the external infrastructure must become."

The balance to be found between support and control depends partly on the quality of the schools and the resources available within the school to improve. Arguably, the transposition of the concept of school evaluation from the developed countries, within a context of a demand for greater public accountability, to developing countries and to underresourced schools, can have adverse effects: the school evaluation strategy which is being promoted, is not appropriate to such schools. They need support, not simply pressure.

Such support will only be significant and lead to sustainable capacities, when it is regular and consistent. That implies that in many countries it cannot be offered to all schools, because resources do not permit to do so. A good argument can be made in any case that support should be extended first of all to the schools most in need of it. This is the principle which has inspired the major reform of the school supervision system in Chile and which has shown a positive impact on individual schools and on disparities between schools.

Central authorities will also continue to play a core role, especially in monitoring the performance of schools and of local offices with a particular concern to redress disparities. SBM indeed carries an evident equity risk: where schools are allowed to select teachers and where parents are given the right to select their schools, it does not take long before the best teachers and the most interested parents choose and are chosen by the "best" schools. The needs of an individual school then come in conflict with those of the system as a whole. Monitoring should therefore cover both quality and equity. This task of monitoring consists of the construction of an information base, the analysis of this information and the definition of actions to be taken in response to problems or weaknesses identified. Analysing the information demands the definition of norms, standards or objectives, which might be more administrative in character or more pedagogical.

The action to be taken can take the form of sanctions, of rewards, or of support and guidance. An essential point is that schools and teachers will need capacity-building. This need to be more than just training; it must include positive working conditions, incentives and the creation of motivating posts. Ideally, different services aiming at improvement in the classroom need to be coordinated and integrated into one global school support programme. Teacher pre- and in-service training, teacher support and supervision could be organised around networks of schools, where a cluster of actors work together to strengthen schools' capacities. It is necessary to develop a flexible policy, which gives autonomy in function of the schools' strengths and needs.

8.6. Conclusion

School-based management is not a "silver bullet" that will deliver the expectations of school reform. When implemented under the right conditions, it is one of several strategies to be addressed simultaneously in a constantly changing mix of strategies that involve different levels of governance in a school system.

SBM is a policy without value to developing societies, neither that it does not carry any promise for quality improvement. Rather its implementation will need to be accompanied by strategies to build capacities of schools, headteachers and communities, inspired by a clear focus on quality improvement and a concern for equity. What is needed perhaps more than School-based management is management focused on school support.

References

Briggs, K. L., & Robertson P. J. "Improving schools through school-based management: An examination of the process of change". *School Effectiveness and School Improvement.* Vol. 9, No. 1, pp. 28-57.1998.

Caldwell, B. J., & Spinks, J. M. *Beyond the Self-Managing School.* London: Falmer Press. 1998.

De Grauwe, A. "The challenges for the school of the future". *IIEP Newsletter.* Vol. XVII, No. 4. 1999.

Dempster, N. "Guilty or not: the impact and effects of site-based management on schools". *Journal of Educational Administration.* vol. 38, no. 1, p. 47-65. 2000.

Fullan, M., & Watson, N. "School-based management: Reconceptualising to improve learning outcomes". *School Effectiveness and School Improvement.* 11(4). 453-474. 2000.

Jesson, D. *Educational Outcomes and Value Added by Specialist Schools.* London: Specialist Schools Trust. 2004.

9

CHANGING PUBLIC SCHOOLING SYSTEMS

9.1. Introduction

Schools and educational institutions must be capable for producing high quality students. It should not be simply a place for transferring knowledge. Instead, it must be able to mould the overall development of a child. Public schools and school systems, as they are presently constituted, are simply not led in ways that enable them to respond to the increasing demands they face under standards based reform.

If schools, school systems, and their leaders respond to standards based reforms the way they have responded to other attempts at broad scale reform of public education over the past century, they will fail massively and visibly, with an attendant loss of public confidence and serious consequences for public education. The way out of this problem is through the large scale improvement of instruction, something public education has been unable to do to date, but which is possible with dramatic changes in the way public schools define and practice leadership.

Most leaders in all sectors of society are creatures of the organisations they lead. Nowhere is this more true than in public education, where principals and district superintendents are recruited almost exclusively from the ranks of practice. As in the military and the church, one does not get to lead in education without being well socialised to the norms, values, predispositions, and routines of the organisation one is leading.

Current education leaders are no better equipped than the organisations they lead to meet the challenges posed by standards-based reform. So relying on leaders to solve the problem of systemic reform in schools is, to put it bluntly, asking people to do something they don't know how to do and have had no occasion to learn in the course of their careers. There are, of course, a few gifted and visionary leaders who are busy inventing solutions to the problems of systemic reform, just as there are a few gifted and visionary leaders at any moment of history in American education. These exceptions prove the rule. Few visionary leaders have had any effect on the dominant institutional patterns of American education.

Society should communicate its expectations for what students should know and be able to do in the form of standards, both for what should be taught and for what students should be able to demonstrate about their learning. School administrators and policy makers, at the state, district, and school level, should regularly evaluate whether teachers are teaching what they are expected to teach and whether students can demonstrate what they are expected to learn. The fundamental unit of accountability should be the school, because that is the organisational unit where teaching and learning actually occurs. Evidence from evaluations of teaching and student performance should be used to improve teaching and learning and, ultimately, to allocate rewards and sanctions.

Over the past fifteen years, the logic of standards-based reform has become, a fundamental part of the architecture of policy and governance in American education. Virtually all states have adopted some form of content and/or performance standards. Most states are moving, in at least a rudimentary way, toward accountability systems that evaluate schools based on student performance. While the design of these policies leaves a great deal to be desired, both in specificity and internal logic, the politics that surround these policies are very energetic and visible. We may get the version of standards-based reform that advocates envision or we may get a corrupted and poorly thought out evil twin. But we will almost surely get some version of standards-based reform in virtually every jurisdiction over the next decade.

The practice of public schooling will respond to standards-based reform in the same way it has responded to virtually every other large scale reform in the twentieth century. It may, in other words, try to bend the logic of the policy to the logic of how the existing institutions function, making the policy unrecognizable upon its arrival in the classroom. If this is the case, the consequences for public education will be severe; the institutions that emerge will look nothing like the present ones, and the idea of a strong basic education system for all children will be lost in all but a rhetorical sense.

Public schools will find a way to incorporate the logic of standardsbased reform into their practice of schooling, in which case the institutions that emerge will probably be very different from what exists today but will perpetuate a strong basic education system for all children. If public schools can adapt to the demands of standards-based reform they will have a better chance of survival.

9.2. Loose-Coupling

United States in early in the development of public schooling opted for a form of organisation based on locally centralised school bureaucracy, governed by elected boards, with relatively low status (mostly female) teachers working in relative isolation from each other under the supervision of (mostly male) administrators whose expertise was thought to lie mainly in their mastery of administrative rather than pedagogical skills.

As the scale of the enterprise grew, the institutional structure grew more elaborate and rigid. School districts expanded to include more schools, schools grew in size and complexity, and the extension of compulsory attendance through the secondary grades resulted in larger, more highly differentiated schools to deal with the diverse populations of previously uneducated students.

The overall administrative guidance of locally centralised systems was safely lodged in the hands of administrative experts; providing local economies with a supply of reasonably qualified labour; holding a large proportion of the youth population out of the labour force; and providing a credentialing system to allocate access to higher education.

The byproducts of this institutional form have been, among other things: relatively weak professionalisation among teachers, since teaching was thought not to require expertise on a level with other, "real" professions and conditions of work were not conducive to the formation of strong professional associations among teachers; a relatively elaborate system of administrative overhead at the district and school level, thought to be necessary for adequate supervision of the relatively low-skill teacher force; and relatively large schools, thought to be a logical extension of principles of scientific management requiring economies of scale to produce efficiencies.

Loose-coupling is derived from institutional sociology. It posits that the "technical core" of education-detailed decisions about what should be taught at any given time, how it should be taught, what students should be expected to learn at any given time, how they should be grouped within classrooms for purposes of instruction, what they should be required to do to demonstrate their knowledge, and, perhaps most importantly, how their learning should be evaluated-resides in individual class-rooms, not in the organisations that surround them.

The model posited that knowledge at the technical core is weak and uncertain. It cannot be clearly translated into reproducible behaviours, it requires a high degree of individual judgment, and it is not susceptible to reliable external evaluation. Therefore, the loose-coupling argument continues, the administrative superstructure of the organisation—principals, board members, and administrators-exists to "buffer" the weak technical core of teaching from outside inspection, interference, or disruption.

Then, administration in education has come to mean not the management of instruction but the arrangement of the structures and processes around instruction. That which cannot be directly managed must, in this view, be protected from external scrutiny. Buffering consists of creating structures and procedures around the technical core of teaching that, at the same time, (a) protect teachers from outside intrusions in their highly uncertain and murky work, and (b) create the appearance of rational management of the technical core, so as to allay the uncertainties of the public about the actual quality or legitimacy of what is happening in the technical core. This buffering creates what institutional theorists call a "logic of confidence" between public schools and their constituents.

Local board members, system-level administrators, and school administrators perform the ritualistic tasks of organising, budgeting, managing, and dealing with disruptions inside and outside the system, all in the name of creating and maintaining public confidence in the institutions of public education. Teachers, working in isolated classrooms, under highly uncertain conditions, manage the technical core. This division of labour has been amazingly constant over the past century. The institutional theory of loose-coupling explains a great deal about the strengths and pathologies of the existing structure of public education.

Most innovation in schools, and the most durable innovations, occur in the structures that surround teaching and learning, and only weakly and idiosyncratically in the actual processes of teaching and learning. Most innovation is about maintaining the logic of confidence between the public and the schools, not about changing the conditions of teaching and learning for actual teachers and students. The theory of loose-coupling explains why schools continue to promote structures and to engage in practices that research and experience suggest are manifestly not productive for the learning of certain students.

They include extraordinarily large high schools that create anonymous and disengaging environments for learning; rigid tracking systems that exclude large numbers of students from serious academic work; athletic programmes that keep large numbers of students from participation in extracurricular activities; grouping practices in elementary school classrooms that provide less stimulation for struggling learners; special programmes that remove students from regular instruction in the name of remediation, instructional aide programmes that are sometimes little more than public employment programmes for community members; and site-based governance structures that engage in decision making about everything except the conditions of teaching and learning.

Loose-coupling also explains why manifestly successful instructional practices that grow out of research or exemplary practice never take root in more than a small proportion of classrooms and schools. Because the administrative structure of schools exists to buffer the instructional core from disruptions and improvements, and because teaching is isolated work, instructional improvements occur most frequently as a consequence of purely voluntary acts among consenting adults. The educational change literature is full of injunctions to respect the autonomy of teaching and the mystery of its fundamental practices-hence the inviolability of individual teachers' choices about what to teach and how. This normative environment is a direct result of an institutional structure that is deliberately and calculatedly incompetent at influencing its core functions.

To improve practice in an organisation in which administrators do not purport to manage the core, volunteerism is the only way. It leads to innovations that are highly correlated with the personal values and predispositions of individual teachers and hence tend to be adopted only by a small proportion of receptive teachers at any given time; and innovations that are largely disconnected from any collective goal or purpose of the school or the school system. Schools are consequently almost always a boil with some kind of "change," but they are only rarely involved in any deliberate process of improvement, where progress is measured against a clearly specified instructional goal.

Loose-coupling explains the elusive and largely unsuccessful quest over the past century for school administrators who are "instructional leaders." Instructional leadership is the equivalent of the Holy Grail in educational administration. Most credentialing programmes for superintendents and principals purport, at least in part, to be in the business of preparing the next generation of instructional leaders.

Majority of professional development for educational leaders makes at least symbolic reference to the centrality of instructional leadership to the work. Insofar as there is any empirical evidence on the frequency of actual instructional leadership in the work of school administrators, it points to a consistent pattern: direct involvement in instruction is among the least frequent activities performed by administrators of any kind at any level, and those who do engage in instructional leadership activities on a consistent basis are a relatively small proportion of the total administrative force. School leaders are hired and retained based largely on their capacity to buffer teachers from outside interference and their capacity to support the prevailing logic of confidence between a school system and its constituencies.

The ethic of volunteerism prevails. Principals who develop the skills and knowledge required to actually do instructional leadership in a serious way do so because of their personal preferences and values, often at some personal cost to their own careers, not because they are expected to do so as a condition of their work. Overall we get about the proportion of instructional leaders in the administrative ranks that corresponds to the proportion of people in the population who are inclined to do that sort of work. The institutional structure does not promote, or select for, knowledge and skill related to instructional leadership; at best, it tolerates some proportion of the population who indulge in it out of personal commitment and taste.

Loose-coupling explains the nervous, febrile, and unstable condition of politics and leadership around most school systems of any size. The governance structure is designed to support the logic of confidence in the institutional structure of public schools, not to provide stability, guidance, or direction for the long-term improvement of school performance. Local politics is usually driven by pluralist imperatives; local factions mobilise by neighbourhood, by racial or ethnic group, or by moral principle, they galvanise electoral support, and they reproduce, not surprisingly, the same political divisions on school boards as exist in the community at large. Since politics is not about the instructional core, but about the logic of confidence between the schools and the community, all policy decisions are essentially about the symbolism of mobilising and consolidating political constituencies.

In this world, a smart board member is one who spends most of his or her time using issues to consolidate political support. A smart superintendent is one who can count the number of board members, divide by two and, if necessary, add one. Superintendents come and go based on their capacity to maintain a working majority on a relatively unstable elected board, rather than on their capacity to focus the institution on its core functions and make steady improvements over time.

9.3. Standard-based Reforms

Standards-based reform creates certain fundamental problems for public schooling-problems that probably can't be solved by tinkering with the existing institutional structure-and why standards-based reform is often greeted with dismay and disbelief by experienced educators, who are battle worn veterans of past educational reform campaigns. The logic of standards-based reform is fundamentally at odds with the logic of loose-coupling, and this difference is not likely to be resolved in the usual way, by simply bending and assimilating the new policy into the existing institutional structure.

Standards-based reform violates the fundamental premise of loose coupling-buffering the technical core from interference by external forces. With standards-based reform, policy reaches, at least in theory, directly into the instructional core of schools, making what actually gets taught, a matter of public policy and open political discourse. Content standards, even in their current somewhat clumsy and over specified form, carry the explicit message that students should receive and absorb instruction in certain subject areas and on certain topics. Performance standards are even more threatening to the technical core because they assert that schools are accountable for what students learn, meaning that someone should manage the conditions of learning in schools so as to produce a given result.

Teachers and administrators who have fully assimilated the norms and values of loose-coupling find these intrusions into the technical core to be both disconcerting and threatening. They often respond with well-known arguments that conjure up the mystery and inviolability of the unique relationship between each student and teacher and its need for distance from bureaucratic or policy controls. What's remarkable in the present political climate is how little weight these arguments now carry in policy discussions. The course of standards-based reform seems largely immune to these traditional arguments.

Standards-based reform hits at a critical weakness of the existing institutional structure, namely its inability to account for why certain students master academic content and can demonstrate academic performance while others do not. When the core technology of schools is buried in the individual decisions of classroom teachers and buffered from external scrutiny, outcomes are the consequence of mysterious processes that no one understands at the collective, institutional level. Therefore, school people and the public at large are free to assign causality to whatever their favourite theory suggests: weak family structures, poverty, discrimination, lack of aptitude, peer pressure, diet, television, etc.

It explicitly localises accountability for student learning with the school and the people who work in it, and it carries the increasingly explicit message that students learn largely as a consequence of what goes on inside schools. Hence, schools are being asked to account for what students are actually taught and what they learn as a consequence of that teaching. And, whatever one may think about this theory—that students generally learn what they are taught, if they are taught with skill and understanding—it has a strong political, economic, and social appeal.

It also undermines a basic premise of local governance of education because it identifies schools, not school districts, as the primary unit of accountability in virtually all state accountability systems. Governors and state legislators are typically polite and indirect about this issue, carefully constructing ways of including local school boards and superintendents in any description of how school accountability works. But the stark reality is that little more than a decade ago most states did not have the capacity to collect, analyse, and report data on individual schools. Now most do, thanks largely to the political imperatives elected officials feel to account for state education expenditures and to the miracles of modern information technology.

When states have the capacity to collect data on individual schools, the individual school becomes the unit of accountability, and the remedies and sanctions that apply to low performance apply to schools. Districts may find a productive role to play in this system of accountability, if they try, but the institutional drift of the system will create increasingly direct relationships between states and schools. The pluralist politics of local boards and administrators will increasingly be played out under a large, dark umbrella of state performance accountability requirements.

It will become increasingly difficult to defend dysfunctional local politics in the face of increasing public scrutiny of individual school performance. Putting schools at the centre of the accountability problem, in other words, has the effect of calling into question the purpose of locally centralised governance and administration. These conflicts between the logic of standards-based reform and the logic of the traditional institutional structure of public education challenge both public schools and the people who work in them.

The traditional arguments that have been used to defend the existing loosely-coupled institutional structure-the mystery and inviolability of teaching and learning, the sanctity of local preferences in the governance of schools, the generally positive support of local schools by their elites, etc.-will probably become weaker and less persuasive as evidence about the performance of schools accumulates over time. The usual process by which public schools deal with these external threats is to bend the new policy requirements to the logic of the existing institutional structure.

The core technology of education is highly uncertain and unspecifiable, and that most matters of instructional quality and performance in education are matters of personal preference and taste, for both educators and their clients. The idea that schools should meet certain specified standards of quality and performance would then recede into the mists of policy history. The problem with this scenario, of course, is that the imperative for school accountability will not go away, even if standards-based reform does, because policy makers are still left with the problem of how to account for the public expenditures they are making and what to do about the governance structure of public education.

9.4. Market Model

School-site accountability for common measures of student performance is the hallmark of standards-based reform is. The standard critique of this model is that it ignores the complexity and idiosyncrasy of teaching and learning and the necessary variability of local and school-site tastes and preferences. Within the current educational reform debate, the governance structure that best fits the view that all matters of quality and performance in education are matters of personal taste, preference, and judgment is, in fact, a market model. The most efficient way to allocate resources around matters of personal taste is to give public money directly to consumers to purchase education based on their own preferences (vouchers), or, in a slightly more domesticated version, to give money directly to schools based on the number of students they attract (capitation grants), or, in an even more domesticated version, to allow educators and their clients to escape the gravitational pull of the existing institutional structure by forming publicly supported schools that operate under independent charters (charter schools).

The existing superstructure of local administration and governance in education becomes increasingly weak, unstable, and irrelevant to many educators and their clients under each of these systems. Active choosers in each of these systems-on both the supply side and the demand side-have very strong incentives to escape the gravitational pull of locally centralised governance and administration. Parents and students with strong tastes and preferences, and the wherewithal to act on them, have little incentive to affiliate with centrally administered schools when they can express their preferences more directly through individual schools. Increasingly, then, the domain of centrally administered and governed public schools, under vouchers, capitation grants, or charters, becomes the domain of the non-choosers and the unchosen.

Schools, and school systems, should be held accountable for their contributions to student learning. The rationale for maintaining local governance and administration of education in the U.S. lies principally in the possibility of using the institutional structure for large-scale improvement of instructional practice and student performance based on standards. In the language of economics, large scale improvement will increasingly be the main comparative advantage of local school districts in the competitive market for clients that will arise as schools and parents increasingly attempt to escape the gravitational pull of local school bureaucracy.

Individual schools, operating largely as individual firms, have difficulty generating surplus resources for use in improving the skills and knowledge of their teachers and administrators. Individual schools that are part of larger corporations also have incentives, in markets largely defined by taste and preference, to under invest in skill and knowledge, since they market their reputations for quality rather than any specific service or result. Most public school systems still have access to resources-largely now spent on non-instructional administrative overhead-that they can capture and invest in improvements in the skills and knowledge of principals and teachers.

These issues of instructional practice and performance are typically left to individuals to decide. Principals and teachers declare whether a given change has worked based on whether they individually think they have altered their practice in useful ways and whether they think students know and can do things they haven't known or done before. Not surprisingly, this situation produces lots of change and not much improvement.

Now add the problem of scale, a key weakness of the existing institutional structure. Improvement implies not just that any given unit in a system is improving (classroom, grade level, school, etc.) but that all units are improving at some rate. In the language of statistics, the mean, or average, of quality and performance in all units is increasing over time, while the variation among units in quality and performance is decreasing.

The problems of the educational system are the problems of the smallest units in that system, and each unit faces a different version of the overall problem of the system. If the overall problem of the system is student performance on higher order cognitive tasks, this problem will be present in very different forms in every classroom where it occurs.

9.5. De-Romanticising Leadership

Students will have different prior knowledge of the basic concepts and different attitudes toward the importance of knowing them. Different groups of students will bring different cultural, linguistic, and cognitive understandings to bear on the problem. At the school level, differences at the classroom level aggregate into differences in the overall culture of expectations for learning, order, and engagement, into the structure of opportunities that determine whether students get access to the content and teaching at all, and into whether they get it in a form that engages them. So the problem of improvement at each location in a system has to be solved in a way that produces results that are roughly consistent across many highly varied contexts.

Feedback is the next problem. Most of what happens in organisations engaged in large scale improvement is collective problem-solving, structured by a common set of expectations about what constitutes a good result. A major source of learning in such situations is analysis and discussion of successes and failures, and feedback about this into the larger pool of knowledge and skill in the organisation. Improvement seldom, if ever, occurs on a straight trajectory; it typically involves bumps and slides, as well as gratifying leaps. Learning about improvement occurs in the growth and development of common understandings about why things happen the way they do.

Learning depends, to a very large degree, on the existence of some variation in the overall system. If everyone is doing exactly the same thing in exactly the same way (a highly unlikely event in a situation where contexts vary dramatically by school and classroom), then we have no internal evidence on which to base judgments about how it might be done better.

Add the problem of benchmarks or standards. Someone usually knows how to do something better than you do, no matter how well you may think you know how to do it. Using variation in practice and performance for purposes of improvement means exploiting situations in which someone, inside or outside the organisation, knows more than you do about what works. Often the knowledge gleaned from other contexts is woefully incomplete; it comes with blank spaces in critical places. So the task of learning from other people in other contexts is an active one of analysing similarities and differences, adapting what make sense, and leaving behind what doesn't.

The knowledge we need to solve problems often doesn't reside close at hand; it has to be found through active inquiry and analysis. Improvement, then, is change with direction, sustained over time that moves entire systems, raising the average level of quality and performance while at the same time decreasing the variation among units, and engaging people in analysis and understanding of why some actions seem to work and others don't.

Leadership is the guidance and direction of instructional improvement. This is a deliberately de-romanticised, focused, and instrumental definition. Leadership tends to be romanticised in American culture, especially in the culture of schooling, both because we subscribe heavily to trait theories of success-people succeed because of their personal characteristics, more than because of effort, skill, and knowledge-and because we like our heroes to have qualities that we think we don't have. The problem with this romanticised theory of leadership is that the supply of character traits we associate with "good" leaders is, by definition, limited, or we wouldn't envy and admire them so much in other people.

Character traits also are much less amenable to influence by education, training, and practice than are knowledge and skill. De-romanticising leadership would have a very positive effect on the quality of schools. A definition of leadership in terms of instruction is also far more focused than most conceptions of leadership in education. Reading the literature on the principalship can be overwhelming, because it suggests that principals should embody all the traits and skills that remedy all the defects of the schools in which they work.

They should be in close touch with their communities, inside and outside the school; they should, above all, be masters of human relations, attending to all the conflicts and disagreements that might arise among students, among teachers, and among anyone else who chooses to create conflict in the school; they should be both respectful of the authority of district administrators and crafty at deflecting administrative intrusions that disrupt the autonomy of teachers; they should keep an orderly school; and so on.

Somewhere on the list one usually finds a reference to instruction, couched in strategically vague language, so as to include both those who are genuinely knowledgeable about and interested in instruction and those who regard it as a distraction from the main work of administration.

In leadership, skills and knowledge have important place. These are those that can be connected to, or lead directly to, the improvement of instruction and student performance. Standards based reform forces this question. It makes leadership instrumental to improvement. The leadership envisioned here differs from that typically described in the literature on management—leaders, or higher level managers, who exercise "control" over certain functions in the organisation. There are, to be sure, certain routine organisational functions that require control-bus schedules, payroll, accounting, etc.

The term "control" applied to school improvement is a dubious concept because one does not "control" improvement processes so much as one guides them and provides direction for them, since most of the knowledge required for improvement must inevitably reside in the people who deliver instruction, not in the people who manage them. Control implies that the controller knows exactly what the controllee should do, whereas guidance and direction imply some degree of shared expertise and some degree of difference in the level and kind of expertise among individuals. It is this problem of the distribution of knowledge required for large scale improvement that creates the imperative for the development of models of distributed leadership.

The basic idea of distributed leadership is not very complicated. In any organised system, people typically specialise, or develop particular competencies, that are related to their predispositions, interests, aptitudes, prior knowledge, skills, and specialised roles. Furthermore, in any organised system, competency varies considerably among people in similar roles; some principals and teachers, for example, are simply better at doing some things than others, either as a function of their personal preferences, their experience, or their knowledge.

Organising diverse competencies requires understanding when the knowledge and skill possessed by the people within the organisation is not equal to the problem they are trying to solve, searching outside the organisation for new knowledge and skill, and bringing it into the organisation. In a knowledge-intensive enterprise like teaching and learning, there is no way to perform these complex tasks without widely distributing the responsibility for leadership among roles in the organisation, and without working hard at creating a common culture, or set of values, symbols, and rituals.

Then, distributed leadership means multiple sources of guidance and direction, following the contours of expertise in an organisation, made coherent through a common culture. It is the "glue" of a common task or goal-improvement of instruction—and a common frame of values for how to approach that task-culture-that keeps distributed leadership from becoming another version of loose coupling.

Performance-based accountability in schools, and good management practice generally, require that certain people be held responsible for the overall guidance and direction of the organisation, and ultimately for its performance. Distributed leadership does not mean that no one is responsible for the overall performance of the organisation. It means, rather, that the job of administrative leaders is primarily about enhancing the skills and knowledge of people in the organisation, creating a common culture of expectations around the use of those skills and knowledge, holding the various pieces of the organisation together in a productive relationship with each other, and holding individuals accountable for their contributions to the collective result.

Seeking or giving collegial advice is not a gauge of relative competence, but rather a professional action viewed as desirable, necessary, and legitimate in the acquisition of new skills. In schools characterised by norms of autonomy, on the other hand, there are ambiguous goals and no attempt to develop a shared teaching technology. There is no agreement among teachers and principals about the outcomes they seek and the means for reaching them. In such settings, therefore, definitions of teaching success and the manner in which it is attained are highly individualistic. Without these commonly held definitions, collegial and principal assistance serves no useful purpose.

9.6. Improving the Performance of School

In the loose-coupling mode, institutional theories of leadership stress the role of leaders as buffers of outside interference and as brokers between the institutions of public schooling and their clients. Political theories of group leadership stress the role of leaders as coalition-builders and brokers among diverse interests. Managerial theories of leadership stress the role of leaders as custodians of the institutions they lead-paterfamilias-and sources of managerial control. Cultural theories of leadership stress the role of leaders as manipulators of symbols around which individuals with diverse needs can rally. None of these theories captures the imperative for large scale improvement, since none of them posits a direct relationship between the work that leaders should be doing and the core functions of the organisation.

Collective learning demands an environment that guides and directs the acquisition of new knowledge about instruction. The existing institutional structure of public education does one thing very well: It creates a normative environment that values idiosyncratic, isolated, and individualistic learning at the expense of collective learning. This phenomenon holds at all levels: individual teachers invent their own practice in isolated classrooms, small knots of like-minded practitioners operate in isolation from their colleagues within a given school, or schools operate as exclusive enclaves of practice in isolation from other schools. In none of these instances is there any expectation that individuals or groups are obliged to pursue knowledge as both an individual and a collective good.

But, the existing system doesn't value continuous learning as a collective good and does not make this learning the individual and social responsibility of every member of the system. Leadership must create conditions that value learning as both an individual and collective good. Leaders must create environments in which individuals expect to have their personal ideas and practices subjected to the scrutiny of their colleagues, and in which groups expect to have their shared conceptions of practice subjected to the scrutiny of individuals. Privacy of practice produces isolation; isolation is the enemy of improvement.

Role-based theories of leadership wrongly envision leaders who are empowered to ask or require others to do things they may not be willing or able to do. But if learning, individual and collective, is the central responsibility of leaders, then they must be able to model the learning they expect of others. Leaders should be doing, and should be seen to be doing, that which they expect or require others to do.

Large scale improvement of schools can be accomplished by recruiting, rewarding, and retaining good people and releasing them from the bonds of bureaucracy to do what they know how to do. Schools get better, in this view, by attracting and empowering good people. It's not hard to see why this view is so widely held among educators. It accords well with the existing institutional structure. The properties of system inhere in the personal qualities of the people in it, not in the system itself. To the minds of these reformers the job of the system is to stay out of the business of the gifted practitioners who work in it and to keep the outside world at bay.

It produces "good" practice and performance only from those people who already embody the personal attributes and characteristics that make good practice and performance possible. We know that this proportion seldom grows larger than about one quarter or one third of the total population of classrooms, schools, or systems.

Experimentation and discovery can be harnessed to social learning by connecting people with new ideas to each other in an environment in which the ideas are subjected to scrutiny, measured against the collective purposes of the organisation, and tested by the history of what has already been learned and is known. The idea of learning to do the right thing-collectively, progressively, cumulatively over time-is at the core of the theory of standards-based reform.

Such reforms must set content and performance targets, open school performance up to public scrutiny and discourse, and, over time, calibrate rewards and sanctions based on the degree to which schools and school systems engage in sustained improvement. There are, to be sure, major problems with the design of most state standards and accountability systems, problems of the sort one would expect with new policies that are discontinueous with past policies and that deal with inherently complex processes and institutions.

The success of these policies will depend, in large part, on the willingness of policy makers to model the kind of learning they are expecting from educators-to scrutinise their own actions and consequences and to modify policies based on their impact on practice and performance. As important as the problems of policy design and implementation are, the problems of institutional design and educational practice embedded in standards-based reform are much, much larger. One can "make" policy by stitching together coalitions of political interests. Redesigning institutions and improving educational practice are massively more complex.

They involve changes of the most fundamental kind in the norms and values that shape work in schools, in the way the resources of the system get used, in the skills and knowledge that people bring to their work, and in how people relate to each other around the work of the organisation. Policy can set the initial expectations and conditions within which large scale improvement will occur, it can set targets for practice and performance, it can open and stimulate public discussion about content and performance in schools, and it can alter the incentives under which schools and school systems work.

The closer policy gets to the instructional core-how teachers and students interact around content-the more policy makers lose their comparative advantage of knowledge and skill, and the more they become dependent on the knowledge and skill of practitioners to mould and shape the instructional core; the more-again, in the words of distributed cognition-knowledge of policy and practice have to be "stretched over" each other in order to be complementary. Issues of institutional design and practice in large scale improvement are the domains where our collective, public knowledge is weakest. There is strong suggestive evidence, both in early research on effective schools and districts and in recent research on the effects of standards-based reform, that some schools and districts are systematically better at the tasks of large scale improvement of instruction and performance than others.

The exact form or wording of the principles is less important than the fact that they are an attempt to derive general guidance from practice and research in a form that can be tried in multiple settings and revised and elaborated with experience.

A major design principle is to organise everyone's actions, at all levels of the system, around an instructional focus that is stable over time. Most low-performing schools and systems start, for example, with a single instructional area-literacy, in most cases-and focus on that area until practice begins to approach a relatively high standard in most classrooms and performance begins to move decisively upward. They then add another instructional area-typically mathematics-and increase the level of complexity they expect of teachers and principals in practice and learning.

Even relatively high-performing schools and districts could benefit from this approach, since the purpose of focus is not just to improve practice and performance but to teach people in the organisation how to think and act around learning for continuous improvement.

Many nominally high-performing schools and districts do well because of the backgrounds of their students and may be just as lacking in organisational resources for learning as low-performing schools. Focus also has to be accompanied by stability-in leadership, in the language that high-level administrators and board members use to describe the goals and purposes of the organisation, and in the commitment to monitoring and redesigning policies and structures that are supposed to enable improvement.

The principle of tight focus and stability in message should apply to everyone. Superintendents and board members should be just as subject to criticism for straying off message as principals and teachers. Another major design principle has to do with the development and conduct of accountability relationships in schools and school systems.

School systems that improve are those that have succeeded in getting people to internalise the expectations of standards based accountability systems, and that they have managed this internalisation largely through modelling commitment and focus using face to face relationships, not bureaucratic controls. The basic process at work here is unlearning the behaviours and normative codes that accompany loose-coupling, and learning new behaviours and values that are associated with collective responsibility for teaching practice and student learning. People make these fundamental transitions, by having many opportunities to be exposed to the ideas, to argue them into their own normative belief systems, to practice the behaviours that go with these values, to observe others practicing those behaviours, and, most importantly, to be successful at practicing in the presence of others.

The most powerful incentives reside in the face to face relationships among people in the organisation, not in external systems. It is the deadliness of life in schools and school systems that sustains loose-coupling. Unless new values and behaviours reach into the deadliness of schools, there will be no change in business as usual. The early evidence also suggests that low-capacity schools and school systems-schools and systems with weak collective values and atomised organisations-tend to try to find the easiest possible way of solving accountability problems with the knowledge they already have.

Schools tend to teach to the test because they have no better ideas about how to improve content and pedagogy. They tend to focus on students who are closest to meeting standards rather than those who are furthest away. They tend to give vague and general guidance about instruction rather than working collectively on learning new instructional practices, etc. Improving school systems override these practices by insisting that the expectations and standards apply to all students, which translates into examining assessment data on individual students in all classrooms and schools, focusing on the particular problems of low-performing students, and avoiding judgments about school performance based on school or grade level averages.

Adults in the organisation all frame their responsibilities in terms of their contribution to enhancing someone else's capacity and performance. System level administrators are judged on the basis of how well they contribute to principals' capacities to work with teachers, principals are judged by how well they contribute to teachers, and teachers are judged for their contributions to students. In very well developed improvement systems, one could imagine the evaluation working the other way too-students being evaluated, in part, on their contribution to improving their teachers' capacities, teachers for principals, principals for superintendents, etc.

Schools and systems that are improving directly and explicitly confront the issue of isolation embedded in loose-coupling. Administrators-both system-level and school-level-are routinely engaged in direct observation of practice in schools and classrooms; they have mastered ways of talking about practice that allow for non-threatening support, criticism, and judgment. Such systems also create multiple avenues of interaction among classrooms and schools, as well as between schools and their broader environment, always focusing on the acquisition of new skills and knowledge. They adjust and adapt the routines of the workplace-teaching schedules, preparation periods, substitute teacher allocations-with the primary purpose of creating settings where teachers, administrators, and outside experts can interact around common problems of practice.

Improving school systems appear not to have been captured by age-old, largely pointless debate about centralisation versus decentralisation. Rather they seem to have developed ways of tailoring system wide strategies of improvement to differences in communities, schools, and classrooms, without losing the overall coherence of system wide standards for content and performance.

Certain school-based management reforms are explicitly designed to push instructional decisions off the policy agenda altogether and focus debate instead on the representation of key constituencies in school governance. It seems clear that administrators in the districts that are improving avoid pointless and distracting debates about centralisation and decentralisation. Instead, they spend a lot of time building a sense of urgency and support in specific schools and communities around issues of standards and performance.

If they communicate that urgency to principals and teachers, as well as to schools collectively, they will have to accept a high degree of responsibility for the detailed decisions required in managing improvement. In so doing they may need to engage in differential treatment of high- and low-performing schools, varying both the content of their oversight and professional development and the process by which they deal with schools, depending on how well a given school is doing on instructional quality and performance.

Schools don't get to choose whether they participate or not. Participation is condition of being in the system. Different schools might get to choose how they will participate. Some systems have allowed schools to enter various phases of an improvement process at different times. Some systems allow schools to choose among an array of instructional approaches as the focus for improvement. There are a variety of ways of introducing choice at the front end of an improvement process. But allowing schools to choose whether they participate is tantamount to returning to the old principles of loose-coupling, in which improvement occurs in small pockets captured by faithful adherents to some instructional approach and never influences the rest of the system.

Local school systems in those states are at various stages of discovering that, in some fundamental sense, they don't have the option of using volunteerism, since ultimately their performance as a system will be based on the performance of all classrooms and schools in the system.

9.7. Conclusion

Design principles derive from the fact that large scale improvement processes run directly against the grain of the existing institutional structure of public education, and therefore it is difficult to do anything consequential about large scale improvement without violating some fundamental cultural or managerial tenet of the existing structure. The proble n, then, is how to construct relatively orderly ways for peop le to engage in activities that have as their consequence the learning of new ways to think about and do their jobs, and how to put these activities in the context of reward structures that stimulate them to do more of what leads to large scale improvement and less of what reinforces the pathologies of the existing structure.

The urgency of learning more about these issues in many school districts and in many different settings is the main point here. This requires pressing hard for more concrete knowledge about how large-scale improvement processes work.

References

Briggs, K. L., & Robertson P. J. "Improving schools through school-based management: An examination of the process of change". *School Effectiveness and School Improvement*. Vol. 9, No. 1, pp. 28-57.1998.

Caldwell, B. J., & Spinks, J. M. *Beyond the Self-Managing School*. London: Falmer Press. 1998.

De Grauwe, A. "The challenges for the school of the future". *IIEP Newsletter*. Vol. XVII, No. 4. 1999.

Dempster, N. "Guilty or not: the impact and effects of site-based management on schools". *Journal of Educational Administration*. vol. 38, no. 1, p. 47-65. 2000.

Fullan, M., & Watson, N. "School-based management: Reconceptualising to improve learning outcomes". *School Effectiveness and School Improvement*. 11(4). 453-474. 2000.

Jesson, D. *Educational Outcomes and Value Added by Specialist Schools*. London: Specialist Schools Trust. 2004.

Elmore, R. F., C. H. Abelmann, et al. *The New Accountability in State Education Reform. Holding Schools Accountable*. H. Ladd. Washington, D.C., The Brookings Institution: 65-98. 1996.

Floden, R., A. Porter, et al. "Instructional Leadership at the District Level: A Closer Look at Autonomy and Control." *Educational Administration Quarterly*. 24: 96-124.1988

Fuhrman, S. H. *The Politics of Coherence. Designing Coherent Education Policy: Improving the System*. San Francisco. Jossey Bass: 1-34.1993.

Hess, F. M. *Spinning Wheels: The Politics of Urban School Reform*. Washington, D.C. The Brookings Institution. 1999.

Lortie, D. "Built In Tendencies Toward Stabilising the Principal's Role." *Journal of Research and Development in Education*. 22(1): 80-90. 1987.

Malen, B., R. Ogawa, et al. What Do We Know About School-Based Management? Choice and Control in American Education. *W. Clune and J. Witte*. 2:289-432. 1990.

10

EMERGING TRENDS IN INDIAN SCHOOLS

10.1. Introduction

India has achieved many milestones in education sector. The recent economic growth rate of this country also evokes positive vibes among social and economic sectors. The country has made encouraging recent progress in raising schooling participation. While the base of India's education pyramid may be weak, it has emerged as an important player in the worldwide information technology revolution on the back of substantial (absolute) numbers of well educated computing and other graduates.

The Indian government is providing primary school education at no cost or negligible cost everywhere in India. India has many schools, enough teachers and facilities for students and teachers. But the great variation in the quality of education is found due to some factors like social background of students, parents, different standards of teaching and teachers training programmes. All teachers cannot deliver the same message to all learners. In the presence of great social diversity in India, it is difficult to change the social background of students, parents and their economical conditions. Therefore the only option left for us is to provide uniform or standardise teaching learning resources or methods. For high quality education throughout India there must be some nation wide network, which provides equal quality education to all students, including the student from the rural areas and villages. The solution to this is Web-Based Learning.

Internet is the ocean of knowledge, therefore it is better to open (introduce) this ocean to all students as early as possible in their life. This can be done by introducing or using Information

Technology and related tools in school education or by using World Wide Web as education delivery medium. The WWW is used not only to disseminate information but it also provides a great opportunity to extend learning outside space and time boundaries. The Web Based Education /Learning has the potential to meet the perceived need for flexible pace, place and face. The web allows education to go to the learner rather than the learner to their education.

10.2. Applications of E-Learning

Internet technology it makes a new revolution in information technology. The wide use of Internet also affected the methods of education. It is a global network and gives the concept of global classroom where any number of students can interact with each other at any time. Goodbye classes, goodbye books and Goodbye teachers' is possible with the webbased education.

There are two different types of web based education in asynchronous the educational module asynchronous and synchronous learning is to be installed from a particular web site and then you can unpack it offline on your machine. In this case there is no mutual interaction of student with teacher. In synchronous type there is synchronisation among the students and teacher on-line. This synchronous Web based education provides the most emerging concept of E-learning.

E-Learning is an interactive experience with access to on line tutors and can be done from any computers once you have your password. Access is through web browsers such as Internet explorer and Netscape Navigator. With E-Learning training is organised in the form of modules. The modules are approximately one hour session that focuses on specific subject of training. Using E-Learning the training can be brought right to your desktop. This makes technical training more convenient. During the live E-Learning module, participants will have the ability to ask the instructor questions, get answers and interact with other students—all on line.

The student, with a very short period of training, can access the learning material when their schedule allows. No separate distribution mechanism needed (WBL), can be accessed from any computer anywhere in the world, keeping delivery costs low, this leads to cost saving.

10.2.1. Enhanced Learning

Cognitively, active and context-based learning activities, the highly interactive nature of well designed online learning, flexibility to review course material at any time, all improve learners' abilities to synthesise and retain information. Many learners also find it easier to ask questions via E-mail because they have the privacy of direct contact with the instructor and avoid the classroom fear of "exposing" ignorance.

10.2.2. Ease and speed of Update

Web based learning allows for efficient and quick updates to course material for frequently changing information. The changes are made on the server programme. Everyone worldwide can instantly access the update.

10.2.3. Uniformity of learning Material

By using WBL, each learner gets identical instructions to ensure the consistency and quality of the message.

10.2.4. Cross Platform

WBL can be accessed by web browsing software on any platform Windows, Mac, UNIX etc. All these factors contribute to improve the quality of school education by overcoming factors like social background of students, parents, different standards of teaching and teachers training programmes, all teachers cannot deliver the same message to all learners. Also by using WBL students can do their self-assessment & management has access to progress reports & assessment data of individual learner.

10.2.5. Useful IT Tools for School Education

The school classrooms, office and training centers are connected through Intranet. This Intranet is connected to the Internet by using network operating system. Firewall is introduced between Intranets and Internet in order to provide security.

10.2.6. System Description

The students are not expert in reading and writing in initial stage of school education. Subject understanding increases if they learn the things through visualisation. With the help of multimedia or Rich Media, which includes, Audio, video, graphics and Java Applets have made WBE very effective. Multimedia database contents the data about educational centers, courses, tutors, students, examinations as well as some story books and games in the form of html pages, audio and video files, Images and Java Applets. Student and teachers can access this database for learning as well as for teaching.

Students don't have good knowledge of English In the primary stage. Therefore the presentation should be available in their mother tongue for the better understanding, which is also helpful in improving their pronunciation. This is possible by developing Natural Language Interface to database. One important device called, as "Tech Commander" is also useful for teachers to identify students' potential by viewing any students computer display on his own monitor. If he finds something that everyone should see he could set everyone's monitor to display it.

10.3. Approaches of Web Based Education

10.3.1. Conversion of Existing Material

We have to convert the existing school educational material to the Web in order to shift from traditional education to WBE. The important points to consider are bandwidth, design, usability, and the necessity of high quality media elements and consistency of material across the mediums.

10.3.2. Authoring for Multiple Delivery

We have to provide consistency of interface and ease of authoring and design of an effective multi-platform course.

10.3.3. Using Web for Student/Teacher Interaction

Website can be used for posting of assignments, student work and marks, along with the ability to submit work on-line through the site, also JavaScript and JAVA applets to demonstrate course concepts interactively. This means that course delivery on the Web must be dynamic and truly interactive between the instructor and the students.

10.3.4. Faculty Support and Training

We have to provide centralised support & training resources for training the teachers initially.

10.4. Implementation of WBE in Schools

We will face some problems while implementing WBE in school education in India. The major problems we will be facing are:

10.4.1. Intensive Training to Schoolteachers

Schoolteachers are not introduced to the web based education. Therefore training should be given in order to create a learning environment that will itself train and spur students on the one hand to turn the learning experience into useful, practical and personal knowledge.

10.4.2. WBL awareness and Workshops

In rural area parents are not much knowing about WBL. So the demonstration, seminars and workshops needs be conducted for society in order to understand the importance of it.

10.4.3. Bandwidth Limitations

Limited bandwidth of Internet connection gives slower performance for sound, video and intensive graphics, causing long waits for downloads that can affect the ease of the learning process. Improved bandwidth will help the teacher to solve his problem.

10.4.4. Effect on Teachers

WBL will lead to reduction in manpower as per as teachers are concerned. This will lead to agitations by teacher's organisation.

10.4.5. Effect on Students

Although the students will be benefited by WBL there will some section of students opposing this introduction of technology in education.

10.4.6. Infrastructure

WBE will primarily require free access to Web to all the learners and hence government of India will have to setup nation wide Fiber Optic Cable network.

10.4.7. Access

Every school will not have equal opportunity to information because of access issues. The schools with fewer budgets will always face this problem. This is the major problem as per as India is concerned, as there is big gap between poor and rich communities in India.

10.4.8. Download

The learning material that appears on web needs to be downloaded will require more time. The speed depends on the transmission methods and bandwidth, which is problem as per as India is concerned.

10.5. Achieving Learning Levels in Primary Education

Workers' productivity and earnings depend not only on years of education acquired but also on what is learnt at school. This literature is summarised in Hanushek. He cites 3 US studies as showing quite consistently that a one standard deviation increase in mathematics test performance at the end of high school in the US translates into 12 per cent higher annual earnings. He also cites three studies from the UK and Canada showing strong productivity returns to both numeracy and literacy skills. Substantial returns to cognitive skills also hold across the developing countries for which studies have been carried out, i.e. in Ghana, Kenya, Tanzania, Morocco, Pakistan and South Africa. Hanushek and Zhang confirm significant economic returns to literacy for 13 countries on which literacy data were available.

This evidence underlines the importance of ensuring that what schools do leads to learning achievement. Unfortunately, no national data on learning achievement levels were available in India until 2006. India's largest educational NGO, Pratham, carried out a survey of learning achievement in 2005 and repeated the survey with a bigger sample of about 330,000 household in 2006. It visited 20 homes each in 30 randomly selected villages in each one of 549 Indian districts, and interacted with all children aged 6 to 16 years old in the sample homes. The Annual Status of Education Report (ASER) 2005 and 2006 reports are published by Pratham. The findings make grim reading. In 2006, nearly 47 per cent of children who were in school and studying in grade 5 could not read the story text at grade 2 level of difficulty.

10.6. Achieving Learning Levels in Secondary Education

Learning levels at the secondary level of education is also poor. In cross-country comparison, achievement levels of Indian students appear to be well below the international average, though the latter does include developed countries. While each Indian state examination board sets its own curricula and examinations and there are no national level data based on a common standardised achievement test in India, the Council of Boards of Secondary Education provides pass rates in the High School and Intermediate (senior secondary) examinations in different states. 2004 pass rates in the High School exam varied from 37 per cent in Manipur to 80 per cent in Andhra Pradesh but such inter-state comparison is meaningless since curricula, exam papers, passing requirements, etc. all differ from state to state.

The high school pass rates cannot be taken at face value as they are much inflated due to the phenomenon of wide-spread cheating, if the experience of Uttar Pradesh can be generalised. While the true levels of learning achievements in secondary education are generally hidden, fortuitously they became visible one year in Uttar Pradesh. When the Kalyan Singh government brought in an anti-cheating rule and installed police at all examination centres in 1992 to prevent the mass-cheating that routinely takes place at board examinations in Uttar Pradesh, the pass rate in the High School exam fell from 57 per cent in 1991 to a pitiful 14.7 per cent in 1992 . This is when the bar for passing is set very low, i.e. a student only needs on average 33 per cent marks in their various subjects in order to pass High School. The true extent of the problem of low achievement levels in secondary education, though it is possible that achievement levels in Uttar Pradesh are lower than those in other states. Moreover, students rely on guess papers, which are prepared and sold a few weeks before the exams. These attempt to anticipate exam question and are often remarkably close to them.

10.6.1. Quality of School

The impact of cognitive achievement on earnings, productivity and economic growth highlights the importance of school quality. The Public Report on Basic Education was the first serious evidence-based study of the state of primary schooling quality in India. It is based on a survey of schooling facilities in 242 villages across five North Indian states, Bihar, Madhya Pradesh, Rajasthan, Uttar Pradesh and Himachal Pradesh in 1996.

District Primary Education Project (DPEP) started with donor assistance in the mid-1990s in districts with below national mean literacy rates. One of the explicit objectives of the DPEP was to construct schooling facilities and upgrade school infrastructures. While DPEP and its successor programme Sarva Shiksha Abhiyan (Campaign for Education for All) have obviously helped, the current state of school facilities is nevertheless clearly far from satisfactory, with substantial proportions of primary schools still without the most basic essentials such as drinking water, toilets, furniture, teaching aids and books, let alone more advanced resources such as fans, playground, computers etc.

Teacher negligence in schools is equally worrying. Firstly, teacher absence rates are high. The extreme cases of teacher negligence were less devastating than the quiet inertia of the majority of teachers. In half of the sample schools, there was no teaching activity at the time of the investigators visit. Inactive teachers were found engaged in a variety of pastimes such as sipping tea, reading comics, or eating peanuts, when they were not just sitting idle. Generally speaking, teaching activity has been reduced to a minimum in terms of both time and effort. And this pattern is not confined to a minority of irresponsible teachers—it has become a way of life in the profession.

10.6.2. Responsibility of Private Schooling

Poorly resourced public schools which suffer from high rates of teacher absenteeism can have encouraged the rapid growth of private (unaided) schooling in India, particularly in urban areas. Private schools divide into two types10: recognised schools and unrecognised schools. Government recognition is an official stamp of approval and for this a private school is required to fulfil a number of conditions. Aided schools are run by private managements but funded largely by government grant-in-aid and are very similar to government schools in many respects. They charge the same fee levels as government schools (now mandated to be nil) and, following centralising legislation in the early 1970s, their teachers are paid directly from the state government treasury at the state teacher salary rates. Schools run by private managements without state aid are private unaided. These run entirely on fee-revenues and have virtually no state involvement. Unaided schools are thus the genuinely private schools and henceforth we refer to these simply as private and refer to private aided schools simply as aided.

Government and aided school teachers have incentives to over-report their enrolments when there is low demand for their services, and this reduces the apparent enrolment share of private schools.

The true size of the private schooling sector is greatly underestimated in official data due to enumerating only the recognised schools. Household survey data give a picture far closer to the truth than official statistics since parents have no incentives to over-report enrolment in publicly funded schools or to report enrolment in recognised schools only.

10.6.3. Development in Private Schooling

The share of private schooling in the total recent is in increase in school enrolment at different levels. This shows the relative growth of private schooling in India. Rural private schools in particular do not easily get government recognition, for which many conditions need to be shown to be satisfied. Given the exacting conditions for and scant rewards of recognition, it is not surprising that most private primary schools remain unrecognised. The growth of private schooling offers a possible explanation for why, despite falling or virtually static per capita public education expenditure in several Indian states and falling share of basic education expenditure in state domestic product, these states have improved their educational outcome indicators in the 1990s.

10.7. Education Initiatives

Teacher absenteeism and school facilities paints quite a grim picture of the state of schooling quality in India, there are several reasons for more optimism about progress of school education in the future. Firstly, a number of recent fiscally-demanding public education initiatives suggest that India has begun in earnest to give greater priority to improving school education. Secondly, a number of educational NGOs have emerged such as Pratham, Digantar, Azim Premji, MV Foundation and others and some have acquired substantial stature both in terms of their contributions to educational improvements in a number of dimensions, as well as in terms of their influence, advocacy voice, public/media profile, research capacity and ability to mobilise funds for education both from individual donors in India and abroad and from the Indian corporate sector. Below we consider some of the important initiatives and their impact on educational outcomes.

10.7.1. Sarva Shiksha Abhiyan

The literal meaning of SSA is Campaign for Universal Education. It is India's flagship programme to universalise elementary education by the year 2010. It is a scheme sponsored by the Central government that is funded out of revenues from a new cess, equal to 2 percent of all taxes, which was introduced in 2004 (increased to 3 per cent in March 2007). SSA provides additional funding to states to enroll out-of-school children and to improve school quality. SSA funds civil works; salaries of additional teachers to reduce whether school and teacher characteristics were included in the achievement equations. The costs of private and public schooling were calculated differently in the different studies.

There is no rigorous evaluation of the impact of this massive intervention or its individual components so far. The treatment intensity of a certain age group in a specific district depended on the years DPEP was in place and on the number of years that the group was in school-going age during this time period. While both studies find substantial programme impacts and find that impacts were greater for low caste children, Schmid finds that effects were stronger for girls but Jalan and Glinskaya find they were negligible, although the latter evaluated the impact of only the first phase of the DPEP while Schmid evaluated the impact of all three phases.

10.7.2. Mid Day Meal Scheme

The Indian Supreme Court directed all states in late 2001 to implement the Mid-Day Meal Scheme by providing every child in every government and government assisted primary school with a prepared mid-day meal with a minimum content of 300 calories and 8-12 grams of protein each day of school for a minimum of 200 days. By 2006, the MDM scheme was near universal in all states, following public mobilisation efforts to encourage states to act. This is a centrally funded scheme in that the central government provides grains, funds transportation and also pays food preparation costs, though the state government is responsible for providing the physical infrastructure for cooking the meals.

Although it is not yet free of problems of quality and corruption, the fact that mid-day meals have become a part of the daily routine in most primary schools across the country is a major achievement. The scheme provides lunch to about 120 million children every school day and, as such, is the largest school meal scheme in the world. Certain states have gone beyond the mandated scope of the scheme, for instance in Kerala and Tamil Nadu the destitute and the aged are allowed to take the MDM and in Gujarat the scheme covers children from Grades 1 to 7 rather than only in the primary grades (1 to 5).

Though there are no rigorous evaluations (e.g. randomised experiment studies) of the impact of this scheme on children's school enrolment and attendance and on nutritional and health status, several micro studies suggest major increases in enrolment immediately after the introduction of mid-day meals, e.g., 23 per cent in Barmer district of Rajasthan, 36 per cent in Madhya Pradesh, and other large increases in Karnataka. However, Deaton and Drèze note that the consumption of mid-day meals in primary schools appears to be heavily under-recorded in the National Sample Survey (NSS) data, making it hard to verify the impact of MDMs on school attendance from NSS surveys.

10.7.3. Para Teacher Schemes

Under Para Teacher schemes, persons with educational qualification requirements below those of government primary school regular teachers are employed on salaries that are one-fifth to one-half of government teacher salaries, in order to (i) expand schooling in a low cost way to small hamlets which are unserved by regular government schools, (ii) to increase the number of instructors in single-teacher schools and (iii) to reduce high pupil-teacher ratios. Although the model varies from state to state, the para-teacher jobs are typically tenable for ten months per year, but are annually renewable.

Para teacher schemes have raised a number of concerns about the ethical, legal, and political difficulties of sustaining two different standards of employment between regular teachers and contract teachers. Some authors have also raised concerns about the quality of teaching provided by these less-qualified instructors. Others have pointed that para-teachers may exhibit greater accountability due to closer community involvement in their recruitment and dismissal and because of the impermanence of their job-contracts.

The contribution of these low-cost schemes so far is uncertain and that it is premature either to applaud or dismiss them. We are not aware of any serious evaluations of these schemes though several micro studies find that learning achievements of 21 Rajasthan had already initiated the Shiksha Karmi (education worker) project in 1987. Several states devised their own versions of Shiksha Karmis in the 1990s.

10.8. Public Private Partnerships

Public private partnership (PPP) is a system of government grant-in-aid to privately managed schools known as aided schools. In 1995-96 the percentage share of aided schools in total schools was 34.0 per cent and 44.3 per cent respectively at the secondary and higher secondary levels, though at the primary and middle levels, it was only 3.4 per cent and 10.1 per cent respectively. However, over time, largely due to successive governments conceding teacher union demands, aided schools have become more and more like government schools: their teachers are now paid directly by the state government treasury at the same uniform salary rates as for government school teachers, and are recruited by a government-appointed selection committee rather than by the school.

Aided schools also have the same fee policy as in government schools. Perhaps not surprisingly, learning achievements in aided schools are similar to those in government schools and significantly lower than in private schools after controlling for student intake and selection bias.

10.9. Role of NGO

Widespread education-related work by a large number of NGOs in India is a relatively new phenomenon but one which has grown rapidly. Their important contribution has been not only in grassroots educational work but also in terms of successful advocacy for education at the macro level by contributing to national educational debates and helping to make education access and quality prominent public issues. For instance, the role of the NGO Right to Food Campaign at both the micro and macro levels was critical in mobilising public opinion and building pressure for the rapid implementation of the school Mid-Day-Meal scheme in Indian states.

Field experiments in education are typically more readily facilitated by educational NGOs on a small scale rather than by governments and, as such, provide invaluable opportunities to test the cost-effectiveness of particular educational interventions.

They can thus inform education policy as to what types of educational innovations and policies give the greatest impacts at lowest costs. NGOs other education activities are far too numerous to summarise but include delivering bridge courses that prepare children who dropped out of schooling earlier to re-join school; arranging for street children to settle with foster parents and attend schools; organising learning camps for girl children and for working children; and many other educational innovations.

10.10. Conclusion

With introduction of Web Based Education at school level our children and youngsters will grow as "Computer kids". Their exposure will get increased due to which the Knowledge level will get definitely improved. Use of Internet for education has a potential to change many aspects of our lives. In conclusion we can say that WBE is platform independent, convenient in access, cost saving, easily updated contents and with emerging technologies it can be made more effective.

Web-Based Learning adds human support through on-line tutor, thereby extending the scope of what can be effectively taught into many new subject areas. In addition more supporting material can be made available through web site links to other documents and systems. With all these important features incorporated in Web-Based Learning system it will enhance the quality of education in our country at all levels i.e. Primary, Secondary and Higher Education.

References

Carr, David. *Making Sense of Education*. RoutledgeFalmer. London. UK. 2003.

Dewan, S. and Vora, N. "Indian Education Sector – Long way from graduation", Sector Report, IDFC-SSKI India Research, Mumbai, India. 2009.

Garg, S. *Four Decades of Distance Education in India: Reflections in Policy and Practice*. Viva Books. New Delhi. India. 2006.

GOI. "National Policy on Information and Communication Technology (ICT) in School Education". Department of School Education and Literacy. Ministry of Human Resources Development. Government of India. New Delhi. 2009.

Keay, F.E. *A History of Education in India*. Oxford University Press. Calcutta. India. 1978.

Kshetrimayum, O. "ICT Integration in School Education – A Sociological Proposition". *Journal of Indian Education*. Vol. 33, No. 1, pp. 62-71. 2007.

Lallana, E.C. "An Overview of ICT Policies and e-Strategies of Select Asian Economies". Asia-Pacific Development Information Programme (APDIP). A division of Reed Elsevier India Private Limited. UNDP-APDIP. ICT-4D Series. 2004.

Mehta, A.C. Elementary Education in India–Progress towards UEE, Analytical Report 2006-07. DISE. National University of Educational Planning and Administration. New Delhi. India. 2009.

Shrimali, K.L. *Education in Changing India* Asia Publishing House, Bombay, India. 1965.

11

QUALITATIVE SCHOOLING FOR ECONOMIC GROWTH

11.1. Introduction

Each year, huge sums of money are spent on education and there are those who ask if it really is necessary for people to have so much education. Although it would seem fairly self evident that education is required if the human capital in a country is to be adequate for the economic tasks required of it, there has been widespread concern that more extensive evidence is required to support this viewpoint.

One of the major impediments to school reform is the lack of regular information about what does, and does not, work. This kind of information needs to be delivered in a timely fashion and must include valid data about student educational achievement and outcomes for new and existing programmes.

Around the world, all governments assume a substantial role in providing education for their citizens. A variety of motivations lead societies to provide such strong support for schooling—some of which come from pure economics and others of which come from ideas of improved political participation, of social justice, and of general development of society.

The underlying notion of human capital is that individuals make investment decisions in themselves through schooling and other routes. The accumulated skills relevant for the labour market from these investments over time represent an important component of the human capital of an individual. The investments made to improve skills then return future economic benefits in much the same way that a firm's investment in a set of machines (physical capital) returns future production and income. In the case of public education, parents and public officials act as trustees for their children in setting many aspects of the investment paths.

Formal schooling is one of several important contributors to the skills of an individual and to human capital. It is not the only factor. Parents, individual abilities, and friends undoubtedly contribute. Schools nonetheless have a special place because they are most directly affected by public policies. The human capital perspective immediately makes it evident that the real issues are ones of long-run outcomes. Future incomes of individuals are related to their past investments. It is not their income while in school or their income in their first job. Instead, it is their income over the course of their working life.

Economic growth determines how much improvement will occur in the overall standard of living of society. Differences in growth rates that appear to be small have huge differences for society if they are maintained over a period of time. It is very easy to see the effect of differences in growth rates on economic well-being. Many factors enter into determining growth. For example, the existence of a strong system of property rights, the ability to develop binding contracts, and the maintenance of relatively free labor and product markets all have been seen to establish the basis for a healthy and growing economy. With these conditions, however, the knowledge and skills of the population have a very powerful impact on national growth rates.

11.2. Economic Growth on School Quality

The human capital of the population, which is enhanced by a strong education system, enters directly and indirectly into economic growth. Education has the possibility of making both the individual receiving it and others better off. Specifically, a more educated society may lead to higher rates of invention; may make everybody more productive through the ability of firms to introduce new and better production methods; and may lead to more rapid introduction of new technologies. These "externalities"—influences on others of individual education outcomes—provide extra reason for being concerned about the quality of schooling.

School quality had a remarkable impact on differences in economic growth. The analysis was very straightforward. All of the available earlier international test scores were formed into a single composite measure of quality. The basic statistical models, which included the level of income, the quantity of schooling, and population growth rates, explained a substantial portion of the variation in economic growth. Most importantly, the quality of the labor force as measured by math and science scores was extremely important. One standard deviation difference on test performance was related to one percent difference in annual growth rates of per capita GDP.

Schooling might not be the actual cause of growth but, in fact, may just reflect other attributes of the economy that are beneficial to growth. Other factors that affect growth such as efficient market organisations are also associated with efficient and productive schools—so that again the test measures are really a proxy for other attributes of the country.

Quality measured by test scores is directly related to individual earnings, productivity, and economic growth. A variety of researchers document that the earnings advantages to higher achievement on standardised tests are quite substantial in the United States and other developed countries. While these analyses emphasise different aspects of individual earnings, they typically find that measured achievement has a clear impact on earnings after allowing for differences in the quantity of schooling, the experiences of workers, and other factors that might also influence earnings. In other words, higher quality as measured by tests similar to those currently being used in accountability systems in various countries is closely related to individual productivity and earnings.

The impact of test performance becomes larger with experience. The labour market experiences that are observed begin in the mid 1980s and extend into the mid 1990s, but other evidence suggests that the value of skills and of schooling has grown throughout that period in many countries of the world (and particularly in the US). Future general improvements in productivity are likely to lead to larger returns to skill.

The effect of quality improvements on school attainment incorporates concerns about drop out rates. Specifically, higher student achievement keeps students in school longer, which will lead among other things to higher graduation rates at all levels of schooling.

A second place where the returns to skills are found is farm productivity. Even in developing countries with relatively small manufacturing and skill-intensive service sectors, skills have been shown to have a strong impact on outcomes. Thus, while much of the quantitative research on the importance of skills has come from developed countries, the qualitative picture appears to hold for a wide range of developing countries.

The frequent focus of governmental programmes has been an increasing school attainment and expanding the years of schooling of the population. The previous discussion, however, highlights the central importance of quality. While years of schooling attainment are important, that holds only if quality is maintained. The impact of improved quality can be obtained from the considerations of how quality affects growth rates for economies.

Commonly identified resources—class size, teacher experience, and teacher salaries—positively influence student performance. Nonetheless, the evidence does not indicate that pure resource policies can be expected to have a significant effect on student outcomes.

Overall resource policies have not led to discernible improvements in student performance. It is important to understand what is and is not implied by this conclusion. It does not mean that money and resources never matter. There clearly are situations where small classes or added resources have an impact. It is just that no good description of when and where these situations occur is available, so that broad resource policies such as those legislated from central governments may hit some good uses but also hit bad uses that generally lead to offsetting outcomes.

This statement does not mean that money and resources cannot matter. Altered sets of incentives could dramatically improve the use of resources. The evidence on resources is remarkably consistent across countries, both developed and developing. Had there been distinctly different results for some subsets of countries, issues of what kinds of generalisations were possible would naturally arise. Such conflicts do not appear particularly important.

The quality of teachers is the key element to improving student performance. But the research evidence also suggests that many of the policies that have been pursued around the world have not been very productive. Specifically, the chosen policies of individual countries may have led to changes in measured aspects of teachers such as degrees or teacher qualifications, but they have not tended to improve the quality of teachers—at least when quality is identified by student performance.

The concern is identifying good and bad teachers on the basis of their performance in obtaining gains in student achievement. An important element of that work is distinguishing the effects of teachers from the selection of schools by teachers and students and the matching of teachers and students in the classroom. In particular, highly motivated parents search out schools that they think are good, and they attempt to place their children in classrooms where they think the teacher is particularly able. Teachers follow a similar selection process. So, it is difficult to sort out the quality of the teacher from the quality of the students that she has in her classroom.

Having a series of good teachers can dramatically affect the achievement of any student. In fact, a series of good teachers can erase the deficits associated with poor preparation for school. The difficulty, as pointed out in the preceding discussion, is that hiring good teachers is not easily done. Teaching ability is not closely related to training or experience. Moreover, common salary systems do not target particularly high quality teachers. From a policy viewpoint the primary objective should be improving the overall quality of the teaching force. If one were simply to redistribute existing teachers, the overall policy goals would not be achieved.

Quality improvements are more likely to come from selecting and retaining better teachers rather from re-training the existing teachers. While some in-service training and development programmes have had success, in general they have been disappointing. Moreover, existing evidence on inservice programmes gives insufficient means for selecting a programme that is likely to yield significant gains in teaching performance.

In other words, research has not established the characteristics of an effective programme.

Concentrating on selecting better teachers appears to be the much better way to go. There are clear limits on how large the changes in the teacher force can be at any point in time. It is simply not feasible to turn over the stock of teachers completely while maintaining a coherent teaching programme. Many nations currently do not have active policies toward retention of teachers but instead leave most of the decision making up to the individual teachers. That is, within broad limits once a teacher is hired into the educational system, decisions about when to leave are made by that teacher and not by the school institutions. This approach would limit the speed of replacement to the existing turnover in teachers. Policy changes may affect this speed—both slowing and speeding up the rate of turnover.

The rate of turnover of teachers essentially establishes a bound on the possibilities for change that exist. Moreover, the ability to improve the teaching force will depend on the types of people who can be attracted into teaching. If the teaching force is to be improved, it is necessary that the hiring selects better teachers or that retention is skewed toward the better teachers. If better hiring is an important element of the plan, it may well take time before new kinds of people are attracted toward teaching. Entering teaching is generally a career choice that requires a prior commitment on the part of prospective teachers. That commitment in turn depends on the career expectations of these people, and expectations take some time to be affected by general policies. This perspective argues for building a plan of improvement over time. One time adjustments or changes in programmes are unlikely to be effective.

The best way to promote improvements in the teaching force depends upon local circumstances. Existing laws, regulations, and policies directly affect the options that are available to improve the quality of the teaching force. Further, since most countries have done little experimentation with alternative policies and approaches, the potential approaches and their effects are generally unknown.

Current knowledge generally will not support aggressive regulatory approaches designed to improve teacher quality. The most feasible approach given the currently available information is to experiment with alternative incentive schemes. These might involve new contracts and approaches to teacher compensation, introduction of parental choice across schools, merit awards for schools, and the like. The unifying theme is that each should be designed to improve student achievement directly.

A major impediment to reform and improvement of schools is a lack of regular information about what is working and what is not working. Too often no regular evaluation of policies and programmes exists. When evaluations are conducted, they frequently focus on inputs to the system and not on student achievement and outcomes.

The previous discussions about the current state of knowledge in key areas underscore the need to assess student outcomes that are related to both new and existing programmes.

Without information about student performance, it is very difficult to alter programmes in ways that will promote truly successful school improvement. Measuring student performance directly is the key element. Without objective data about student achievement, programmes and policies often proceed in unproductive directions.

Specifically, past research amply demonstrates that many good guesses about policies do not prove successful. Thus, regular monitoring is essential.

11.3. Evaluation of Educational Programmes

The economic impact of reforms that enhance student achievement will be very large. Reform must be thought of in terms of both the magnitude of changes and the speed with which any changes occur. Based on current knowledge, the most productive reforms are almost certainly ones that improve the quality of the teaching force; and, fourth, such policies are likely to be ones that improve the hiring, retention, and pay of high quality teachers, i.e., selective policies aimed at the desired outcome.

Countries always face limited budgets in making decisions about schools. If there are the commonly accepted two objectives of expanding access and of improving quality, these objectives will conflict because they must compete for the same budget.

Thus, by this standard policy makers are faced with a particularly unpleasant dilemma: choose between broad availability of schools and good schools. An alternative view, while apparently different, is actually quite closely related. Analyses of labour market implications and the rate of return to schooling in developing countries suggest strongly that schooling is a very good investment.

School quality may be an important explanation for the "strange" investment behaviour that does not take advantage of the available high returns. School quality is directly related to decisions about attending schools and to promotion through schools. High quality schools raise student achievement and speed students through primary (and perhaps secondary) schools, thus limiting costs. Additionally, students respond to school quality in deciding whether or not to drop out of school. They tend to stay in high quality schools and drop out of low quality schools.

Studies of the rate of return to schooling which only consider quantity of schooling produce a misleading estimate of the potential gains. Estimation of the rate of return to schooling that does not account for quality differences will systematically overstate the productivity gains that are associated with additional years of schooling, because the estimates will include quality differences that are correlated with quantity. If policy simply pushes people to stay in school longer, without changing the fundamental quality of the schools, the newly-induced school completers will only get the returns associated with years of schooling and not with quality. Thus, they will not be able to gain as much as the rate of return estimates suggest.

Existing research strongly points to focusing policies on quality improvements in schools. National growth plus individual earnings respond strongly to increased school quality.

11.4. Educational Quality and Economic Growth

Most attention to the value of schooling focuses on the economic returns to different levels of school attainment for individuals. These studies have uniformly shown that more schooling is associated with higher individual earnings. Educational quality is directly related to school attainment. Lower quality schools, measured by lower value added to cognitive achievement, lead to higher dropout rates in Egyptian primary schools. Thus, as for developed countries, the full economic impact of higher educational quality comes in part through greater school attainment. This complementarity of school quality and attainment also means that actions that improve quality of schools will boost attainment goals. Conversely, attempting to simply expand access and attainment-say through opening a large number of low quality schools-will be self-defeating to the extent that there is a direct reaction to the low quality that affects actual attainment.

Education can increase the human capital in the labour force, which increases labor productivity and thus leads to a higher equilibrium level of output. It can also increase the innovative capacity of the economy-knowledge of new technologies, products, and processes promotes growth. And it can facilitate the diffusion and transmission of knowledge needed to understand and process new information and to implement new technologies devised by others, again promoting growth.

The majority of the macroeconomic literature on economic returns to education employs the quantitative measure of years of schooling, now averaged across the labour force. Using average years of schooling as an education measure implicitly assumes that a year of schooling delivers the same increase in knowledge and skills regardless of the education system. This measure also assumes that formal schooling is the primary source of education and that variations in the quality of nonschool factors affecting learning have a negligible effect on education outcomes.

This neglect of cross-country differences in the quality of education is the major drawback of such a quantitative measure. The standard method of estimating the effect of education on economic growth is to estimate cross-country growth regressions where average annual growth in gross domestic product (GDP) per capita over several decades is expressed as a function of measures of schooling and a set of other variables deemed important for economic growth.

Education is important in facilitating research and development and the diffusion of technologies, with initial phases of education more important for imitation, and higher education more important for innovation. So, a focus on basic skills seems warranted for developing countries. But reverse causation running from higher economic growth to additional education may be at least as important as the causal effect of education on growth in the cross-country association. It is also important-for economic growth-to get other things right as well, particularly the institutional framework of the economy.

The returns to increased years of schooling increase with the quality of the education. Once there is a high-quality school system, it pays to keep children in school longer—but it does not pay if the school system does not produce skills. The results are very robust to alternative specifications of the growth relationships. First, the impact of cognitive skills remains qualitatively the same when measured just by the tests performed at the level of lower secondary education, excluding any test in primary schooling or in the final year of secondary education. Given differing school completion rates, the test for the final year of secondary schooling may imply cross-country samples with differential selectivity of test takers.

11.4.1. Educational Quality and Economic Institutions

The role of economic institutions as the fundamental cause of differences in economic development, emphasised in recent literature, raises the possibility that the effect of educational quality on economic growth may differ depending on the economic institutions of a country. The institutional framework affects the relative profitability of piracy and productive activity. If the available knowledge and skills are used in the former activity rather than the latter, the effect on economic growth may be very different, perhaps even turning negative. The allocation of talent between rent-seeking and entrepreneurship matters for growth: countries with more engineering students grow faster and countries with more law students grow more slowly. Education may not have much impact in less developed countries that lack other facilitating factors such as functioning institutions for markets and legal systems.

Due to deficiencies in the institutional environment, cognitive skills might have been applied to socially unproductive activities in many developing countries, rendering the average effect of education on growth across all countries negligible. Social returns to education may be low in countries with perverse institutional environments-a point certainly worth pursuing. Adding the interaction of educational quality and one institutional measure-openness to international trade-to the growth specification suggests that both have significant individual effects on economic growth and a significant positive interaction.

Both the quality of the institutional environment and the quality of education seem important for economic development. Furthermore, the effect of educational quality on growth seems significantly larger in countries with a productive institutional framework, so that good institutional quality and good educational quality can reinforce each other. Thus, the macroeconomic effect of education depends on other complementary growth-enhancing policies and institutions. But cognitive skills have a significant positive growth effect even in countries with a poor institutional environment.

11.5. Educational Quantity and Quality

The quantity and quality of education are two educational challenges for developing countries. For countries with both reliable attainment data from the household surveys and data from international student achievement tests, educational attainment of 15-19-year-olds from the latest available year is combined with test scores at the end of lower secondary education (eighth grade or 15-year-olds) from an adjacent year close by. This allows calculation of rough shares of recent cohorts of school-leaving age: how many were never enrolled in school, how many dropped out of school by grade 5 and by grade 9, how many finished grade 9 with a test-score performance below 400 (signalling functional illiteracy), and how many finished grade 9 with a test-score performance above 400. Only the last group can be viewed as having basic literacy in cognitive skills.

Lack of any systematic relationship between student achievement and resources raises the question of whether there is some minimum required level of resources even if impacts are not evident at higher levels. This almost certainly is the case. It is consistent with the few "resource findings" about the availability of textbooks, the importance of basic facilities, the impact of having teachers actually show up for class, and similar minimal aspects of a school.

There is little evidence for any serious notion of resource needs. One might suspect that resource effects would appear to be nonlinearly related to achievement such that, there is a strong relationship between added resources and student outcomes. There is little evidence supporting this kind of relationship. Part of the difficulty arises from the inference that teacher quality is the most important school element but that teacher quality is unrelated to common measures of salary, education, experience, certification, and the like. This implies that resources, at least as currently spent, are not effective in improving teacher quality. Rather than a necessary condition, this is merely an observation about how the current institutions translate resources into results.

Good teachers, defined in terms of student learning, are able to move the achievement of their students far ahead of those of poor teachers. Yet the identification of good teachers has been complicated by the fact that the simple measures commonly used-such as teacher experience, teacher education, or even meeting the required standards for certification-are not closely correlated with actual ability in the classroom. Much of this evidence comes from research in developed countries, but there is strongly consistent work from a number of developing countries.

It is difficult if not impossible to identify aspects of teachers that could form the basis for policies and regulations encouraging good teachers in the classroom. This difficulty of regulating the employment of high-quality teachers suggests that the institutional structure of the school system must be designed to provide strong incentives for improving student achievement.

11.6. Educational Incentives

National economies are dependent on the quality of their economic institutions. It is hard to have a strongly growing economy without complementary institutions in the labour and product markets, without openness to trade and investments from the outside, and without effective systems of laws and property rights. It is difficult to have a well-functioning education system without a supportive institutional structure. On this matter, however, there are more different opinions and perhaps wider divergence in outcomes. Part of the reason for the different opinions is simply a lack of experience, analysis, and evidence. This said, some clear general policies are important. Foremost among them, the performance of a system is affected by the incentives that actors face. If the actors in the education process are rewarded for producing better student performance, and if they are penalised for not producing high performance, this will improve performance.

The incentives to produce high-quality education, in turn, are created by the institutions of the education system-all the rules and regulations that (explicitly or implicitly) set rewards and penalties for the people involved. A significant aspect of such incentives involves either getting better performance out of existing teachers or improving the selection and retention of high-quality teachers. So, one might expect that institutional features impact student learning. Three institutional features may be part of a successful system for providing students with cognitive skills:

- Choice and competition.
- Decentralisation and autonomy of schools.
- Accountability for outcomes.

11.6.1. Choice and Competition

Choice and competition in schools were proposed a half century ago. The simple idea: parents, interested in the schooling outcomes of their children, will seek productive schools. This demand side pressure will create incentives for each school to produce. These incentives will also pressure schools to ensure high-quality staff and a good curriculum. In developed countries, a number of privately managed schools provide alternatives for students.

The benefits of competition are so well documented in other spheres of activity that it is inconceivable that more competition would not be beneficial. Choice and competition are very broad terms that can encompass many different programmes. The specific design of any choice programme will be important, particularly in distributional outcomes, because programmes might segregate the school population in various ways that might not be desirable. There is a need for greater experimentation and experience, given the current levels of uncertainty.

11.6.2. School Autonomy

Several institutional features of a school system can be grouped under autonomy or decentralisation, including local decision-making, fiscal decentralisation, and parental involvement. Almost any system to improve incentives for schools depends on school personnel being heavily involved in decision making. It is difficult to compile evidence on the impact-of autonomy because the degree of local decision making is most generally a decision for a country (or state) as a whole, leaving no comparison group within countries.

11.6.3. School Accountability

Many countries have been moving toward increased accountability of schools for student performance. One institutional setup that combines accountability with parental choice is a system that gives students in schools that repeatedly do badly on the accountability test a voucher to attend private schools.

Given the importance of high teacher quality, aiming incentives directly at teachers is promising. While convincing evidence on the effects of performance-related teacher pay is scarce, the more rigorous studies in empirical identification find a positive relationship between financial teacher incentives and student outcomes. Monetary incentives for teachers based on their students' performance have improved student learning in Israel immensely.

11.7. Need to Alter Institutions

Education matters but focuses most attention on ensuring that everybody is in school-regardless of the learning that goes on. Relatedly, it assumes that the prime constraint is resources-those needed to provide broad access to basic schooling. Because of these distortions, the results in terms of measurable economic circumstances have been disappointing. The accumulated evidence from analyses of economic outcomes is that the quality of education-measured on an outcome basis of cognitive skills-has powerful effects. Individual earnings are systematically related to cognitive skills. The distribution of skills in society appears closely related to the distribution of income.

Economic growth is strongly affected by the skills of workers. Other factors also enter into growth and may well have stronger effects. For example, having well-functioning economic institutions-such as established property rights, open labor and product markets, and participation in international markets—have clear importance for economic development and may also magnify the benefits of quality education.

However, quality of education independently affects economic outcomes, even after allowing for these other factors. Moreover, the existing research provides strong reasons to believe that quality of education is causally related to economic outcomes. To be sure, quality may come from formal schools, from parents, or from other influences on students. It may result from policies that maintain and enhance health and nutrition, allowing students to learn effectively. But a more skilled population—almost certainly including both a broadly educated population and a cadre of top performers-results in stronger economic performance for nations.

Available measures of school attainment uniformly indicate that developing countries lag dramatically behind developed countries. This fact has driven a variety of efforts to expand schooling in developing countries, including the Education for All initiative. Yet much of the discussion and much of the policymaking has tended to downplay the issues of quality. International testing indicates that, even among those attaining lower secondary schooling, literacy rates are very low in many developing countries.

Some basic resources in the least developed schools, such as textbooks for all students, have a reliable impact. But these situations have been documented just in the poorest schools and, even there, just in limited areas. There is also evidence that some schools use added resources better than others, although research does not characterise these different situations well enough to build them into overall resource policies. There is mounting evidence that the quality of teachers is the key ingredient to student performance. But the characteristics of good teachers are not described well, making it impossible to legislate or regulate good teachers.

In terms of overall changes, more choice and competition among schools leads parents to be directly involved in evaluating the performance of schools. While experiments in various choice plans have been limited, the existing evidence suggests that they do tend to lead to better student outcomes. The best way to introduce choice in rural systems within resource-constrained developing countries is not fully known now, but it appears clear that the existing system is not working.

Uncertainty about the best design of incentive programmes for schools is most acute in developing countries, largely due to lack of relevant experience. For this reason, it is especially important to implement a programme of experimentation and evaluation-a key missing aspect of policymaking in most developing countries. Education policy must be viewed as evolutionary, where ongoing evaluation permits discarding policies that are ineffective while expanding those that are productive.

The binding constraint seems to be institutional reform-not resource expansions within the current institutional systems. For educational investments to translate into student learning, all people involved in the education process have to face the right incentives that make them act in ways that advance student performance.

11.8. ICT, Education Reforms and Economic Growth

Global economic and social trends over the past several decades have profound implications for educational reform and the use of technology in schools. The convergence of these trends has created significant economic and social opportunities but also enormous challenges. The pervasiveness of information and communication technologies (ICT)-from cell phones, to low-cost video cameras, personal digital assistants, and laptops wirelessly connected to the Internet-has changed the way people live, work, and play.

New knowledge and the use of new technologies have resulted in the creation of new products, services, and jobs, some of which were unimaginable only a few decades ago. At the same time, trade agreements and the reduced costs of communication and transportation have increased the flow of capital, goods, services, knowledge-and jobs-between countries. The result has been significant worldwide economic growth but also considerable social turmoil and dislocation. These converging trends have put tremendous stress on educational and other social systems responsible for preparing society for the future and moderating the adverse impact of social and economic change.

Countries are confronted with the need to rethink their educational systems in order to prepare students for the global economy, to maintain economic progress, and to assure that their citizens will benefit equitably from this growth. To participate in this economy and to improve their standard of living, students need to leave school with a deeper understanding of school subjects, particularly science, mathematics, and technology, and with the skills needed to respond to an unbounded but uncertain 21st century-skills to use their knowledge to think critically, to collaborate, to communicate, to solve problems, to create, and to continue to learn.

Development in economic output can occur with an increase in input factors: more equipment is purchased and more workers enter the labour force, what economists call capital accumulation. Or it can occur with an increase in the economic output per person, that is, an increase in productivity. Growth based on capital accumulation is subject to diminishing returns; additional increases in input result in smaller and smaller increases in output. Increased productivity is the key to raising the standard of living and to sustained growth. Economic theory describes three factors that can lead to increased productivity: capital deepening, higher quality labour, and technological innovation-the creation, distribution, and use of new knowledge.

Education has a high economic value. This is supported by the results of both international micro and macro-economic studies. Microeconomic studies focus on the benefit of educational investments to individuals while macroeconomic studies focus on returns to the economy more generally.

The limitation of both microeconomic and macroeconomic studies is that they treat the educational system as a black box. They do not describe how curriculum, teaching, assessment, teacher quality, or the use of ICT can actually influence what it is that students know and are able to do as a result of their educational experience or how these education factors contribute to economic growth and social development. Yet the details of these connections are very important to educational policymakers who are charged with trying to prepare citizens to participate in the knowledge ICT, Education Reform, and Economic Growth White Paper economy and information society and create a workforce that is globally competitive.

Students will need to understand what they learn deeply enough to use it to solve the complex problems they will encounter in the real world. They will also need to be able to use technology, manage information, communicate effectively, think critically, work well in teams, and produce new intellectual and creative works that have value to others. Perhaps most importantly, they will need the skills to continuously learn and create new knowledge throughout their lives. These are the skills that students will need in the 21st century.

Some educational reform focuses on improving education by increasing knowledge acquisition. The emphasis in this approach is on quantity rather than quality. The goal is to boost enrollments, decrease dropouts, extend the school day, and increase the amount of knowledge that students acquire, particularly in reading and math. But few other things change in the system. Knowledge is still compartmentalised by traditional subjects and measured on standardised tests that include simple one-part problems with one correct answer. Higher scores on these are equated with more learning.

However, it is not clear how these traditional school subjects and assessment tasks correspond to situations and problems that students will encounter when they leave school and enter the real world. This approach does not include the learning of 21st century knowledge and skills that would make students more productive and innovative. So the connection between increased knowledge acquisition and a higher performing economy and more equitable society is unclear.

There are two ways in which education reform can develop 21st century skills and contribute to economic growth and an increased standard of living. One is through what can be called knowledge deepening. The traditional curriculum is bounded by school experience; knowledge of school subjects remains inert and cannot be applied outside the class or contribute to productivity or innovation. But the knowledge deepening approach leads to the improved economic productivity of students by deepening their understanding of school subjects and making these subjects more relevant to the problems and challenges of the real world. Learning inside school is connected to out-of-school examples and experiences.

Knowledge deepening also goes beyond the memorisation of isolated facts and the solution of simple problems that permeates the standard curriculum to emphasise the learning of complex concepts, principles, and procedures that lead to a higher quality, better prepared workforce and higher value jobs. Rather than the superficial "coverage" of a large number of topics, the curriculum focuses on a smaller number of key concepts, principles, and procedures and on how these ideas are organised and interconnected within and across subject areas to form complex knowledge systems. Extended assessments consisting of several parts parallel the complex tasks students will encounter in the real world and these assessments call for the adaptive application of concepts, principles, and procedures that cut across subject domains to fit the circumstances of novel problem situations mathematics, science, language, and reasoning are all used together rather than tested separately.

11.9. Conclusion

Policymakers and ministry officials face many important decisions, as they cope with sweeping global trends. None is more important to economic and social development than those they make in education policy. By examining the relationships between reforms in curriculum, teaching, assessment, the use of ICT, teacher training, and school organisation, and by aligning these changes with important economic and social goals, policymakers can leverage public investments to move from knowledge acquisition to knowledge creation. Early gains in deepening the knowledge of students and teachers can be leveraged to transform schools into learning communities and provide students with 21st century skills. The widespread ability to think critically, communicate effectively, use technology, work well in teams, learn continuously, and produce new intellectual and creative works is the basis for sustained and equitable economic growth.

References

Acemoglu, Daron, Simon Johnson, and James A. Robinson. "The Colonial Origins of Comparative Development: An Empirical Investigation." *American Economic Review*. 91 (5): 1369-1401. 2002.

Angrist, Joshua D., Eric Bettinger, Erik Bloom, Elizabeth N. King, and Michael Kremer. "Vouchers for Private Schooling in Columbia: Evidence from a Randomised Natural Experiment." *American Economic Review* 92 (5): 1535-58. 2002.

Barro, Robert J. "Human Capital and Growth." *American Economic Review* 91 (2): 12-17. 2001.

Bedi, Arjun S., and Ashish Garg. "The Effectiveness of Private versus Public Schools: The Case of Indonesia." *Journal of Development Economics* 61 (2): 463-94. 2000.

Benhabib, Jess, and Mark M. Spiegel. "Human Capital and Technology Diffusion." In Philippe Aghion and Steven N. Durlauf, eds., *Handbook of Economic Growth*. Amsterdam: North Holland. 2005.

Betts, Julian R., and Tom Loveless, eds. *Getting Choice Right: Ensuring Equity and Ef. ciency in Education Policy*. Washington, D.C.: Brookings. 2005.

Bils, Mark, and Peter J. Klenow. "Does Schooling Cause Growth?" *American Economic Review* 90 (5): 1160-83. 2000.

Bishop, John H. "The Effect of National Standards and Curriculum-Based Examinations on Achievement." *American Economic Review* 87 (2): 260-64. 1997.

12

GRADE REPETITION IN SCHOOLS

12.1. Introduction

Grade repetition means the students are held in the same grade for an extra year rather than being promoted to a higher grade along with their age peers. In some school systems grade repetition is seen as a valid corrective action that should be taken in cases of academic failure. In other school systems grade repetition is not permitted, and instead the policy for all pupils is "social promotion" whereby students pass automatically to the next grade with their peers and—if required—receive remedial academic assistance.

The reasons for applying grade repetition often differ across developed and developing countries. The effects of grade repetition have three important dimensions:

i) *The effects on academic achievement*—where research has indicated short-term gains and long-term problems because grade-repeaters eventually fall further behind;

ii) *The effects on student self-esteem, peer relationships, and attitudes towards school*—with negative outcomes in these areas leading to increased risks of dropping out; and

iii) *The effects on school operations*—whereby high levels of grade repetition can lead to increased class sizes and classroom management problems .

The application of grade repetition brings extra costs and long-term negative academic and social consequences. However, this should not be taken as a signal to approach policy development on the basis of a simplistic "grade repetition versus social promotion" dichotomy. Rather, the strategy should be to prefer automatic promotion—provided that this is supplemented with a range of initiatives (early intervention, remedial instruction, parent involvement, etc.) that are specifically designed to help struggling students to achieve at acceptable levels.

The voluntary form of grade repetition occurs primarily when students want to continue schooling but do not have access to a school that offers the next grade. In remote regions of developing countries, schools sometimes only teach the first few grades.

Some families think that the student did not learn much the previous year and therefore ought to repeat the grade. This type of grade repetition is most common in developing countries in areas where attendance is sporadic because schooling itself is sporadic or because many children spend much of their time working rather than attending school.

Another form of repetition occurs in areas where the language used at school differs from the language that many students speak at home. Repeating early grades may enable these students to gain fluency in the language of instruction so that they can begin to learn efficiently. Grade repetition for this reason is often family-initiated in developing countries but school-imposed in developed countries.

The repetition also occurs at higher grade levels in countries that require students to pass examinations to qualify for secondary or post-secondary education. Students who fail to qualify must either drop out of school and enter the workforce, pursue vocational training, or prepare to retake the examination. The latter students might work with tutors, take test preparation classes, or voluntarily repeat the previous grade.

Moreover, there is also involuntary form of repetition. This is initiated by the school rather than students or their families. It is most common in developed countries where school attendance is mandatory until some point in the adolescent years. Here, schools sometimes require or at least strongly advise failing students to repeat the grade.

12.2. Policy Issues in Grade Repetition

Schooling is most efficient if every student moves up a grade every year. Each student who repeats has the economic effect of adding a new student (at that grade and subsequent grades). This translates into larger class sizes and the need for additional desks and supplies. If many students repeat each year, the school system will need more teachers and classrooms.

Repetition also represents wastage of resources. The society provides schools, teachers, and other resources presumed sufficient to enable all students to make expected advances in achievement. Failures to do so suggest that these resources were insufficient or that some students failed to take advantage of the opportunities provided.

Though macro-level economic analyses depict repetition as undesirable, micro-level psychological analyses suggest a mixed picture. Voluntary repetitions that enable students to pass examinations or learn content that was not learned the year before will be viewed by students and their families as rational decisions that led to desired outcomes. However, school-imposed grade repetition has negative effects on achievement and is associated with social adjustment problems and increased likelihood of school dropout.

Automatic promotion is often opposed by people who believe that it lowers school expectations and student achievement. They want to allow or even to require schools to retain in grade all students who fail to meet specified promotion criteria. Analyses typically conclude that neither automatic promotion nor grade repetition addresses the problems of low achievers satisfactorily, so that potential solutions lie in providing these students with more and better learning opportunities.

Except for countries with enforced automatic promotion policies, grade repetition occurs with sufficient frequency to merit research attention and potential policy formulation in both developing and developed countries. Eisenmon reported that repetition rates in developing countries often are quite high. The highest rates were in the sub-Saharan African countries, where each year, about 22 percent of primary students and 21 percent of secondary students were repeating their grade.

The low achievement patterns of grade repeaters tend to be associated with poverty indicators, at both the school and the family levels. Schools in poor areas (especially remote rural areas) often feature limitations: short school years, frequent teacher absence, limited supplies, poorly qualified teachers, large classes, multi-age classes, or double shifts. Within any given school, students from the poorest families are more at risk for repetition because their home backgrounds leave them less well prepared to succeed and because they are likely to miss more school days.

12.3. Grade Repetition in Developing Countries

In developing countries, repetition occurs more frequently and is more likely to be initiated or at least accepted by the family rather than imposed by the school. There are other differences as well. In developed countries, students ordinarily are not absent from school more than a few days each year (mostly due to minor illnesses). However, in developing countries (especially rural areas), many children miss many days of school because of more serious health or nutrition problems or because their families require them to assume child care or work responsibilities.

Many students repeat a grade because they did not attend school frequently (if at all) the previous year. Although the situations that create them are undesirable from a societal perspective, these repetition choices are understandable, even productive, from the family's perspective.

Grade repetition is associated with low achievement and early dropout. Yet, needless repetition persists because many school administrators, teachers, and parents believe that repeating the grade is preferable to promotion when students have achieved poorly. Teachers in developing countries ordinarily are not trained to make promotion/repetition decisions and do not have access to detailed achievement standards and aligned assessment instruments, so concerns have been expressed that many decisions may be based on arbitrary observations or beliefs rather than justified criteria.

Repetition occurs because accessible schools only offer a few grades. This problem will disappear as developing countries become able to offer instruction in all grades at all elementary schools. Repetition that results from sporadic school attendance related to health or nutrition problems or family work expectations also should recede as developing countries make improvements in general health, nutrition, and economic opportunities. Pending such improvements, repetition appears productive for students who did not experience enough of the previous grade to enable them to acquire the expected learning. Grade repetition also appears to make sense for students who come to school with little exposure to the language of instruction, if it enables them to develop fluency in that language. A bilingual programme targeted to their needs would be preferable, but in its absence, grade repetition appears to be a viable strategy.

For students who miss school because their families want them to earn money, a simple but effective approach is to provide cash stipends to the families in exchange for ensuring their child's school attendance. Voluntary grade repetition undertaken as preparation for qualifying examinations will recede as countries provide more opportunities for secondary and post-secondary education. However, this depends not only on what countries can afford, but on their public education policies.

Any imposed qualification standards must be realistic rather than overly stringent, especially standards for promotion through the primary cycle. Given the relationship between grade repetition and school dropout, policies that increase repetition in these grades are counterproductive for countries that aspire to universal basic education.

Grade repeaters are more likely to come from families that rank lower on measures of socioeconomic status and related variables (income, parental years of education completed, etc.). They also are more likely to be male than female. Their parents are less likely to be involved with the school and to advocate effectively for their children. Repetition occurs most often at kindergarten or first grade. Subsequently, it occurs more often at grades preceding transitions to middle school, junior high school, or high school than at other grades. Repetition decisions are almost always initiated by the school rather than the parents, although they may be communicated as recommendations rather than requirements.

Preschool or kindergarten children repeat a grade are usually based on teachers' assessments of intellectual and social maturity (attention span, direction following, social adjustment), whereas retention recommendations in first grade and beyond are usually based mostly on indicators of achievement progress. Grade repeaters tend to be younger than their classmates and more often absent from school. Otherwise, however, comparisons of repeaters with other low-achievers who either were promoted or recommended for placement in special education usually do not show significant group differences in intelligence, achievement, or even social competence.

12.4. Grade Repetition and Academic Achievement

In developing countries, grade repetition is primarily involuntary, imposed by the school on students who have made unsatisfactory achievement progress. Most research relating repetition to achievement has been done in the United States, although researchers from other developed countries such as Belgium and France have reported similar patterns and concerns. The American findings seem to conflict at first, because different research designs yield contrasting outcomes. When placed into perspective, however, the findings converge on the conclusion that school-imposed grade repetition is counterproductive.

Involuntary grade repetition also has negative effects on social, emotional, and behavioural aspects of adjustment to school. Although their teachers and sometimes even their parents view it as an enabling opportunity, students experience it as a personal punishment and social stigma. From the beginning, but increasingly with age, they view "flunking" or "being held back" as embarrassing and stressful. By the time they are sixth graders, they rate it as among the most stressful things they can imagine.

Reduced self-esteem, impaired peer relationships, and increases in behavioural problems, negative attitudes toward school, and absences from school are commonly reported problems associated with involuntary grade repetition. The combination of low achievement and alienation from school makes grade repeaters much more likely than other students to drop out of school once they become old enough to do so.

Grade repeaters literally repeat the same lessons and activities they experienced the previous year, and teachers at the next grade do not make adjustments based on the notion that their classes are now more homogeneous. Except in schools where repetition is very rare, any potential advantages to increased homogeneity are likely to be nullified by grade repetition's collateral effects. First, class sizes throughout the school will be larger than they would have been if promotion were automatic. Second, although teachers in the next grade do not get the students who are held back this year, they will get them next year.

12.5. Reasons for Grade Repetition

12.5.1. Background and Experiences

The background and experiences of each primary school student is different—some will have benefited from pre-primary education or regular pre-school attendance and may be quite advanced socially and educationally, being able to read and write, while others may not have had any of these opportunities so will appear to be struggling by comparison. In addition, some children will have special educational needs including learning difficulties and behavioural problems. Conflict, economic difficulties affecting the time parents or other careers are able to spend with children, migration, natural disasters, health and nutrition problems or other interruptions may have had an impact on children's pre-school cognitive development. The social environment of school may also be very different from a child's previous social experience and acclimatisation to the social codes in school may take varying times. Another contributory problem may be that the language of instruction (LoI) is often a child's second or even third language.

12.5.2. Formative Versus Summative Evaluation

Formative and summative evaluations are the two main approaches to evaluating the progress of learners through an education system. A summative evaluation that involves testing at the end of a certain period and seeing if the child has reached the necessary 'normative' standard assuming that there is a certain standard that every child should meet; or a formative evaluation which looks more at how an individual child is responding to new educational ideas and ensuring that the child is growing in knowledge relative to his or her initial starting point, regardless of whether the child has reached the standard that another child has reached.

In summative evaluation, selection of children and who progresses from one year or level to the next is more important than ongoing development at a child's own pace. The outcome of this approach for any child who is perceived as struggling is repetition. For those believing formative evaluation is a better approach, the focus will be on how each individual child is progressing year by year, providing additional support where an individual may need it, rather than on setting certain standards each year that have to be reached and if not, to fail the child. Thus, there is an individual dimension to learning under formative evaluation and the outcome is one in which each child receives positive feedback about at least some of their capabilities, rather than sensing they are a failure.

12.6. Grade Repetition—Issues and Concerns

Repetition mostly takes place in the first and last years of primary school. It is seen by some protagonists as being important and its practice is seen as advantageous under certain conditions:

i) Where students are falling behind and do not have the expected knowledge of their peers and the necessary knowledge to be promoted to the next cycle, they will benefit from going over the material another time to bring them up to the necessary level;
ii) Where students are immature or very young for their year, an additional year in the same class is viewed as giving them the option to feel more secure and settled;
iii) Where there is a wide variety of ability in a class, it benefits the teacher and the remaining students if the weaker pupils are made to repeat, thus creating a more homogenous year group.

Repetition is the easiest and most visible response to the learning difficulties of certain pupils, but that it is a 'false thermometer' of school failure, since a repeating pupil who has encountered difficulties learning is more susceptible to ongoing difficulties, thus stigmatising these difficulties by making the pupil repeat the year in the same way rather than providing supplementary support to assist the pupil.

Although, there are clearly some circumstances where to deny a child the chance to repeat is fundamentally disadvantageous. The most obvious is in the last year of schooling, where, if a child fails their leaving certificate, they should be allowed the chance to re-sit the examinations and, should they fail again, repeat the whole year. This is usual practice in both developed and developing countries.

Repetition is enabled by educational policy at national level. Its continued popularity in developing countries can be seen partly as a response to limited resources. Automatic promotion of children is assumed to imply a greater range of abilities in a class. Nevertheless, the need for differentiated resources and a teaching methodology that takes adequate account of a range of abilities in the class is clear. So too is the need for a supportive teaching and learning style, personal knowledge by the teacher of an individual child's specific learning needs, and the ability to address those needs adequately. Even in well-resourced classes of 30 in a developed country, providing this sort of teaching environment is often considered one of the greatest challenges a teacher faces, and the debate about the benefits of mixed-ability classes remains contentious.

12.6.1. Grade Repetition and Dropout

Both developed and developing countries across the world, research shows that there are strong links between repetition and dropout, with repeating children being more likely to drop out of school in later years. American research is mostly focused on high school level. Some may counter argue that the pupils who drop out were poor learners who could not keep up with others and were thus doomed to fail irrespective of being made to repeat.

However, many children are made to repeat without objective evaluation of their performance, and children who are weak but promoted go on to do better than those who have been forced to repeat, so this counterargument is not strongly supported by pedagogical evidence.

12.6.2. Financial Impact of Grade Repetition

In economic point of view, the practice of repetition is extremely inefficient. Where repetition rates are significant, it means that additional teachers and classrooms are needed to cater not only for the regular cohort of children, but also for those who repeat and spend longer in the system. Furthermore, for each additional year that a child repeats, the public purse must pay what it would not normally have to in a more efficient system.

In the longer term, each extra year a child spends in school through repetition is one year less they will spend in the labour market in the future. Also, given that repeaters are more likely to drop out, school dropouts generally earn lower wages than those who leave with a diploma.

There is little empirical evidence to support the view that repetition increases learning outcomes, with more crowded classrooms and little, if any, additional support being made available to repeating learners, educational quality is not improving. Certain groups are more vulnerable to repetition and subsequently to dropping out, meaning that the inequalities among different beneficiaries of the education system worsen.

Repetition is very costly, as the public purse and additional family support have to pay for the additional years of schooling, whereas this money could be used more effectively in other ways to improve quality and enable more children in a cohort to complete primary schooling. Repetition also has a significant impact on the primary school completion rate, a key component of UPE. The higher the repetition rate, the fewer the children that complete primary schooling and the more likelihood there is of some children who have repeated going on to drop out.

12.6.3. Supporting Weaker Children

One of the keys to successful support to weaker children and those most at risk of repeating is early intervention. Interventions like tutoring, summer schools and individualised instruction either in the classroom or for some lessons outside the classroom are more effective and less costly than making children repeat the grade. Interventions such as reading programmes, encouraging greater parental involvement in the school through regular meetings, training programmes and discussing behaviour management strategies in the case of disruptive children had also been successful.

12.6.4. Role of Teacher Trainers

TTCs, in-service teacher training programmes and distance learning teacher education institutes have two main roles to play in teacher education: one is to train teachers in the philosophy of education (teaching and learning), and the other is to help them gain sufficient subject knowledge coupled with practical skills to teach that subject in the classroom. These two roles are important in creating effective teachers.

12.6.5. Subject Knowledge and Practical Skills

An important aim of teacher trainers is to produce teachers who have sufficient subject knowledge and practical skills to create stimulating, critical thinking oriented learning environments; environments which prioritise quality and access through individualised support, a diverse range of teaching and learning strategies, differentiated lessons and resources, systematic and progressive planning, and developmental assessment. A strong focus on supported and monitored teaching practice should be developed in TTCs to facilitate this.

In some countries this will require more of a focus on gaining sufficient subject knowledge, and in others a focus on practical skills, sharing good practice, preparation for classroom realities, and teaching trainees how to be flexible and adaptable in the way in which they teach the curriculum so that it meets the specific needs of a given group of children. TTCs are also obviously the primary site of learning for teachers about mixed-ability and multigrade teaching. In countries where these are particularly relevant approaches, training on these areas and self supported learning methodologies in pre- and in-service teacher training should be prioritised.

One approach would be for trainers to offer a core set of modules covering essential competencies including subject knowledge and basic teaching approaches, with additional optional modules covering practical skills of particular relevance to a specific teaching and learning environment. If teacher trainers are able to help trainee teachers see their role as not being limited to the confines of the school, but also as resources available for the community, this would enhance the integration between the formal and non-formal learning environments and between the school and the community. This would also result in more accountable schools and improvement in the understanding of the community of the potential value of education, which in turn would contribute towards reduced irregular attendance of children.

12.7. Repetition Reform Plan

Automatic promotion can have potentially disruptive effects on classroom practice, implying as it does a wider variation of ability in a class and the expectation that the class teacher will need to use different pedagogical, assessment and classroom management techniques. As a result, it will be important to build the capacity of teachers and schools to offer children appropriate support in class. It is important to note at this point that even in developed countries it is acknowledged that creating a fully differentiated lesson is much more time consuming than creating one which is not, and the debate about mixed-ability classes is not over yet.

Reform may be aided by the recruitment of volunteers from the community who, with appropriate training, could act as teaching assistants. A programme in Togo called 'Students' Tutoring for Achievement and Retention' has succeeded in reducing repetition rates. In recognition of the extra preparation time which is necessary for delivering lessons in a differentiated teaching style, teachers' terms and conditions should be amended to include a minimum 10 per cent of planning, preparation and assessment (PPA) non-contact time. Safeguards should be put in place to make sure that this time is actually used for PPA, and support structures should be instituted to maximise the effective use of this time.

School management committees, together with community stakeholders, parents/careers, teachers and children, develop a repetition reform plan (RRP) which sets out how they will implement the process of reform from repetition to automatic promotion. This will require clear policy directives from government to provide the framework for the plan. The plan should include advocacy for the change, such that all stakeholders possess sufficient evidence-based knowledge to make informed choices about the process. The plan should also identify learning needs among the stakeholders and identify how these learning needs might be met.

In exceptional circumstances, such as where a child has missed the greater part of a year's schooling, repetition may well be the preferred option and in the best interests of the child. The flexibility to keep repetition where appropriate should therefore be retained, and should be seen as one way of keeping children in school in order to meet the EFA targets. Once the RRP has been developed, schools should ensure that, where repetition is allowed, all teachers are making decisions on repeating students informed by a reliable, objective and evidence-based assessment of a child's learning made in accordance with national standardised criteria. The decision about whether a child should repeat or not should be taken with the child and his or her parents/ careers. An appeals process, to an independent mediator, should be available in case of disagreement.

To avoid repetition as a result of irregular attendance, schools will need to monitor attendance closely and keep written, accurate records for each child. Irregular attendance should be investigated at an early stage with schools having a coherent strategy for tackling irregular attendance based on a sympathetic and informed assessment of a child's individual situation rather than an authoritarian response. This might include providing financial assistance, working with community members who can monitor the situation, and raising awareness about special needs and disability issues in order to reduce stigmatisation and allow early detection of problems.

The criteria of school inspection should include identification of the rate of repetition, investigation into the factors influencing it, and an assessment of the work the school is doing to address them. DEOs should play an important role in assisting school to develop an RRP, monitoring how the school is implementing this plan, and working with community leaders to address issues of irregular attendance, feeding information into decentralised planning structures to enable appropriately targeted interventions where necessary.

12.8. Conclusion

Repetition is an option which works to the benefit of children, their families, their schools or the African continent as a whole. On the contrary, the empirical evidence suggests that the effects of repetition on children are deleterious and have a negative impact on the availability of limited government resources. This implies that, in those countries where a high percentage of children currently repeat, reform is necessary for both pedagogical and financial reasons. Such reform will need to focus firstly on addressing the multiple issues which lie behind irregular attendance causing the very real need for repetition due to the amount of schooling that has been missed. The reform will need to focus on increasing the quality and relevance of teaching and learning and providing teachers with the necessary support to teach a mixed-ability group.

School-imposed grade repetition is harmful to grade repeaters and does not benefit non-repeaters. Even the most recent research continues to show that it is counterproductive. It is not justifiable except for students who have missed a great deal of schooling due to illness or injury. Automatic promotion is clearly preferable. It does not help low achievers catch up to their peers, but it spares them the self-esteem and social adjustment problems associated with retention.

Automatic promotion is more feasible than it may seem at first, because there is considerable overlap from one grade to the next. Also, two key assumptions underlying arguments for imposed retention do not hold up. First, most students failing in school are low achievers who must work hard even to make the progress they are able to make, not underachievers who do not apply themselves and need the threat of retention to motivate them to do so. Threats of punishment are actually demotivating to students who are failing despite persistent efforts. Second, repeating the grade does not confer the assumed benefits on retained students.

References

Eide, E., & Showalter, M. "The effect of grade retention on educational and labor market outcomes". *Economics of Education Review, 20*, 563-576. 2001.

Eisenmon, T. *Reducing repetition: Issues and strategies*. Paris: IIEP-UNESCO. 1997.

Karweit, N. *Grade retention: Prevalence, timing, and effects* (Report No. 33). Baltimore: Center for Research on the Education of Students Placed at Risk, Johns Hopkins University. 1999.

Owings, W., & Kaplan, L. *Alternatives to retention and social promotion*. Bloomington, IN: Phi Delta Kappa International. 2001.

Smith, M. "Teachers' beliefs about retention". In L. Shepard & M. Smith (Eds.), *Flunking grades: Research and policies on retention* (pp. 132-150). London: Falmer. 1989.

13

FINANCING OF SCHOOL EDUCATION

13.1. INTRODUCTION

Lack of rigorous impact evaluation is one of the main constraints to better programmes. While the number of evaluations is growing rapidly over time, it is important to consider this key factor early on in the planning stages. More information about how the programme operates, the problems it faces, and the impacts it produces can be used to improve its delivery, modify and expand it as necessary, and disseminate results. All this should be done throughout the life of the programme, including the all-important pilot phase.

The principle of channelling education resources through students and their parents or basing school funding on enrolments or attendance is demand-side financing. It has been proposed for a number of reasons in different countries. Supply-side financing usually refers to funding inputs such as human and material resources based on formal sector planning by technical planners and managers. However, ensuring the supply side is, in many cases, not enough. Thus, there may be good equity and access reasons to consider demand-side financing.

Since the demand for schooling is often influenced by economic, political, social and cultural factors, in many cases it is not sufficient merely for a school to exist in order for parents to enrol children. Even free education may not entice poor families.

There are reasons to think that demand-side financing may be more efficient, for example, by empowering parents. Demand-side financing includes a range of interventions. The focus is on putting the resources in the hands of those who demand education and not those who supply it. The goal is to bring down the barriers that prevent children from continuing their education. Some of the benefits of demand-side financing are said to include schooling gains, in terms of higher enrolments, attendance, completion and achievement. Demand-side financing should also make it easier to institute school choice plans. Relating resources to the ultimate beneficiaries—students and their families—and close monitoring of those resources could lead to considerable efficiency gains to the system, thus increasing the cost-effectiveness of education programmes.

Around the world, the governments spend significant resources on education. While such outlays have led to a tremendous expansion of schooling, they have not reduced the level of disadvantage for many groups, especially those in rural areas, including the poorest of the poor, women, ethnic or religious minorities and indigenous peoples. Even in countries where the overall enrolment rate is high, there are still areas with little access to education. Often this is the poorest segment of the population. In some countries there is a sizeable portion of the least wealthy where access to schooling is slight, if not at the primary school level, then certainly at the secondary school level.

Even at the primary school age level, the gap in enrolment rates between the poorest and the richest is high. At the secondary school level, the poorest 20 percent are especially disadvantaged. In an attempt to improve the delivery of basic services and the equity with which public funds are disbursed, some governments are experimenting with new ways of channeling public funds. One such mechanism is demandside financing, whereby public funds are channeled directly to individuals or to institutions based on the characteristics of users such as income. In the last few years, some very important demand-side financing initiatives in education have been implemented in a number of countries.

There is significant interest in benchmarking government efforts to provide universal primary education. The role of public financing of education is crucial. For most countries, the state plays the predominant role in the management and financing of the education system. How governments fund educational institutions is central to a number of important policy debates that have gained greater attention in the last decade, such as decentralisation and privatisation.

The inequalities are even sharper within countries because children and young people do not have equal access to education. Some children never enter school and therefore receive no benefit from public funding for education. According to entry rates, one out of three children in sub-Saharan countries does not have access to school and, thus, public resources for education. Many other children enter school but then drop out before completing primary education. So they only benefit from a few years of public spending. On the other hand, the small group of students who go on to secondary or tertiary education receive the greatest benefit from public education funds.

International financial statistics are often criticised for shortcomings in comparability. While there is still much room for improvement, the UIS has reinforced initiatives with individual Member States to improve the quality of these data, particularly in terms of public expenditure on education. The UIS has made greater efforts to document data sources underlying finance indicators and to identify problems with definitions, as well as data gaps and areas requiring further development.

Furthermore, the UIS collects data to monitor progress towards the international education-related targets, such as EFA and the Millennium Development Goals. The Institute undertakes a number of activities across countries which seek to improve the timeliness, comparability, completeness and reliability of data. For example, a series of regional workshops on education statistics are taking place in 2007 for statisticians and policymakers in Member States. These intensive exchanges lead to improvements in the scope and comparability of data by implementing international measurement standards.

Financing of Education for All (EFA) has become a key issue in national and international efforts to achieve universal primary education by 2015. Basic education is widely recognised as an essential human right and a key to poverty alleviation and sustainable human development. Yet, some governments are unable to provide sufficient resources to provide free basic education for all. This, in turn, has highlighted the role of the international donor community in closing the gap. Measures must first better assess the capacity of governments (and societies) to mobilise needed resources. They must also reflect the demographic constraints and policy trade-offs that influence a government's ability to achieve EFA goals.

The level of public funding alone does not indicate good outcomes. Successful governments also find a balance between private and public education costs as they improve efficiency and prioritise primary school expenditure. For most countries, the state plays the predominant role in the management and financing of the education system, especially at the primary level. Governments must often make difficult decisions about mobilising and allocating these resources, especially in light of rising demand from other public service sectors, such as infrastructure or health care. There is also competition within the education system.

Universities and secondary schools often vie for the same funding as primary schools. Policymakers also face other trade-offs when setting goals for their education systems. Crossnational comparisons can help authorities to assess whether they are adequately investing in education and using these resources in the most effective, efficient and equitable manner. It is difficult to link resource levels to potential educational outcomes. It is clearly not enough to simply change spending patterns to bring about a desired outcome. Education financing must be used in an effective and efficient manner for positive change. Moreover, system-level indicators do not provide a clear picture of the effective use of resources and their impact on learning.

13.2. Typology of Demand-side Financing

A number of demand-side financing mechanisms exist. Stipends may be thought of as cash payments, including scholarships and conditional cash transfers, made to families to offset schooling-related costs for a child. Scholarships have been around for a long time. Conditional cash transfers are relatively newer and have a twist: they are also designed to alleviate short-term poverty and the payment is conditional upon the child attending school and achieving certain performance targets, such as a minimum number of days of attendance each month. Targeted vouchers, or cash payments given directly to families or schools based on enrolments, allow for attendance in private (or public) schools for a select number of students based on some sort of income or poverty measures. Student loans are used to help defray costs to the state and help a greater number of students to access education; these are not reviewed here since they are usually for higher education.

Demand-side financing programmes are used to improve the efficiency and effectiveness of the overall system of education. In developed countries, especially in the OECD, the trend in recent years has been to increase public funding of private school attendance. In many European countries, historical compromises allow parents today to choose from a number of alternative or religious schools that are financed by the state, and increasingly through direct funding formulas, or demand-side financing.

Demand-side interventions aim to change behaviour. The specific objective may be to increase school attendance, reduce repetition or drop-out, or increase achievement. The idea is to support families through a financial incentive tied to a schooling outcome. The interventions address the main schooling problem and focus on the demand side. One of the main barriers to school attendance, especially regular attendance, is family income and the opportunity costs of schooling. The demand-side subsidy is designed to substitute for the child's work that the family might otherwise rely upon.

The existing impact evaluations on enrolment and performance use panel data at the student level from a randomised rural sample. Evaluations consistently find significant increases in enrolments, especially for girls at the secondary school level.

Conditional cash transfer programmes improve educational indicators and outcomes. Demand-side programmes appear more effective at the secondary school level. The direct costs of secondary education (tuition, school supplies, uniforms, and transportation) act to reduce enrolment, especially for girls. In Bangladesh, one year of tuition alone is equivalent to half an average family's income. In addition to direct costs, the opportunity costs associated with schooling are significant. These increase over time as children become more productive and have a greater negative impact at the secondary than at the primary school level. Bangladesh's female secondary school scholarship programme led to considerable schooling gains at the secondary level because they directly addressed the costs associated with school attendance. While getting children to enroll is very important, keeping them in school longer is even more important. Demand-side financing programmes have been shown to have an impact on school completion rates.

13.2.1. Demand-side Financing

Most demand-side financing programmes focus on income constraints associated with school attendance, thus providing cash incentives for enrolment or attending a minimum number of days each month. Most of the time school quality—or learning outcomes—is not a central condition, except in some cases indirectly.

However, demand-side programmes can be effective in raising scores but there is a danger of lowering average scores if the programme brings in more marginal students and does not include special measures to reach those students—such as compensatory education. Therefore, setting conditions on cash transfer programmes that require achievement score gains requires caution. Achievement targets may be unrealistic if the programme is very successful in increasing enrolments of weaker students without adding special compensatory measures, since many factors outside the control of the school are responsible for determining academic achievement.

13.2.2. Outcomes of Labour Market

Labour market success is another outcome of education. If the demand-side programmes are successful in significantly increasing the quantity of schooling, then individuals' earnings rise as a result. Rates of return to education are higher in lower income countries. Thus, increasing schooling attainment should increase labour market earnings in the future. Returns to another year of schooling are typically above 10 percent a year in most countries and higher for lower levels of schooling. In cases where evaluations have projected future earnings, the gains are highly significant. The rate of return year to an additional year of schooling is significant in many developing countries, especially low income countries.

Parental education is a key determinant of their children's educational attainment. Demand-side financing programmes can help break the vicious cycle by accelerating educational attainment in the current generation, thus ensuring even higher attainment levels for their children.

Education contributes to social benefits, such as consumers that are more informed, technological progress, better health outcomes, and so on. Education is also important to economic growth and poverty reduction. The implication is clearly that increasing the accumulation of education by the poor will increase their incomes and well-being. Therefore, the social benefits of demand-side financing programmes should consider future earnings gains and other benefits.

13.2.3. Choice of the School

Voucher programmes are meant to increase choices for the population. Programmes can be used to increase the supply of education by enticing non-traditional providers to cater to the poor. Both the highest quality private schools and low-quality schools focused largely on profit decided not to participate in the programme. Participating schools were predominantly of average quality, charging low fees. Voucher recipients at these schools typically came from amongst the poorest. Demand-side financing programmes such as Colombia's targeted vouchers can be a cost-effective way to increase educational attainment and achievement in countries with a weak public school system and a well-developed private education sector.

The programme affected outcomes by enabling voucher recipients to attend private schools that may be better than comparable public schools, and giving stronger incentive for voucher recipients to devote more efforts to school, because failing a grade would disqualify them from keeping the voucher. The programme shows how vouchers can allow, in principle, a central funding body to complement local resources and private education providers to address public sector constraints. Adoption of the programme was most likely in municipalities where pre-existing private schools could expand capacity, where a large proportion of students were already enrolled in private schools, and where there were a limited number of under-served students.

Municipalities with very large numbers of under-served students or with relatively little preexisting private school capacity chose not to participate, presumably because the total cost to them of the voucher system would exceed the cost of building additional public schools.

Community grants can be an effective way to create new private schools in underserved areas. Income levels higher than those found in remote rural villages will allow fees to be set at a self-sustaining level. This pilot design does not appear to be appropriate for small rural villages. Not all demand-side programmes, of course, lead to private sector provision. In some cases, they offer opportunities for parents to send their children to a local school, which is often a public school.

13.2.4. Efficiency

Demand-side financing programmes not only help increase schooling; they are also cost-effective. Although demandside financing is not a panacea, it appears to increase education more effectively than popular alternatives. This is especially the case at the secondary level. Depending on the design, targeted programmes can increase educational costs. Administration and monitoring costs can significantly increase the total cost of the programme.

13.3. Importance of Evaluation

There are many theoretical arguments as well as some empirical evidence to show that demand-side financing programmes in education can work. They can help reduce repetition and drop-out and increase schooling attainment. If targeted correctly, they can even improve learning outcomes. However, few of the programmes have been subject to rigorous impact evaluation. Evaluations not only help justify continuing a programme or scaling it up; they can also provide valuable lessons that can be used in other contexts. For example, a good evaluation can help guide how much such programmes should cost.

So, if the aim is to increase enrolment, then one would know how much it would cost per student, compared with, say, supply-side interventions. Given that local problems require local solutions, then small pilots—preferably with a randomised rollout, properly identifi ed treatment and control groups, baseline and follow-up surveys—can be used to inform policymakers about what works and how.

If the quality of schooling is very poor, simple cash transfers could simply make everyone worse off. In such cases, it would be better to combine demand-side programmes with a quality intervention, or to design a very different demand-side programme. An alternative would be a targeted voucher to allow parents to choose better performing non-public schools; or school-based management initiatives that channel more resources to schools and generate parental participation and heightened levels of accountability.

It is important that programmes experiment with different approaches and combinations. That is, implement different demand-side financing programmes, such as scholarships, targeted vouchers, conditional cash transfers, and so on, depending on the educational problem being addressed. In some cases, it might be useful to combine with quality interventions such as compensatory education, teacher training, or female empowerment, among other interventions.

Besides, to the extent possible, demand-side programmes should be rolled out over time in a randomised manner. For example, if 1,000 villages are set to be beneficiaries in the next three years, then it would make sense to randomly select 500 as the treatment group and the rest become the control group for the next two years, at which time they too become beneficiaries. The pilot should have proper treatment and control groups, with baseline and follow up surveys, rigorous evaluation and dissemination of results. All this should be done before deciding when to scale up.

13.4. Commitments in Financing

National governments, international organisations and donors must assess the levels of resources currently invested in EFA and those required to actually achieve the goals. In particular, there is growing attention to benchmarking the efforts by governments in terms of resources devoted to universal primary education. This section looks at two main indicators used to measure government commitment to education. The first consists of education expenditure as a share of national wealth or gross domestic product (GDP) per capita. This represents the available resources for education in the broadest sense. It is then possible to better gauge government commitment by the second indicator, which represents the share of the total public budget devoted to education. It reflects the commitment of governments to education and the extent to which the sector can compete with other public spending priorities.

These indicators only reflect public education expenditure—not private investment. Only one-quarter of the world's countries are able to provide internationally comparable data on private education expenditure. They are typically among the world's most developed countries.

13.4.1. Government Spending on Education

The overall level of funding for education is an important issue facing policymakers. Global and regional averages for education indicators help to provide a context for analysing country-level data.

The public sector plays a role in the provision of goods and services helps to account for differences in public education expenditure levels across countries. When governments actively finance and provide such services, public expenditure plays a redistributive role in society.

The rise in national income in many countries could potentially lead to more resources for education. But this ultimately depends on a government's ability to mobilise additional revenue, which almost all countries succeeded to do, except for Argentina, Guyana and Saint Lucia. In a number of countries, public budgets grew more slowly than GDP.

The widespread growth in GDP and the even more rapid growth in public expenditure provided a good basis for expanding education budgets in many countries. In general, growth in the economy and public expenditures corresponded to increased education expenditures. Thus, while available resources help to define the parameters for public education spending, the political will to redistribute income and allocate investment in the sector differs broadly across countries.

13.4.2. Investment in Primary Education

Investment at the primary level is the focus of several international education goals. Relatively few children and young people pursue higher levels of education. The allocation of public budgets is ultimately the result of competing demands for limited resources. Countries with rising demand for education are compelled to keep costs per student low. But other governments are less constrained by this demographic pressure and can, therefore, seek to improve the quality of education provision more broadly. To explore these policy choices, this section will present indicators that reflect both perspectives: the cost of educating a student and the resources invested in the education system.

Public expenditure per student reflects the investments and costs associated with education. It covers the public contributions to the full range of expenses, including school construction and maintenance, teacher salaries, learning materials, as well as loans and scholarships for tuition and student living costs.

13.4.3. Expenditure on Educational Institutions

Educational institutions include public and private teaching institutions and non-teaching institutions, such as ministries, local authorities, curriculum development or student welfare institutions. Expenditure includes teacher and staff salaries, as well as pensions and allowances, school buildings, teaching materials, books, student welfare and administration of schools. At the tertiary level, expenditure also includes research and development performed at higher education institutions.

13.4.4. Public Subsidies to the Private Sector

This includes scholarships, grants and loans to domestic students and those abroad for tuition and living costs. In addition, there are child allowances and special public subsidies, in cash or in kind, which are contingent upon student enrolment.

13.4.5. Private Expenditure

This funding is limited to expenditure on educational institutions and excludes costs occurring outside institutions (e.g. school uniforms, transport, private tutoring, student living expenses and opportunity costs).

13.4. 6. Capital Vs Current Expenditure

Current expenditure is used on the basis for calculating expenditure per student. It does not include capital costs, which are generally associated with infrastructure (such as school construction, maintenance and rental fees). By excluding these costs, current expenditure better reflects the actual resources invested in pupils. However, many countries only report total expenditure that includes capital costs.

By expressing expenditure as a percentage of GDP per capita, education budgets can be compared in relation to national income level, which is a proxy for a country's ability to generate education financing. Low public expenditure does not necessarily mean that schools or universities are underresourced. In many countries, the contributions of students, families and others are extremely important, especially at the tertiary level. Due to limited data coverage at the country level, it is not possible to calculate regional averages. However, the median provides a good indication of regional patterns in education spending.

Expenditure may be overstated for countries that subsidise internationally mobile students. Even when taking into account differences in national income when comparing expenditure per student across countries, the results show that poorer countries tend to provide substantially less funding per student than richer countries.

Annual spending on primary students in poorer countries represents a relatively smaller share of an already low level of GDP per capita. The previous indicator reflects spending patterns in relative terms, but it is revealing o also consider the absolute values of these investments. By converting expenditure per student into PPP$, it is possible to compare the purchasing power of these resources in absolute terms. Any discussion on the absolute levels of education investments must also consider the impact of private contributions. In many less developed countries, parents and communities directly pay for teacher salaries. In addition, schools often rely on tuition and other types of fees in diverse countries.

Public spending on education varies widely across countries of the world, reflecting great divides in national wealth. Yet, these imbalances pale in comparison with those facing children and young adults in countries with limited resources. It is tempting to assume that resources are allocated evenly among young people, but the opposite is true: disparities within countries are stronger than those between them. Two factors contribute to the inequalities within countries. First of all, children and young people do not have equal access to education. Some children never enter school and, therefore, receive no benefit from public funding for education.

The children, who enter school but then drop out before completing their primary education, only benefit from a few years of public spending. On the other hand, students who continue to secondary or tertiary education derive much greater benefit from public education funds. The varying extent of these benefits is amplified by the increase in costs when students reach higher levels of education. Typically, expenditure per primary student is substantially lower than that at the secondary or tertiary level.

For most countries with low participation rates, both levels of education follow a similar pattern of large cost increases relative to primary education. Therefore, these governments invest the most in the relatively few students who continue their education. Yet, less than one-half of the school-age children actually benefit from the increased investment, with gross enrolment ratios below 50 per cent in these countries.

The association between education spending and participation levels is even more marked at the tertiary level, where expenditure per student tends to rise dramatically. In countries with gross tertiary enrolment ratios above 35 per cent, the annual public funds used to educate a tertiary student never exceeds 275 per cent (or 2.75 times) the amount spent per primary student. Yet, in countries with tertiary enrolment ratios below 10 per cent, the spending gap explodes: annual spending is between 5 and 50 times (5000 per cent) more for a tertiary student than a primary student.

It is important to consider that expenditure per tertiary student may be overstated for countries that subsidise internationally mobile students, namely Belize, Botswana, Gambia and Lesotho. Unfortunately, the exact number of mobile students receiving state subsidies is unavailable. But, in the unlikely event that all mobile students are subsidised by their countries of origin, expenditure per tertiary student would still range from 8 to 30 times more than the annual expenditure per primary student in these countries.

Many countries aim to meet their commitment to universal primary education (UPE) by improving the coverage and quality of educational provision. However, they face very different contexts which underlie the potential to finance these goals. At the level of the education system, they represent important contexts for resource mobilisation and allocation which, in turn, shape the challenges and opportunities to improve the delivery of education services. The demand for primary education stems from population growth and efforts to expand school systems in order to serve all schoolaged children.

The share of the school-age population is an important determinant of resource levels for education. The school-age dependency ratio reflects a country's share of the population which is not of age to work and pay taxes yet is the target of public education expenditure. The higher the ratio, the smaller the number of taxpayers to provide funds for the population in need of education. An overall dependency ratio would also include those considered beyond the age to work and, thus, in need of social support. The variation in the level of spending on primary education is largely due to differences in the relative size of the youth population. A country with a large proportion of school-age children will spend a higher share of its resources on education than a country with fewer children given equivalent unit costs.

13.5. Efficient Use of Resources

The costs of education are influenced by how efficiently education is provided. The discussion will turn now to student progression and completion, and the financial implications associated with children who start school but repeat grades. The indicators presented reflect how resources invested in primary education relate to the efficiency of primary schools, but do not examine the effectiveness of education systems, i.e. whether they are delivering good learning outcomes.

The education system does not have the capacity to enroll the whole school-age population. The proxy for primary completion rates is the gross intake ratio to the last grade of primary, which represents the proportion of the school-age population who complete primary education at the intended graduation age. There are basically two groups of countries facing problems related to resources. The first group can be characterised by insufficient levels of capacity and low completion rates.

The quality of education appears to be an issue, given the repetition and retention rates. This means that considerable resources are being used on students outside of the intended school-age population, without achieving the desired results. These children appear to be leaving school without attaining basic literacy and numeracy skills.

13.5.1. Sources of Education Funding

International debates concerning education financing have focused largely on public expenditure by governments and, to some extent, development agencies and donors. This is especially true for efforts to determine the resources required to achieve Education for All or the education-related targets of the Millennium Development Goals. In this context, the public sector focus is justified for it is the government's responsibility to provide access to compulsory or basic education. However, public funds reflect only part of what society as a whole invests in education.

The private sector plays a significant role in financing schooling at all levels in many countries. However, the level of this investment is often difficult to identify and compare across countries. Many countries provide estimates of the amounts spent by households on education. But, they employ different definitions of 'education costs' and a variety of data sources, ranging from national accounts to household and school surveys. Despite these limitations, the available data reveal considerable differences in private contributions to educational institutions across countries and by education levels.

A proportion of public funding goes towards private schools in many countries. At the same time, many public schools rely considerably on the private contributions of families. In addition, governments also indirectly fund educational institutions by providing subsidies to households.

13.5.2. Investment of a Society in Education

For education and measure this investment using a consistent framework, it is essential to consider all sources of funding. To do so, it is necessary to identify what is meant by sources, flows and destinations of funding. There are three main sources of funding for education: the public sector, the private sector and international sources. Public sector expenditure refers to funds spent by governments on educational institutions. This source can be further divided into responsibilities by different levels of government.

The private sector includes contributions from individuals, households and other private entities (e.g. religious groups, firms, associations). International sources of funding include loans and grants from multilateral organisations (e.g. development banks), bilateral aid and cooperation, and funds from international non-governmental organisations (NGOs). Typically, funds are provided through governments, but on rare occasions financing may go directly to educational institutions. Globally, international or external support comprises a small proportion of total education expenditure, although it can account for a considerable share of education resources in certain countries.

The state provides a subsidy to a household which is used to pay for tuition or other fees at an educational institution. Policymakers must balance the cost of providing quality education with available resources. Therefore, it is essential to consider all of the financial resources invested by society in education. The issue of private contributions raises important questions concerning the equity of education systems. Heavy reliance on private contributions is often an indication that some students may be denied access to education or specific educational services because their families are unable to pay for them.

13.5.3. Private Provision and Education Expenditure

Public and private schools are often represented as a clear dichotomy. Yet, in reality, the boundaries between public and private sectors are blurred. In terms of funding, some private schools receive public funds, which in some countries contribute to the provision of basic education. On the other hand, public—as well as private—institutions can require payment of tuition fees and other costs. The term private sector encompasses very different types of institutions. It is often assumed that for-profit companies account for the largest share of private education provision. Yet, the opposite is true with mostly non-profit civil society organisations involved in most countries. Many private schools are run by religious organisations, while others respond to specific preferences of parents and students.

Besides, some private schools are designed for communities under-served by public education systems. There are also a complex set of relationships between the state and education provider in terms of financial and regulatory requirements.

In order to compare schools around the world, UNESCO distinguishes between public and private education according to whether a public agency or a private entity has ultimate control over the institution, regardless of the source of funds. Ultimate control is decided with reference to who has the power to determine the general policies and activities of the institution and to appoint the officers who manage it.

Therefore, private schools are further classified into government dependent and independent institutions. In the case of government-dependent private schools, governments provide the majority of the budget. In both private and public schools, families must purchase textbooks, supplies and uniforms, which account for one-half of household expenditure on education. Enrolment levels are low in tertiary education, thus private spending is concentrated at the primary and secondary levels.

13.6. Conclusion

Demand-side programmes produce benefits beyond immediate schooling goals, such as the ability to tie together short-run assistance and long-run human capital formation to fight poverty. They address gender issues by giving incentives to girls and/or by making mothers the recipients of the transfer. Demand-side programmes help improve educational outcomes. In most cases, they lead to higher school attendance rates and lower school drop-out rates.

The most comprehensive programmes contribute to the reduction of child labour, increased educational attainment, and improved health and nutrition for the poor. The phased implementation of such programmes makes it easier to evaluate their impact, and the dissemination of results helps justify their continued growth. However, few programmes are rolled out this way and, therefore, very few are subject to this level of evaluation. Since fiscal affordability will remain an issue, then it is doubly important that they be properly evaluated.

Besides rigorous evaluation, demand-side programmes should be reviewed for needed modifications and expansion. Since most poor children already get primary education in middle-income countries, as well as some lower income countries, then the cost per child of bringing new children into the system among the difficult-to-reach is high. In such cases, it might make sense to expand to lower secondary and even the upper secondary school level. Demand-side programmes require complements such as good physical access and quality of services to ensure schooling.

Conditional cash transfer programmes in education may be best suited to settings where poverty is chronic and human capital outcomes continue to be low despite efforts to provide extensive and good quality services on the supply side. If the outcomes associated with the few programmes that have been rigorously evaluated continue, then demand-side financing might be the key to achieving an important part of the Millennium Development Goals. That is, demandside financing could be used to provide an important strategy for achieving universal primary education in the near future.

References

Hanushek, E.A., & Luque, J.A. Efficiency and equity in schools around the world. *Economics of Education Review.* 22(5), 481-502. 2003.

Gold, Steven D., David M. Smith and Stephen B. Lawton. *Public School Finance Programs of the United States and Canada 1993-94.* New York: American Education Finance Association. 1995.

Riddle, W. *Expenditures in Public School Districts: Why Do They Differ?* Washington: Congressional Research Service. 1990.

Swanson, Austin D. and Richard A. King. *School Finance : Its Economics and Politics.* New York: Longman Publishers. 1997.

Wong, Kenneth K. *Funding Public Schools: Politics and Policies.* Lawrence, KA: Kansas Press. 1999.

14

CONCERNS OF QUALITY EDUCATION

14.1. Introduction

A literate society has enormous gains over an illiterate society and no illiterate society has ever been able to modernise and progress. We are now transiting to a knowledge society where the quality and relevance of education would play a crucial role in economic development. Poor quality of teaching learning and systemic level inefficiencies affect the learners as well the society in many ways. The long-term implications include lower productivity levels of the perspective workforce, resistance to modernisation and perpetuation of inefficient production systems where cost benefit ratio adversely affect the economic sustainability of production processes.

14.2. Attaining Educational Quality

Improving educational quality requires reforms in teacher training; improvements in the facilities and infrastructure in schools; teachers' motivation; and a change in the style of teaching to make it attractive to the students. However, in actual practice, there has always been a trade-off between quality and quantity, in favour of the latter. This not only affected the internal efficiency of the educational system but also resulted in a situation where only a few graduates of the school and higher education system could attain the expected skills and competencies.

Policies in labour market and predominance of public sector employment opportunities did not put enough pressure on the educational systems to change as the degree was more important than the acquired knowledge and skills. The gap between the planned and the realised goals of education continues be so large that even the basis of educational planning and underlying assumptions can be easily challenged. The basic educational planning models have gone off the trajectory both at the central as well in the states. Bringing it back on the tracks remains a serious challenge for the development planners.

The inter-state and intra-state variations in school facilities, quality of teachers and learning outcome are large and so are social and economic conditions of the areas where the primary schools operate. While indicators to measure the access, retention and internal efficiency of the educational system in terms of participation rate, accessibility, repetition rates, promotion rates, dropout rates and input-output ratio have been developed, but little information is available about the learners' achievement of cognitive and non-cognitive competencies. Under the no detention policy, followed by most of the states, a child is not even tested on the learning outcomes for many years after entering the school. The no detention policy prohibits the use of examinations in first few years of schooling. The proposed system of continuous and comprehensive evaluation is yet to be implemented on sustainable basis. Reforms in the quality of education have not received serious attention of many states.

Assessment may be defined as 'any method used to understand the current knowledge that a student possesses. The idea of current knowledge implies that what a student knows is always changing and that we can make judgment about student achievement through compares on over a period of time. Good assessment techniques provide accurate estimates of student performance and enables teachers and decision-makers to make appropriate decisions. The current debate about the determinants of student achievement, specifically the contributing effect of teacher variables, has its origin primarily in the findings of the Coleman Report.

In developing countries, the examination results are often used as a proxy for the quality of education. However, such a method is fraught with great problems, as the examination system is limited in scope and coverage as far as learning is concerned. The research has established that acquiring both cognitive and non-cognitive competencies are necessary for a child's overall development.

Nonetheless, most of the research in learning achievement has focused on the assessment of cognitive skills acquired by the students. An equally reliable measure of quality of education is whether pupils are learning effectively, improving their knowledge, skills and abilities; widening their experience and growing socially and morally or not. Ability to work with others, readiness to accept responsibility and to work for public good are highly praised characteristics among school leavers.

But assessment tools do not test for such skills. While there is no consensus among educationists regarding the definition of the quality in education but there are several ways of measuring quality in education. In the context of school effectiveness, the concept of quality is linked to the efficiency of teaching learning processes. Quality is a relative concept and not something that is absolute. One useful approach could be to select a range of educational indicators that are explicit and measurable representing various facets of quality.

Educational quality and its determinants remain a topic of interest since the beginning of formal education. It is possible to develop indicators to measure learning along important dimensions, closely related to the curriculum, both in standardised assessment instruments and in alternative for ms of assessment. Non standardised assessment refers to the traditional form of assessment by teachers on regular basis through classroom interaction, questions, assignment of homework and other such techniques. The results of such assessment may be accurate or faulty, depending upon the teachers' skill as a judge of various indicators and their applicability in a given situation.

In comparing, generalising and indicating levels of attainment based on pre-defined standards, standardised tests have proved useful. It is assumed that levels of learners' achievement are assessed at best through standardised achievement tests. Since the beginning of sixties, the measurement of students' academic performance on regular basis has been an ongoing effort in the advanced countries. Based on these results policy level interventions are made so that the deficiencies in learners achievement can be overcome.

In India, the large scale achievement studies were conducted only in the recent years for primary education. The methods and tools for assessing learning outcome at other levels of education are yet to be put in place. The country is yet to evolve a policy for periodic collection and analysis of learners achievement data and using it for monitoring the quality of education at various levels. Considerable research is needed to improve the achievement testing methodology, achievement tests and tools of analysis. The analysis and feedback from achievement studies must be used for curriculum reforms and for restructuring of teacher training contents and methodology of training.

International organisations like the World Bank, UNICEF, UNESCO and UNDP have produced valuable studies on educational assessment and measurement. The Fourth Survey on Research in Education in India identified many studies, essentially at the M.Phil. and Ph.D. level, addressed to the achievement of primary school children. These researches are more of conceptual nature and their use in policy planning was practically nil.

The learning achievements are not significantly different between rural and urban schools. However, a significant difference was observed among the schools belonging to different management agencies. Similar studies were also conducted in many states as a part of the DPEP baseline learners' studies. The type of management of the school is not an influencing factor in learning achievement. The study found that the level of school infrastructure and variations in the availability of teaching-learning materials is not clearly related to learning achievement.

14.2.1. Success of Learners

The interest among developing and developed countries to compare information and experience about achievement in terms of both the standards which are prescribed and the standards that are actually achieved by the learners is indicated by the growing number of countries participating in the cross-national comparative studies on learning achievement. At the international level, the International Evaluation Agency (IEA) has developed achievement tests which are administered across the participating countries and used for establishment and comparison of learning outcome of children of specified age groups in developed and developing countries. The OECD has a long tradition of assessing achievement level in various countries and providing comparative statistics.

Many countries have also adopted a unique approach for assessing learning outcomes at various levels on regular basis. In France, for example, the focus of external assessment is to provide information on the attainment of individual pupils so that teachers can respond effectively to specific weaknesses or strengths as revealed through assessment studies. The information on achievement of pupils is made available to the schools and public.

The public has the right to know about the performance of schools and be able to make comparative judgements between schools. In Ontario, Canada, all grade 3 pupils (8-9 year olds) are assessed on various literacy and numeracy tasks in a comprehensive testing programme. The programme is designed to set benchmarks for achievement at this level. In Australia, some states such as Victoria and New South Wales, test all students of a similar age. The information on performance of pupils is made available to the pupils and schools and not to the public. New South Wales conducted state-wide tests in literacy and numeracy at years 3 and 5 for many years. The common element of all these tests has been to help teachers improve their programmes.

14.3. Dimensions of Quality in Education

Quality of education plays pivotal role in the process of development of nations. Hence, quality concerns in education are national priorities for all nations. Quality is multiple perspectives and is not a unitary concept. The dimensions of quality in education include achieving pre-determined targets and objectives. Concerns for ensuring quality level has arisen out of factors such as decline in percentage of grants from the government sources due to sharp rise in number of institutions, students and teachers, dilution in quality of PG courses that produce higher education teachers, dilution in intake standards in PG courses, as talented ones join professional courses, low standard of members of teaching profession as non-teaching jobs fetch more income, The details of expectations from quality education differ from one situation to another. A Report of the Higher Education Academy of UK states that "among the general public and media commentators there does not appear to be a common understanding of what the terms 'academic standards' or 'academic quality' mean".

The Communiqué of the World Conference on Higher Education 2009 states that "Quality criteria must reflect the overall objectives of higher education, notably the aim of cultivating in students critical and independent thought and the capacity of learning throughout life. They should encourage innovation and diversity".

Quality of an institution or a programme is generally considered on the basis of placement of its products. It is ascertained from quality of material and human resources. Various factors that affect quality are: finance, sincerity of faculty and students and management, skills of management, skills of teaching of faculty members, and quality of brain of students. Finance is a serious concern. Rapid growth rate of higher education has created problems in acquiring appropriate infrastructure.

Although national governments fail to provide adequate amount of funds, private initiatives have made education a huge industry. Profit from educational institutions in certain cases is much higher than one can expect from a small scale industry. Concern for making quality education available to their children has made parents go for private and high fee charging institutions, expected to be of high quality. The next level students go to next level institutions on the basis of their capacity to pay. Some of them also go abroad. Search for quality in higher education has upshot the concept of world class universities.

In the past decade, the term "world-class university" has become a catch phrase, not simply for improving the quality of learning and research in tertiary education but also, more important, for developing the capacity to compete in the global tertiary education market place through the acquisition, adaptation, and creation of advanced knowledge.

Not only developed nation, but also developing nations have started making attempt to create world class universities. "No longer are countries comfortable with developing their tertiary education systems to serve their local or national communities. Instead, global comparison indicators have gained significance in local development of universities. At the national level, appropriate bodies take care of quality.

A large element of private and voluntary enterprise is a healthy element in the provision, of education. It is necessary for variety, life and progress as State control of generality and a high standard of efficiency. The Communiqué of the World Conference on Higher Education 2009 states that

> "Expanding access poses challenges to the quality of higher education. Quality assurance is a vital function in contemporary higher education and must involve all stakeholders. Quality requires both establishing quality assurance systems and patterns of evaluation as well as promoting a quality culture within institutions. Regulatory and quality assurance mechanisms that promote access and create conditions for the completion of studies should be put in place for the entire higher education sector."

14.4. Quality Assurance in Education

Efforts to improve quality have resulted in establishment of agencies at national, regional and global level for assuring quality. Concern for high quality in higher education programmes has given rise to new bodies. International Network of Quality Assurance Agencies in Higher Education established in 1991 with 8 members, has 200 members in 2009. In 2000, the European Association for Quality Assurance in Higher Education was established as the European Network for Quality Assurance in Higher Education. In 2004, it was transformed into an association. In 2005, the European Ministers adopted Standards and Guidelines for Quality Assurance in the European Higher Education Area.

In UK, in 1997, Qualification Assurance Agency for Higher Education was established to take care of quality and standards in higher education. In 2001, it brought out a national framework for higher education qualifications. Its Code of Practice for the Assurance of Academic Quality and Standards in Higher Education Institutions has 10 sections, which are:

1. Postgraduate research programmes (2004),

2. Collaborative provision and flexible and distributed learning (including e-learning) (2004),
3. Students with disabilities (1999),
4. External examining (2004),
5. Academic appeals and student complaints on academic matters (2007),
6. Assessment of students (2006),
7. Programme design, approval, monitoring and review (2006),
8. Career education, information and guidance (2001),
9. Work-based and placement learning (2007), and
10. Admissions to higher education (2006).

There have been attempts to rank higher education institutions. World rankings made by the Academic Ranking of World Universities (ARWU) of Sanghai Jia Tong University of China (since 2003) and World University Rankings (THE-QS) of Times Higher Education- Quacquarelly Simonds (since 2004) have wider acceptance. Both the rankings made in 2009 had Harvard University of USA as No. 1. THE-QS ranked Stanford University as 16, whereas ARWU ranked Stanford University as 2. Most of the top 20 universities were from USA. THE-QS ranked University of Oxford as 4, whereas ARWU did not include it in top 20. There was none from India.

The ranking indicators of ARWU are:

1. Alumni of an institution winning Nobel Prizes and Fields Medals (Alumni) - 10%,
2. Staff of an institution winning Nobel Prizes and Fields Medals (Award) - 20%,
3. Highly cited researchers in 21 broad subject categories (HiCi) - 20%,
4. Papers published in Nature and Science (N&S) -20%,
5. Papers indexed in Science Citation Index-expanded and Social Science Citation Index (PUB) - 20% and
6. Per capita academic performance of an institution (PCP) 10%.

In case of THE-QS, the ranking indicators are:

1. Academic Peer Review score- 40%,
2. Employer Review score - 10%,
3. International Faculty score -5%,
4. International Students score – 5%,
5. Faculty / Student score -20% and
6. Citations/Faculty score-20%.

14.5. International Assessments of Student Performance

There have been international assessments of student performance that gives indicators of quality of school education in countries included in the assessment. Programme for International Student Assessment (PISA) conducted by the Organisation for Economic Co-operation and Development surveys key competencies of 15-year-old students in OECD member countries and a group of partner countries. These surveys are administered every three years. In case of PISA 2006, on the science scale, Finland ranked No. 1, followed by Hong Kong-China, Canada, Chinese Taipei, Estonia and Japan. USA ranked 18. Since 1995, the International Association for the Evaluation of Educational Achievement (IEA), an international organisation of national research institutions and governmental research agencies has been bringing out The Trends in International Mathematics and Science Study (TIMSS). It assesses the mathematics and science knowledge and skills of Fourth and Eighth-graders of the participating countries. TIMSS 2007 covered 58 countries.

International Association for the Evaluation of Educational Achievement stated that "Across both disciplines, Asian countries had the highest percentages of students reaching the advanced International Benchmark, representing fluency on items involving the most complex topics and reasoning skills." Highlighting position of USA, the Institute of Educational Sciences stated that "At eighth grade, the average U.S. science score was higher than the average scores of students in 35 of the 47 other countries, lower than those in 9 countries (all located in Asia or Europe), and not measurably different from those in the other 3 countries." Such types of international assessments have facilitated efforts for innovation in school education.

14.6. Student Performance Assessment in India

In India, the National Assessment and Accreditation Council (1994) of the University Grants Commission accredits institutions in general higher education. National Board of Accreditation (1994) of the AICTE accredits programmes related to Applied Arts & Crafts, Architecture, Hotel Management & Catering Technology (HMCT), Engineering & Technology, Master in Business Administration (MBA), Post Graduate Diploma in Management (PGDM), Pharmacy, Master in Computer Application (MCA).

There are a number of Government controlled/created organisations for taking care of quality in education. National level organisations are: Indian Council for Agricultural Research (1929), Medical Council of India (1933), All India Council of Technical Education (1945), Dental Council of India (1948), Pharmacy Council of India (1948), Institute of Chartered Accountants of India (1949), University Grants Commission (1956), Institute of Costs and Works Accountants of India (1959), Bar Council of India (1961), Central Council of Indian Medicine (1970), Council of Architecture (1972), Central Council of Homoeopathy (1973), Institute of Company Secretaries of India (1981), Veterinary Council of India (1984), Distance Education Council (1992), Rehabilitation Council of India (1992), and National Council for Teacher Education (1995). Government departments also control quality in education. The Directorate General of Shipping takes care of merchant navy courses. Department of Electronics takes care of computer related courses.

At the State level, there are State Government Departments which take care of quality. State Councils of Higher Education cover higher education and State Councils for Educational Research and Training cover education of school teachers. Sarva Shiksha Aviyan scheme takes care of quality of school education.

In order to accelerate qualitative improvement in higher education, National Knowledge Commission recommended establishment of 30 new Central universities, 16 in States where they do not exist and 14 as World class universities (all India admissions, course credits, regular syllabi revision, incentives for faculty, strong linkage with industry and research institutions, no affiliated colleges, outsource nonteaching functions). The Central

Government has started the process of establishment of central Universities. NKC also recommended increase in number of high quality institutions. It suggested establishment of new Indian Institutes of Technology - 8, Indian Institutes of Management - 7, National Institutes of Technology - 10, Indian Institutes of Science Education and Research - 3, Indian Institutes of Information Technology -20, and Schools of Planning Architecture - 2.

As part of attempt to provide school education of high quality to rural talented children, the Central Government had established one Navodaya Vidyalaya in each district. National Knowledge Commission recommended establishment of 6,000 model schools, one in each block, It also recommended ICT based pedagogy and learning aids and broadband connectivity to all the Government and Government aided secondary schools.

14.7. Teacher Quality Assessment

Existing quality assurance agencies assess teachers on the basis of their achievements in terms of qualifications and publications. It does not assess their teaching skills. Existing assessment indirectly gives credit to teachers for performance of their students, whereas, paid private tutoring might have contributed more to student performance. Quality of higher education teachers is promoted by making teachers participate in orientation and refresher courses. Such courses are offered by not only Academic staff Colleges, but also by many Departments of universities. However, the nation needs to improve quality of such courses.

Any attempt to develop a new curriculum or improve existing curriculum requires a strong research base. High quality curriculum development process carries out comparative studies of different aspects of curricula in India with those of developed countries. Comparative study of the efficiency of the products of various education programmes and case studies of high quality institutions and their programmes are of great help. Examining bodies generally do not give stress on contact hours in an academic session. In an autonomous college, it was observed that the Ist year PG students had to go for hunger strike, when the principal decided to have their annual examination only after 5 working months. Neither the examining bodies nor the State Governments enforce the UGC circular for minimum number of

180 teaching days in an academic session. For effective transaction of curriculum, the quality of teaching is more important than the level of publication and research capabilities of teachers. The quality assurance agencies need to give stress on evaluation of teaching skills. Quality of teaching also depends on certain physical resources such as provision for power point presentation, separate cubicle or room for each teacher and facility for internet browsing, taking print out, Xeroxing therein. Availability of such facilities motivates the teachers to become more effective that upgrades the level of curriculum transaction.

School education employs a large number of para teachers, who have neither qualification nor experience. In case of a large number of private schools, teachers are low paid – a meagre amount of one thousand rupees per month. Hence, quality is far of from such institutions. There are government schools, which have such categories of teachers on a monthly remuneration of Rs. 2, 000/- only. Such types of situation portray lack of concern for quality. In 2006, the Government of India set up National Testing Service-India at the Centre for Testing and Evaluation of the Central Institute of Indian Language at Mysore, Karnataka. Its objectives include creation of a variety of measurement frames (aptitude, achievement, and proficiency) for assessing learner growth at every level of education for the courses of study / programmes of education (in terms of content inputs and consequential effects) etc.

Human resources include managers, heads of the institutions, students and teachers. Teachers play paramount role in national development. Teacher quality is an overall concept that comprises not only knowledge and skills, but also personal qualities (respect, care, courage, empathy, etc.) and personal values, attitudes, identity, beliefs, etc.. The efforts to have high quality teachers have made many developed nations formulate standards for teachers of specific subjects and specific classes and also standards for institutions. USA has many non governmental organisations such as National Council for Accreditation of Teacher Education (1954), National Board for Professional Teaching Standards (1987), Teacher Education Accreditation Council (1998), etc. In order to improve quality of teacher education, the Centrally Sponsored Scheme of Teacher Education huge amount of funds are being spent for improving human and material resource. A few existing Departments of Education in universities and teacher training colleges have been designated as Institutes of

Advanced Study in Education that could offer doctoral research and other types of programmes. A few other training colleges have been designated as Colleges of Teacher Education. One elementary teacher training institution in every revenue district has been designated as District Institute of Education and Training. The Government of India takes burden for a few years, after which the concerned State government takes over. In most of the cases, the scheme reflects a huge wastage of material as well as human resources. While some of these institutions do not function with heads and faculty members having at least B. Ed. qualification, a few function without adequate work load, as the concerned State governments do not give funds for conducting in-service programmes for school teachers. The scheme also gives support to State Councils of Educational Research and Training that even has Directors without a B. Ed. qualification or school teaching experience.

The dismal status of teacher education in India has been stated in the National Knowledge Commission's final report which states that "The training of teachers is a major area of concern at present, since both pre-service and in-service training of school teachers is extremely inadequate and also poorly managed in most states". Hence, it is imperative that appropriate agencies take immediate steps to improve initial teacher training curricula. Recently, in one AIAER Workshop on Developing Skills for Writing Scholarly Articles and Research Papers, which had more than 40 Lecturers and Readers in Education, it was found that no participant was aware of 86th amendment of the constitution that made elementary education a fundamental right. Hence, the Central as well as State governments need to take steps for continuous updating of knowledge and skills of teachers. They may follow the pattern of ERIC in USA. There may be State level agencies for quality assurance in education which may develop and operationalise resource centers for continuous updating of knowledge and skills of teachers.

14.8. Ensuring qualitative improvement

Open and Distance Learning is the modern tool for accentuating self-initiated lifelong learning efforts. A new policy on distance learning in higher education sector of the Government of India focuses on encouragement to Open University and distance education systems in the educational pattern of the country, coordination and determination of the standards in such systems and promises to set up a Standing Committee on Open and Distance Education as part of the proposed National Commission for Higher Education and Research, to undertake the job of coordination, determination and maintenance of standards of education through the distance mode.

In many nations, including India, pupils receive fee-free education in government and government aided schools and then supplementary tutoring in the same subjects on a fee-paying basis. Private supplementary tutoring has raised problems of equity. No doubt, this has created a supplementary school system and employment opportunities. In India, this practice has affected government run and government aided schools and colleges including professional institutions. Teachers in these institutions are found giving coaching in morning and evening hours and getting fainted in classrooms during day hours for which they are officially paid. Unscrupulous teachers do not teach in their regular classes, so that the students have to attend their private coaching on payment basis.

Government funded coaching classes for students from disadvantaged population benefit students from the said group, who have learning problems. In the days of privatisation and self-financed programmes in government run and government managed institutions, the availability of quality education for the poor is a serious issue, not only in India but also in rich nations.

14.8.1. Funding and Management

Out of various factors that obstruct quality in education, funding and management pattern are crucial. One Central University was found conducting a PG course without having any regular faculty. Guest teachers came from far away places for the purpose. A few years ago, neither concerned quality control agencies of the Central Government nor the State government could stop one private university have nearly two thousand students in an academic session for a PG course run by its Department of

Education. The Regional Colleges of Education of the National Council of Educational Research and Training have been running their courses with the help of contract teachers who are paid on hourly basis. This is not a case of paucity of fund, but a case of ineffective management.

Growth in literacy coupled with rise in economic level, has led to growth in percentage of students and corresponding increase in number of institutions. The nation has to take immediate steps for improving quality of educational programmes, so that it can contain rush of rich Indian parents to foreign countries to provide quality education to their children. Assessing quality is an important task of the national as well as State governments.

Although, indicators of quality can be ascertained from recruitment tests and entrance tests conducted by various agencies, there is a necessity for national level tests. It is expected that the new Tests can be developed by CIIL within a short period. There may be subject specific tests at various levels at intervals. This may accelerate the process of improving quality of programmes and management of institutions.

14.9. Conclusion

The concern for quality of education has been voiced from time to time in India. Quality can not improve by itself. It requires multi-pronged and strategic reforms in teacher training; improvements in the facilities and infrastructure in schools; teachers' motivation; and a change in the style of teaching to make it attractive to the students. The policy also recommended that a system of continuous and comprehensive evaluation would be established. Besides the state level schemes to improve access and quality of education, a number of Centrally Sponsored Schemes and externally funded projects, undertaken in the recent years, are experimenting with various models of bringing about increased coverage, retention and improvement in quality.

In the recent years, a number of new approaches have been developed to assess the achievement levels. In India, some of these methods have yet to be tried to establish their applicability. Assessment should be viewed as a tool for improving educational standards, provide information to educators to determine which practice has resulted in desired outcomes and to what extent. Ensuring qualitative improvement is not only the responsibility of the government; it is also the responsibility of the teachers.

References

Bollart, F. et al. (Eds.) *Embedding Quality: Culture in Higher Education (A Selection of Papers from the 1st European Forum for Quality Assurance)*,14-20. European University Association, Brussels.

Bray, M. *Confronting the Shadow Education System: What Government Policies for What Private Tutoring?* IIEP/UNESCO, Paris. 2009.

Central Institute of Indian Languages. *National Testing service-India.* Mysore. 2008.

Chapman, D. & Adams, D. *The Quality of Education: Dimensions and Strategies.* IIEP, Paris. 2002.

DEC. *New Policy on Distance Learning in Higher Education Sector.* New Delhi. 2009.

National Knowledge Commission *Final Report (2006-09).* Govt. of India, New Delhi.2009.

Salimi, J. *The Challenge of Establishing World Class Universities.* World Bank, Washington DC. 2009.

UNESCO. *World Conference on Higher Education : The New Dynamics of Higher education and research for Societal Change and development: Communiqué.* Paris. 2009.

BIBLIOGRAPHY

Arnove, Robert F., Philip G. Altbach, and Gail P. Kelly (eds.). *Emergent Issues in Education: Comparative Perspectives*. Albany: State University of New York Press, 1992.

Aungles, P., Karmel, T., & Wu, T. *Demographic and Social Change: Implications for Education Funding*. Department of Education, Training and Youth Affairs, Canberra. 2000.

Bullock, A & Thomas, H. *Schools at the centre? a study of decentralisation*, London. Routledge. 1997.

Bürger, S. et al. "International Study on Transnational Mobility in Bachelor and Master Programmes". In: German Academic Exchange Service (ed.). *Transnational Mobility in Bachelor and Master Programmes*. Bonn: DAAD, pp. 1-98. 2006

Caldwell, B. J., & Spinks, J. M. *Beyond the Self-Managing School*. London: Falmer Press. 1998.

Carr, David. *Making Sense of Education*. RoutledgeFalmer. London. UK. 2003.

Castells, M.*The Rise of the Network Society*. London: Blackwell. 1996.

Chapman, D. & Adams, D. *The Quality of Education: Dimensions and Strategies*. IIEP, Paris. 2002.

Clune, W H & Witte, P. *School-based management: Institutional variation, implementation, and issues for further research*. New Brunswick, NJ, Eagleton Institute of Politics. Center for Policy Research in Education. 1997.

DEC. *New Policy on Distance Learning in Higher Education Sector*. New Delhi. 2009.

Delpit, L. *Other peoples' children: Cultural conflict in the classroom*. New York: The New Press.1995.

Dempster, N. "Guilty or not: the impact and effects of site-based management on schools". *Journal of Educational Administration*. vol. 38, no. 1, p. 47-65. 2000.

Eisenmon, T. *Reducing repetition: Issues and strategies*. Paris: IIEP-UNESCO. 1997.

Elmore, R. F., C. H. Abelmann, et al. *The New Accountability in State Education Reform. Holding Schools Accountable*. H. Ladd. Washington, D.C., The Brookings Institution: 65-98. 1996.

Farkas, S., Johnson, J., & Foleno, T. *A sense of calling: Who teaches and why*. New York: Public Agenda. 2000.

Feiman-Nemser, S. "What new teachers need to learn". Educational Leadership. 60 (8). 25-29.2003.

Floden, R., A. Porter, et al. "Instructional Leadership at the District Level: A Closer Look at Autonomy and Control." *Educational Administration Quarterly*. 24: 96-124.1988

Fuhrman, S. H. *The Politics of Coherence. Designing Coherent Education Policy: Improving the System*. San Francisco. Jossey Bass: 1-34.1993.

Fullan, M. *The new meaning of educational change*. Toronto, OISE Press. 1991.

Garg, S. *Four Decades of Distance Education in India: Reflections in Policy and Practice*. Viva Books. New Delhi. India. 2006.

Giles, C. *School development planning: a practical guide to the strategic management process*. Plymouth. UK. Northcote House Publishers. 1997.

Gold, Steven D., David M. Smith and Stephen B. Lawton. *Public School Finance Programs of the United States and Canada 1993-94*. New York: American Education Finance Association. 1995.

Grace, G. *School leadership: beyond education management*. London. Falmer Press. 1995.

Hanushek, E.A., & Luque, J.A. Efficiency and equity in schools around the world. *Economics of Education Review*. 22(5), 481-502. 2003.

Hativa, Nira, & Becker, Henry. J. "Problems and Potential Benefits." *International Journal of Educational Research*. 21 (1), 113-119. 1994.

Hausman, C S. "Principal role in magnet schools: Transformed or entrenched?". *Journal of Educational Administration*. 38(1), pp 25-46. 2000.

Hughes, Barry B. *International Futures*. Boulder : Westview Press, 1999.

Huisman, J. and van der Wende, M. (eds.) *On Cooperation and Competition: National and European Policies for the Internationalisation of Higher Education*. Bonn: Lemmens.2004.

James, R., Wyn, J., Baldwin, G., Hepworth, G., McInnis, C., & Stephanou, A. *Rural and isolated school students and their higher education choices*, AGPS, Canberra. 1999.

Jesson, D. *Educational Outcomes and Value Added by Specialist Schools*. London: Specialist Schools Trust. 2004.

Karweit, N. *Grade retention: Prevalence, timing, and effects* (Report No. 33). Baltimore: Center for Research on the Education of Students Placed at Risk, Johns Hopkins University. 1999.

Keay, F.E. *A History of Education in India*. Oxford University Press. Calcutta. India. 1978.

Kehm, B.M. and Teichler, U. "Research on Internationalisation in Higher Education". *Journal of Studies in International Education*. Vol. 11. 2007.

Knight, J. "Internationalisation: Concepts, Complexities and Challenges". In: Forest, J.J. and Altbach, P.G. (eds.). *International Handbook of Higher Education*. Dordrecht: Springer, pp. 207-227.2006.

Kshetrimayum, O. "ICT Integration in School Education – A Sociological Proposition". *Journal of Indian Education*. Vol. 33, No. 1, pp. 62-71. 2007.

Lortie, D. "Built In Tendencies Toward Stabilising the Principal's Role." *Journal of Research and Development in Education*. 22(l): 80-90. 1987.

Lucas, Robert E. "On the Mechanics of Economic Development". *Journal of Monetary Economics*, 22: 3-42. 1988.

Malen, B., R. Ogawa, et al. What Do We Know About School-Based Management? Choice and Control in American Education. *W. Clune and J. Witte*. 2:289-432. 1990.

Means, B. *Technology and education reform: the reality behind the promise*. San Francisco, CA: Jossey-Bass. 1994.

Owings, W., & Kaplan, L. *Alternatives to retention and social promotion*. Bloomington, IN: Phi Delta Kappa International. 2001.

Psacharopoulos, George and Maureen Woodhall. *Education for Development: An Analysis of Investment Choice*. New York: Oxford University Press. 1985.

Riddle, W. *Expenditures in Public School Districts: Why Do They Differ?* Washington: Congressional Research Service. 1990.

Romer, Paul M. *Human capital and growth: theory and evidence*. Carnegie-Rochester Conference Series on Public Policy, 32:251-286. 1990.

Sagna, O. and S. D'Antoni, eds. "The Virtual University Models and messages". UNESCO (IIEP).2006.

Salimi, J. *The Challenge of Establishing World Class Universities*. World Bank, Washington DC. 2009.

Schultz, T.W. "Education and Economic Growth". In *Social Forces Influencing Economic Growth*, ed., N.B. Henry. Chicago: National Society for the Study of Education. 1961.

Selwyn, Neil "Promoting Mr Chips: The construction of the teacher / computer relationship in educational advertising," *Teaching and Teacher Education.* Vol. 17, pp3-14. 2001.

Shrimali, K.L. *Education in Changing India* Asia Publishing House, Bombay, India. 1965.

Smith, M. "Teachers' beliefs about retention". In L. Shepard & M. Smith (Eds.), *Flunking grades: Research and policies on retention* (pp. 132-150). London: Falmer. 1989.

Solow, Robert. "A Contribution to the Theory of Economic Growth." *Quarterly Journal of Economics,* 70:65-94. 1956

Sprague, T. "Explanation of a new formula for interpolation."*Journal of the Institute of Actuaries,* Vol. 22. 1881.

Stevenson, S., Maclachlan, M. & Karmel, T. 'Regional Participation in Higher Education', *Higher Education Division Occasional Paper Series,* AGPS, Canberra. 1999

Swanson, Austin D. and Richard A. King. *School Finance : Its Economics and Politics.* New York: Longman Publishers. 1997.

UNESCO. *World Conference on Higher Education : The New Dynamics of Higher education and research for Societal Change and development: Communiqué.* Paris. 2009.

Wheeler, D. "Human Resource Development and Economic Growth in Developing Countries: A Simultaneous Model". World Bank Staff Working Paper No. 407. Washington D.C. 1980.

Wong, Kenneth K. *Funding Public Schools: Politics and Policies.* Lawrence, KA: Kansas Press. 1999.

World Bank. Improving educational quality through interactive radio instruction: A toolkit for policy makers and planners. Washington, DC. Africa Region Human Development Working Paper Series. 2004.

Index